C000147120

READERS' GUIDES TO ESSENT

CONSULTANT EDITOR: NICOLAS TR

Published

Lucie Armitt	George Eliot: *Adam Bede – The Mill on the Floss – Middlemarch*
Paul Baines	Daniel Defoe: *Robinson Crusoe – Moll Flanders*
Richard Beynon	D. H. Lawrence: *The Rainbow – Women in Love*
Peter Boxall	Samuel Beckett: *Waiting for Godot – Endgame*
Claire Brennan	The Poetry of Sylvia Plath
Susan Bruce	Shakespeare: *King Lear*
Sandie Byrne	Jane Austen: *Mansfield Park*
Alison Chapman	Elizabeth Gaskell: *Mary Barton – North and South*
Peter Childs	The Fiction of Ian McEwan
Christine Clegg	Vladimir Nabokov: *Lolita*
John Coyle	James Joyce: *Ulysses – A Portrait of the Artist as a Young Man*
Martin Coyle	Shakespeare: *Richard II*
Michael Faherty	The Poetry of W. B. Yeats
Sarah Gamble	The Fiction of Angela Carter
Jodi-Anne George	Chaucer: The General Prologue to *The Canterbury Tales*
Jane Goldman	Virginia Woolf: *To the Lighthouse – The Waves*
Huw Griffiths	Shakespeare: *Hamlet*
Vanessa Guignery	The Fiction of Julian Barnes
Geoffrey Harvey	Thomas Hardy: *Tess of the d'Urbervilles*
Paul Hendon	The Poetry of W. H. Auden
Terry Hodgson	The Plays of Tom Stoppard for Stage, Radio, TV and Film
Stuart Hutchinson	Mark Twain: *Tom Sawyer – Huckleberry Finn*
Stuart Hutchinson	Edith Wharton: *The House of Mirth – The Custom of the Country*
Betty Jay	E. M. Forster: *A Passage to India*
Elmer Kennedy-Andrews	The Poetry of Seamus Heaney
Elmer Kennedy-Andrews	Nathaniel Hawthorne: *The Scarlet Letter*
Daniel Lea	George Orwell: *Animal Farm – Nineteen Eighty-Four*
Philippa Lyon	Twentieth-Century War Poetry
Merja Makinen	The Novels of Jeanette Winterson
Jago Morrison	The Fiction of Chinua Achebe
Carl Plasa	Tony Morrison: *Beloved*
Carl Plasa	Jean Rhys: *Wide Sargasso Sea*
Nicholas Potter	Shakespeare: *Antony and Cleopatra*
Nicholas Potter	Shakespeare: *Othello*
Berthold Schoene-Harwood	Mary Shelley: *Frankenstein*
Nick Selby	T. S. Eliot: *The Waste Land*

Nick Selby	Herman Melville: *Moby Dick*
Nick Selby	The Poetry of Walt Whitman
David Smale	Salman Rushdie: *Midnight's Children – The Satanic Verses*
Patsy Stoneman	Emily Brontë: *Wuthering Heights*
Susie Thomas	Hanif Kureishi
Nicolas Tredell	Joseph Conrad: *Heart of Darkness*
Nicolas Tredell	Charles Dickens: *Great Expectations*
Nicolas Tredell	William Faulkner: *The Sound and the Fury – As I Lay Dying*
Nicolas Tredell	F. Scott Fitzgerald: *The Great Gatsby*
Nicolas Tredell	Shakespeare: *Macbeth*
Nicolas Tredell	The Fiction of Martin Amis
Angela Wright	Gothic Fiction

Forthcoming

Pascale Aebischer	Jacobean Drama
Simon Avery	Thomas Hardy: *The Mayor of Casterbridge – Jude the Obscure*
Annika Bautz	Jane Austen: *Sense and Sensibility – Pride and Prejudice – Emma*
Matthew Beedham	The Novels of Kazuo Ishiguro
Justice Edwards	Postcolonial Literature
Jodi-Anne George	*Beowulf*
Louisa Hadley	The Fiction of A. S. Byatt
William Hughes	Bram Stoker: *Dracula*
Aaron Kelly	Twentieth-Century Irish Literature
Matthew Jordan	Milton: *Paradise Lost*
Sara Lodge	Charlotte Brontë: *Jane Eyre*
Matthew McGuire	Contemporary Scottish Literature
Timothy Milnes	Wordsworth: *The Prelude*
Steven Price	The Plays, Screenplays and Films of David Mamet
Stephen Regan	The Poetry of Philip Larkin
Mardi Stewart	Victorian Women's Poetry
Michael Whitworth	Virginia Woolf: *Mrs Dalloway*
Gina Wisker	The Fiction of Margaret Atwood
Matthew Woodcock	Shakespeare: *Henvy V*

Readers' Guides to Essential Criticism
Series Standing Order
ISBN 1–4039–0108–2
(*outside North America only*)

You can receive future titles in this series as they are published by placing a
standing order. Please contact your bookseller or, in the case of difficulty, write
to us at the address below with your name and address, the title of the series and
the ISBN quoted above.

Customer Services Department, Palgrave Macmillan Ltd
Houndmills, Basingstoke, Hampshire RG21 6XS, England

Daniel Defoe

Robinson Crusoe
Moll Flanders

PAUL BAINES

Consultant editor: Nicolas Tredell

First published 2007 by
PALGRAVE MACMILLAN
Houndmills, Basingstoke, Hampshire RG21 6XS and
175 Fifth Avenue, New York, N.Y. 10010
Companies and representatives throughout the world

PALGRAVE MACMILLAN is the global academic imprint of the Palgrave
Macmillan division of St. Martin's Press, LLC and of Palgrave Macmillan Ltd.
Macmillan® is a registered trademark in the United States, United
Kingdom and other countries. Palgrave is a registered trademark in the
European Union and other countries.

ISBN-13: 978–1–4039–8988–8 hardback
ISBN 10: 1–4039–8988–5   hardback
ISBN-13: 978–1–4039–8989–5 paperback
ISBN 10: 1–4039–8989–3   paperback

This book is printed on paper suitable for recycling and made from
fully managed and sustained forest sources. Logging, pulping and
manufacturing processes are expected to conform to the environmental
regulations of the country of origin.

A catalogue record for this book is available from the British Library.

A catalog record for this book is available from the Library of Congress.

10   9   8   7   6   5   4   3   2   1
16   15 14 13 12 11 10 09 08 07

Printed and bound in China

Contents

CHAPTER ONE

Introduction

Daniel Defoe came to the writing of fiction from an unusually varied career which was not on the face of it likely to produce enduring literary monuments. He was about 60 when *Robinson Crusoe* was published in 1719, and after an astonishing burst of fiction over the next five years, he more or less stopped writing full-length stories, though he lived a further seven years. Nor was Defoe really known in his time for these fictions (which were all published anonymously, claiming to be the authentic stories of the people after whom they are named): he would have been astonished to find himself spoken of as a 'novelist', for that identity was not available to writers in 1719, though Defoe is often credited with having made it available to later writers. To his contemporaries he was a journalist, a writer on trade, a spy, a turncoat, a party hack. Because he wrote anonymously, contemporaries could not be sure which side he was writing for, or whether he was writing on behalf of both sides, or neither. He was not, in short, seen as a literary artist of the kind we take for granted in modern critical discussions. After his death it took many generations to sort out the most basic biographical facts, and the compass of what he actually wrote is still a matter of controversy.

Defoe was born in 1660, in London, in the year that saw Charles II (1630–85) restored to the throne after eleven years of Puritan government. Defoe's father, James Foe, was originally a tallow-chandler but had, by then, become a merchant with various interests. The family became Presbyterians in 1662 when the Act of Uniformity, requiring adherence to the Church of England, was passed; repressive measures against the dissenters began shortly afterwards. The universities being closed to dissenters, in the 1670s Defoe attended a dissenting academy at Newington Green, with a view to becoming a clergyman. But by 1683 he was established as a London merchant; the following year he married Mary Tuffley, the daughter of a dissenting wine-cooper. He traded in tobacco, wine, hosiery, and marine insurance, and prospered for a while, travelling in Europe on business. In 1685, on the accession of Charles II's Catholic brother James II (1633–1701; reigned 1686–8), Defoe joined the disastrous Protestant rebellion led by Charles II's illegitimate son, the Duke of Monmouth (1649–85), and though, unlike many others, he escaped without serious complication or punishment, this extremely risky venture cast a long shadow.

When James was removed in 1688 in favour of the Protestant William III, known as William of Orange (1650–1702; reigned 1689–1702), Defoe again joined the anti-Catholic side, which now gained the ascendant. But Defoe's various businesses (including the breeding of civet cats for perfume, and investment in diving equipment) collapsed in 1692. He was bankrupted for the enormous sum of £17,000 and imprisoned, never really escaping the shame and anxiety of this early disaster. Government friends helped him to start again, and he added the aristocratic-sounding 'De' to his surname 'Foe' in 1695, perhaps as a means of reassuming status. His first significant publication was the *Essay upon Projects* (1697), which advanced a number of possible schemes for economic advancement, which prefigure some of Crusoe's expansive spirit of accumulation and design. He published *The True-Born Englishman* (1701), a verse satire in support of the 'foreign' (Dutch) William III, whose government he advised in various matters. After William's death in 1702, harassment of dissenters became more extreme and Defoe wrote *The Shortest Way with Dissenters*, an all-too skilled impersonation of High-Tory intolerance towards those of his religious persuasion, which managed to annoy everyone: Tories were furious at the skill of the impersonation, Whigs and dissenters because Defoe, one of their own, seemed to have given the opposition a usable manifesto. Defoe was imprisoned, fined, sentenced to stand in the pillory, and bankrupted once more. He published a *Hymn to the Pillory* (1703) and an authorised collection of his writings by way of response, but another business, making bricks and tiles, collapsed while he was in jail. He was rescued by the politician Robert Harley (1661–1724), who employed him as a writer and spy for the government for the next decade. During that period he published a journal, *The Review*, which discussed politics and social and economic matters from a moderately Tory perspective, and travelled extensively in England and Scotland as part of the government's attempts to promote the Act of Union (1707). He was in trouble repeatedly during the difficult last years of the reign of Queen Anne (1665–1714; reigned 1702–14), writing provocatively during political uncertainty about the succession. After Harley's fall, on the death of Tory-inclined Anne in 1714 and the accession of the hard-line Whig Hanoverian George I (1660–1727; reigned 1714–27), Defoe continued to write extensively on social affairs through didactic manuals such as *The Family Instructor* (1715; second volume, 1718), but also continued to work for the new government as a propagandist and agent.

Several of Defoe's social pamphlets and journalism had contained elements of fiction: dialogues, conversations, short narrative examples. In 1719, however, the course of Defoe's literary career changed radically with the publication on 25 April of

■ *The Life and Strange Surprizing Adventures of Robinson Crusoe, of York. Mariner: Who lived Eight and Twenty Years, all alone in an un-inhabited Island on the Coast of America, near the Mouth of the Great River of Oroonoque; Having been cast on Shore by Shipwreck, wherein all the Men perished but himself. With An Account how he was at last as strangely deliver'd by Pyrates. Written by Himself.* □

In the absence of dust-jackets or any extensive promotional media except newspapers, booksellers and writers tended to turn title pages into this kind of rather breathless package. As an additional inducement, opposite the title page appeared an engraving of what soon became an iconic image: Crusoe standing on the sea-shore in his goatskin outfit, complete with cap, guns on each shoulder, pistol in his belt, a huge sword hanging from his waist. Commercial success was immediate: a second edition appeared on 9 May; a third came on 4 June, and the fourth, map included, about 7 August. A reduced but regular flow of 'authorised' editions (that is, issued by the publishers who held the copyrights) followed. It was soon pirated in Dublin, where the writ of copyright did not run, and an abridged version was published in August 1719. The rival publishers squabbled over the rights in newspapers. Defoe took up the hints of more to come that he had left in the final paragraph of the book by producing a sequel, *The Farther Adventures of Robinson Crusoe*, in which the story of Crusoe's island colony is developed. This came out on 20 August 1719, with a second edition appearing in the same year; a third, with six plates, and a fourth, in small format, came out in 1722. A serial version, abridged but encompassing both parts, was published in *The Original London Post or Heathcot's Intelligence* from 7 October 1719 to 20 October 1720. The final instalment of the Crusoe epic was a book of essays, *Serious Reflections during the Life and Surprising Adventures of Robinson Crusoe: with his Vision of the Angelick World*, which emerged on 6 August 1720. This contained 'Robinson Crusoe's Preface', and chapters on solitude (the most cited essay), honesty, conversation, religion, the voice of providence, relations between the Christian and non-Christian world, together with the 85-page 'vision'. Neither sequel was as popular as the original story, which turned into one of the most influential and widely read books there has ever been: by 1900 there had been at least 200 editions, 110 translations, over 115 revisions or adaptations and nearly 300 imitations.[1]

Defoe's career as a writer of adventure stories was now launched. In 1720 he published *The Life, Adventures, and Pyracies of the Famous Captain Singleton*, the memoirs of a not very repentant pirate who, amongst other exploits, managed to walk across Africa. The same year saw publication of a historical fiction, *Memoirs of a Cavalier*. In January 1722 came the other novel we focus on in this Guide:

■ *The Fortunes and Misfortunes of the Famous Moll Flanders, &c. Who was Born in Newgate, and during a Life of continu'd Variety for Threescore Years, besides her Childhood, was Twelve Year a Whore, five times a Wife (whereof once to her own Brother), Twelve Year a Thief, Eight Year a Transported Felon in Virginia, at last grew Rich, liv'd Honest, and died a Penitent. Written from her own Memorandums.* □

Here the memoirist is for the first time a woman, cast adrift in English society with nothing but her body and her intelligence to support her. *Moll Flanders* was in one sense Defoe's true sequel to *Robinson Crusoe*, using the same individual focus for what is essentially a narrative of vicissitude and adventure, but switching gender, social orientation, and relationship model: where Crusoe has shipwreck and cannibals, Moll has incest and the criminal law. The sex that is so conspicuously lacking in Crusoe is here generously supplied, as the title page racily indicates. The novel was successful enough to require two further editions in the same year, but its success was on nothing like the scale of *Robinson Crusoe*; it was not often reprinted, spawned fewer adaptations, and had little initial vogue in translation.

The year 1722 also saw the publication of *A Journal of the Plague Year*, a historical reconstruction of the great plague of 1665, and *The History and Remarkable Life of the Truly Honourable Colonel Jacque, commonly call'd Colonel Jack*, a sort of male version of *Moll Flanders*. Two years later Defoe took another look at the situation of women, in *The Fortunate Mistress*, better known today as *Roxana*, a harder, darker take on the life of the courtesan; its famously abrupt and inconclusive ending has seemed a fitting termination for Defoe's novelistic endeavours. However, *A New Voyage round the World, by a Course Never Sailed Before* (dated 1725 but published in November 1724) might be taken as Defoe's valediction to fiction, a return to Crusoesque adventuring. Defoe continued to write: a huge, three-volume *Tour Thro' the Whole Island of Great Britain* (1724–6); some criminal biographies, though the authenticity of these is often disputed; further books on family life (*Conjugal Lewdness*, 1727) and trade (*The Complete English Tradesman*, 1725–7). But the novels were all completed in one remarkable six-year outburst. Defoe died, in hiding from his creditors, in 1731.

Of all Defoe's novels, *Robinson Crusoe* was by far the most commercially successful, and it was the first to be established within the canon of English literature. Most modern critics, in speaking of *Robinson Crusoe*, mean the *Life and Strange Surprizing Adventures*, that is, the first part, setting out the legend-forming shipwreck, solitary life on the island, cannibal terrors and advent of Friday; modern editions reprint only this, though Victorian ones commonly included the *Farther Adventures*.[2] Critics do, however, mine the *Farther Adventures* and *Serious Reflections* for material that might reflect on the first instalment. *Moll Flanders* has always been a kind of Eve to Crusoe's Adam, a secondary figure. The novel spawned no sequel and was less readily absorbed into mainstream culture. *Moll Flanders* has its share of iconic and much-discussed moments to set against Crusoe's shipwreck, footprint, parrot, unmoveable canoe, cannibal wars and Friday: her first seduction; the discovery of incest; the theft of the necklace from the child; the arrest and the scenes in Newgate; the recovery of the lost son. But the book does not have *Robinson Crusoe*'s feel of myth, nor the sense that it is about to tip into allegory. And for early readers especially, Crusoe's tale was that of a wayward but eventually solid British businessman; Moll was a whore and a thief. *Robinson Crusoe* was the book named as favourite childhood reading by Victorian readers and writers; *Moll Flanders* was a more guilty, underground pleasure. As late as 1916, William Trent excluded *Moll Flanders* (and *Roxana*) from his *Daniel Defoe: How to Know Him*, on the grounds that it was 'not a book to be recommended to young readers' – or perhaps to anyone. Trent thought the full title of *Moll Flanders* was unprintable. In the twentieth century, however, these moral positions became less important; *Moll Flanders* was very highly regarded by Virginia Woolf (1882–1941) and E. M. Forster (1879–1970), and as Crusoe has become more subject to hostile critique for his colonial endeavours (he is shipwrecked in the course of a voyage to buy slaves), so Moll's powerful self-assertion in a sexualised economy has become more open to liberal and feminist appreciation. (*Roxana* has also benefited from this critical turn, as well as from an enhanced appreciation of its unresolved darkness.) For some commentators, indeed, *Moll Flanders* is more like what a novel is now conceived to be: Defoe's touch was surer, he was less ambivalent about fiction, and more concentrated on psychological sequence, than he was in his first miraculous effort.

I include in the second chapter a selection of comments from the (often hostile) earliest readers of the novels, from Romantic marginalia, and from Victorian autobiographical accounts and critical essays, concluding with some pronouncements by early twentieth-century authors. At that point, formal academic research has begun, and the following three chapters chart the main directions of such criticism from about 1925 to about 1985. After that, work on Defoe shows a marked increase in awareness of more radical versions of literary theory and I have felt it necessary to adopt a slightly different, less chronological approach. However, it has not seemed helpful to divide the account of Defoe criticism that follows into a series of recognised schools of critique – the well-worn path through Marxism, psychoanalysis, feminism, and on to deconstruction and the postcolonial. Not much criticism from the 1980s onwards is unaware of the challenges posed by these methods and positions; at the same time, in

Defoe's case, less is formally attached to any one type of theory than might be supposed, though allegiances can be discerned. Adherents to the idea of the 'rise of the novel' might be said loosely to have a kind of Marxist orientation, going back in some sense to Karl Marx (1818–83) himself, who contributed some famous remarks on *Robinson Crusoe*. Despite the invitations that might appear to be offered by such elements of plotting as Crusoe's alarming solitary footprint, the narcissistic parrot and the defiance of his father, and Moll's incest, psychoanalytic criticism has tended to be incorporated rather loosely into mainstream readings of the novels, though there are some exceptions to this. Some work on Defoe, like John Bender's analysis of Crusoe's island as a prison, clearly owes much to theories on the disposition of power advanced by the French philosopher Michel Foucault (1926–84). Work on narrative voice sometimes shows the influence of the Russian theorist Mikhail Bakhtin (1895–1975); postcolonial theory has certainly prodded a re-examination of Defoe's fiction. Defoe has never really seemed in need of deconstruction: the internal contradictions and the ambiguities of his truth claims have been obvious since Charles Gildon pointed them out in 1719.

If anything, the main effort of criticism in the twentieth century has been to reconstruct Defoe, to set his fictions into a coherent history, or artistic technique, or mode of thinking, and this continues to be a major aspect of what constitutes Defoe research, albeit with greater theoretical inflection. Accordingly, I have found it more productive to think of modern Defoe research in broadly thematic areas rather than in terms of theoretical category, and Chapter 6 is divided into themes such as crime, gender, politics and economics, the rise of the novel, and the exotic. These categories are about as watertight as Crusoe's first pots, which is to say, not very. There are obviously strong correlations, at times, between politics, economics, and the colony, not to mention social issues regarding the position of women; I have also referred back, occasionally, to earlier criticism on these themes. Nonetheless there is some sense in trying to follow what appear to be fairly consistent threads of interest in recent work on Defoe, and this approach may assist some readers to concentrate on particular aspects.

Literary criticism on the novels comes in a wide variety of forms: biographies of Defoe, critical studies of his fiction in general, book-length studies of either novel, monographs which attempt to link the fiction to specific categories of thought or literary tradition, briefer specialist articles focusing on particular aspects. Defoe is treated extensively in large-scale histories of the novel and small-scale analyses of eighteenth-century writing, in anthologies of essays and in special issues of journals. Some writing concentrates on one novel, some on the other, some on both. I have tried to take account of these varying forms and balances. Readers will find something on both novels in each chapter and section, though especially in the latter thematic arrangement, one or other tends to predominate. An appendix lists adaptations and appropri- ations of the two novels, in illustrations, popular abridgements, poetry, drama, music and film, mediations which have acted as part of the cultural presence of Defoe's fiction through the centuries.

CHAPTER TWO

Early Responses

FIRST READINGS

Robinson Crusoe appeared in bookshops on 25 April 1719 without anything extraordinary in the way of pre-publication promotion. There was no book-signing tour, no interview with the author, and no series of reviews in the papers: such things did not happen in 1719, and in any case the book was anonymous, not clearly categorised as either fiction or fact, still less a 'novel' in the sense now understood. The quick succession of editions, however, shows that the book sold well from the start. Defoe's sequel, *The Farther Adventures of Robinson Crusoe*, which appeared in August of that year, contains in the preface the first printed comment on the success of the first instalment, as well as addressing some grievances which were, apparently, lodged against it:

■ The Success the former Part of this Work has met with in the World, has yet been no other than is acknowledg'd to be due to the surprising Variety of the Subject, and to the agreeable Manner of the Performance.

All the Endeavours of envious People to reproach it with being a Romance, to search it for Errors in Geography, Inconsistency in the Relation, and Contradictions in the Fact, have proved abortive, and as impotent as malicious.

The just Application of every Incident, the religious and useful Inferences drawn from every Part, are so many Testimonies to the good Design of making it publick, and must legitimate all the Part that may be call'd Invention, or Parable in the Story. □

Defoe seems to be shifting here from a position announced in the brief preface to *Life and Strange Surprizing Adventures*, in which an unnamed 'editor' shufflingly 'believes the thing to be a just history of fact; neither is there any appearance of fiction in it', to one in which the charge of 'Romance' is rebutted by reference to a religious standard: the parable. The 'sober and ingenious reader' is expected to understand this argument, but the truth claims of the book would continue to be a focus for criticism.

There was no institutionalised form of book reviewing in Defoe's day: criticism was largely left to word of mouth in the coffee houses of London, which is what Defoe must be referring to as 'the Endeavours of envious People'. The first published criticism of *Robinson Crusoe* that we have is a hostile pamphlet. No doubt it was partly the success of the novel that prompted a savage assault on its author within the year, in Charles Gildon's *The Life and Strange Surprizing Adventures of Mr. D... De F...*, *of London, Hosier* (1719).[1] Gildon, a fellow toiler in the literary marketplace, takes the title and rewrites it as if Defoe were his own hero, in the process drawing contemptuous attention to the writer's 'low' business status, as 'hosier'. A preface makes clear some of the grounds of Gildon's antagonism to Defoe, who figures as an unprincipled writer for hire on all sides, and fundamentally unstable: 'The Fabulous Proteus of the Ancient Mythologist was but a very faint Type of our Hero, whose Changes are much more numerous, and he far more difficult to be constrain'd to his own Shape.' In the first part of the main structure, 'D...l' meets with Crusoe and Friday, who subject him to a hostile interview about their appearance in his best-seller. Defoe appears submissive and cowardly in the face of their threats to shoot him 'for making us such Scoundrels in thy writing'. Crusoe complains that Defoe has made him 'a strange whimsical, inconsistent Being, in three Weeks losing all the Religion of a Pious Education; and when you bring me again to a Sense of the Want of Religion, you make me quit that upon every Whimsy; you make me extravagantly Zealous, and as extravagantly Remiss [. . .]'. Friday in his turn complains that Defoe makes him able to understand English 'tolerably well' in a month, but still talk in pidgin English twelve years later. Defoe is made to respond by flattering Crusoe with his popularity among the lower classes: 'there is not an old Woman that can go to the Price of it, but buys thy Life and Adventures, and leaves it as a Legacy, with the *Pilgrims Progress*, the *Practice of Piety*, and *God's Revenge against Murther*, to her Posterity'. To be lumped in with such petty street literature only inflames Crusoe more, so Defoe confesses that Crusoe is his 'dear Son', 'a greater Favourite to me than you imagine; you are the true Allegorick Image of thy tender Father [. . .] I drew thee from the consideration of my own Mind; I have been all my Life that Rambling, Inconsistent Creature, which I have made thee'.[2] Defoe presents a drastic travesty of his life-story by way of proof. Crusoe and Friday are not convinced and force Defoe to eat both volumes of the adventures, thereafter tossing him in a blanket, a kind of rough justice with crude consequences for the author.

The main part of the pamphlet, a nitpicking and literal-minded 'Epistle', accuses Defoe of inculcating very bad morals through his fable. Englishmen will be put off going to sea, which is against the national interest; Crusoe's continual invocation of providence as particularly interested in his fate tends towards Popish (Catholic) superstition; Defoe is guilty of 'Burlesquing the Sacred Writ' in the use Crusoe makes of his bible. 'To me the Impiety of this Part of the Book, in making the Truths of the Bible of a Piece with the fictitious Story of *Robinson Crusoe*, is so horribly shocking that I dare not dwell upon it.'[3] Gildon highlights several errors and contradictions: Crusoe says he stuffs his pockets with biscuits when he has previously said he took off his clothes to swim; he sees a goat's eyes in the pitch darkness of a cave; he demands written agreements when he has run out of ink; Friday knows about bears despite living in a region where there are no bears, and so on. A post-script, added after the *Farther Adventures* appeared, continues the assault. Envious and distorted as the pamphlet is, it raises themes, especially in respect of Crusoe's conversion, that resonate through to modern criticism. It perhaps also had the effect of suggesting a line to Defoe in his dilemma about the status of the fiction.

Defoe's *Serious Reflections during the Life and Surprising Adventures of Robinson Crusoe* (1720) includes an encounter between Crusoe and an old lady who has read the earlier volumes, indicating that Defoe thought seriously about how his fictions were read. The book is prefaced by a rebuttal of Gildon ('a malicious, but foolish Writer') and revisits the objection that 'the Story is feign'd, that the names are borrow'd, and that it is all a Romance; that there never were any such Man or Place, or Circumstances in any Mans Life; that it is all form'd and embellish'd by Invention to impose upon the World':

■ I *Robinson Crusoe* being at the Time in perfect and sound Mind and Memory [. . .] do hereby declare, their Objection is an Invention scandalous in Design, and false in Fact; and do affirm, that the Story, though Allegorical, is also Historical; and that it is the beautiful Representation of a Life of unexam-pled Misfortunes, and of a Variety not to be met with in the World, sincerely adapted to, and intended for the common Good of Mankind [. . .] □

'Crusoe' also refers to 'a Man alive, and well known too, The Actions of whose Life are the just Subject of these Volumes, and to whom all or most Part of the Story most directly alludes, this may be depended upon for Truth, and to this I set my Name'. This has often been taken to be a reference to Defoe himself, who would thus appear as the historical foundation for the fictional or allegorical adventures which translate the facts into morally meaningful form. Defoe does not quite argue this: he says that all the famous incidents such as the footprint on the shore and the terrifying dream and the rescue of Friday 'are all Histories and real Stories' and 'literally true', while at the same time presenting them as having been worked up into the fable that is *Robinson Crusoe*'s book. It is not a wholly lucid or satisfactory explanation, though it offers consider-able material for certain kinds of modern critical analysis.

The preface to *Moll Flanders* (1722), with its careful emphasis on the editorial role in cleaning up Moll's manuscript, and its potential for moral reading, can be considered as a further document in this debate, just as the story itself can be seen as a kind of comment on the earlier novel, with a female survivor encountering social and legal rather than elemental hostility and savagery. But the literary world was not yet ready for Defoe's fictions. The preface to a picaresque criminal biography of 1723 declares:

■ It is not a romantic Tale that the Reader is here presented with, but a real History; not the adventures of a *Robinson Crusoe*, a *Colonel Jack*, or a *Moll Flanders*, but the actions of the *Highland Rogue*, a Man that has been too notorious to pass for a mere imaginary Person [. . .][4] □

A couplet in the *Flying Post* of 1 March 1729 seems to indicate that *Moll Flanders* was considered to be reading for the lower orders, a common anxiety in the period:

■ Down in the kitchen, honest Dick and Doll
Are studying Colonel Jack and Flanders Moll. □

But another writer was worried about the effect of these fictions on middle-class readers:

■ Your *Robinson Crusoe*'s, *Moll Flanders*'s, *Sally Salisbury*'s and *John Shephard*'s, have afforded notable Instances how easy it is to gratify our Curiosity, and how indulgent we are to the *Biographers* of *Newgate*, who have been as greedily read by People of the better sort, as the Compilers of *Last Speeches* and *Dying Words* by the Rabble.[5] □

The preface to the 1734 edition of Captain Richard Falconer's *Voyages* complained that *Robinson Crusoe* and *Colonel Jack* were displacing the works of William Shakespeare (1564–1616) and Ben Jonson (1572–1637), while *Moll Flanders* and *Sally Salisbury* were pushing out those of the poet and dramatist John Dryden (1631–1700) and the playwright Thomas Otway (1652–85): '*Shakespear*, and *Ben Johnson*, must give way to *Robinson Crusoe* and Colonel *Jack*; as well as Dryden and Otway to *Moll Flanders* and *Sally Salisbury*.' In the engravings based on the series of paintings *Industry and Idleness* (1747) by William Hogarth (1697–1764), the doomed Tom Idle begins his fatal path to the gallows by reading a story or poem based on *Moll Flanders*, rather than tending to his loom.

Defoe, educated outside university and lacking the gentlemanly classicism of most writers of the day, was held to be corrupting literature with his low subject matter. Alexander Pope (1688–1744) himself pictured Defoe 'Earless on High', that is, punished in the pillory, in Book Two of his epic of Grub Street writers, *The Dunciad* (1728).[6] Jonathan Swift, another Tory, who referred contemptuously to Defoe as 'the Fellow that was *pilloryed*, I have forgot his Name', seems clearly to have *Robinson Crusoe* in his sights during *Gulliver's Travels* (1726). Crusoe's materialism, empiricism, egocentricity, lack of historical perspective and naïve verisimilitude are parodied in Gulliver's deadpan narration of fabulous travels. In particular, the bitter closing assault on European colonialism, as largely a matter of piratical rapine under a cloak of divine right, can hardly fail to remind readers of Crusoe's blithe assumption of sovereignty over his island and his 'subjects'. As Pat Rogers puts it, Swift satirically strips Gulliver, while Defoe 'gives mankind a recoat' in Crusoe's goatskin garb; for Michael Seidel, 'Swift charts in Defoe's Crusoe a kind of formalized egomania, and Gulliver is a Crusoe figure who comes apart at the subjective seams, an adventurer whose ego destroys him, whose self-absorption is a mental travesty, whose compulsion is a human failing, whose neuroses take him right out of body and mind.'[7]

Defoe died in 1731. Oddly enough, the earliest known positive remark on Defoe's fiction probably comes from Pope, who around 1742 told his friend Joseph Spence in conversation: 'The first part of *Robinson Crusoe*, good. DeFoe wrote a vast many things, and none bad, though none excellent. There's something good in all he has writ.'[8] By midcentury Defoe's reputation was beginning to recover from political sniping as the fictions proved resilient and were increasingly absorbed into mainstream literature. In a biographical dictionary of English writers published in 1753, the 'Defoe' entry contained high praise for his natural abilities in political and economic writing, and added: 'His imagination was fertile, strong, and lively, as may be collected from his many works of fancy, particularly his *Robinson Crusoe*, which was written in so natural a manner, and with so many probable incidents, that, for some time after its publication, it was judged by most people to be a true story.' The status of the fictions had ceased to be a problem, and indeed 'realism' had become a point of critical interest.[9]

In addition, Crusoe was beginning to colonise the European imagination. *Émile* (1762), by the French writer Jean-Jacques Rousseau (1712–78), promoted *Robinson Crusoe* as the ideal children's book, which it seems to have been for very many male readers, at least. The island experience has the great initial merit (for the primitivist Rousseau) of stripping away social prejudice. His ideal child will read nothing else to begin with; Émile will even dress like Crusoe, and think of nothing but what is necessary to furnish the island; the novel functions as a kind of purgation of accumulated social knowledge, a fresh start for the blank mind of the child. Another French writer of the period, Jean-François Marmontel (1723–99), apparently declared that *Robinson Crusoe* 'is the first book I ever read with exquisite pleasure, – and I believe every boy in Europe might say the same thing'.[10]

By the late eighteenth century *Robinson Crusoe* had become canonical. Samuel Johnson (1709–84) went so far as to draw up a list of Defoe's 'works of imagination', which he gave to a leading woman intellectual, Elizabeth Montagu (1720–1800). Part of Johnson's respect for Defoe was based on class fellow-feeling (Johnson's father was a provincial bookseller, who may have handled Defoe's work through his shop). According to his biographer James Boswell (1740–95), Johnson awarded 'a considerable share of merit to a man, who, bred a tradesman, had written so variously and so well. Indeed, his *Robinson Crusoe* is enough of itself to establish his reputation.' In a further comment, Johnson ranked *Robinson Crusoe* with *Don Quixote* (Part 1, 1605; Part 2, 1615) by the Spanish writer Miguel de Cervantes (1547–1616) and *The Pilgrim's Progress* (Part 1, 1678; Part 2, 1684) by John Bunyan (1628–88): 'Was there ever yet anything written by mere man that was wished longer by its readers, excepting Don Quixote, Robinson Crusoe, and the Pilgrim's Progress?'[11] Hugh Blair, in a series of academic lectures at Edinburgh, declared that while *Robinson Crusoe* was

■ carried on with that appearance of truth and simplicity, which takes a strong hold of the imagination of all Readers, it suggests, at the same time, very useful instruction; by showing how much the native powers of man may be exerted for surmounting the difficulties of any external situation.[12] □

In 1783 James Beattie (1735–1803), a Scottish poet and clergyman, categorised *Robinson Crusoe* under the heading of 'serious romance':

■ Some have thought, that a lovetale is necessary to make a romance interesting. But *Robinson Crusoe*, though there is nothing of love in it, is one of the most interesting narratives that ever was written; at least in all that part which relates to the desert island: being founded on a passion still more prevalent than that of love, the desire of self-preservation; and therefore likely to engage the curiosity of every class of readers, both old and young, both learned and unlearned [. . .] it sets in a very striking light [. . .] the importance of the mechanick arts, which they, who do not know what it is to be without them, are apt to undervalue: it fixes in the mind a lively idea of the horrors of solitude, and, consequently, of the sweets of social life, and of the blessing we derive from conversation, and mutual aid: and it shows how, by labouring with one's own hands, one may secure independence, and open for oneself many sources of health and amusement. I agree, therefore, with Rousseau, that this is one of the best books that can be put into the hands of children. □

Conceivably he would have disagreed had he known that some children of the period, such as the future engraver Thomas Bewick (1753–1828), ran naked through the hills in imitation of the savages in the book.[13]

Clara Reeve (1729–1807), herself a novelist, became the first woman to record a comment on Defoe, in her *Progress of Romance* (1785). 'Euphemia' recommends *Robinson Crusoe* to her group of friends for its 'natural and probable' manner of putting an exotic scene before the reader and its promotion of the causes of virtue and religion. It is safe 'to be put into the hands of youth'; indeed 'Such books cannot be too strongly recommended, as under the disguise of fiction, warm the heart with the love of virtue, and by that means, excite the reader to the practice of it.' Hortensius, one of the friends, confesses that he read it too young and has forgotten it; Euphemia assures him that if read at the right time it can never be forgotten. But she counsels him against reading the *Serious Reflections*, which she takes to be an interpolation, *Robinson Crusoe* being 'one of the books, which *Fanaticism* has laid her paw upon, and altered it to her own tenets'.[14]

This error, along with the misdating of the novel (to 1720) and an account of Defoe's plagiarism of material from a (quite mythical) manuscript by the marooned sailor Alexander Selkirk (1676–1721), indicates the huge gap between estimation of the novel and knowledge of its author. In the same year as Reeve's book, the Scottish antiquary George Chalmers (1742–1825) began to remedy the situation by producing the first serious *Life of Daniel De Foe*, appended to editions of Defoe's *History of Union* (1786) and *Robinson Crusoe* (1790). This also contained the first published attempt to provide a bibliography of Defoe's writings; his researches produced 80 items, a long way short of even the most conservative modern count but still a major advance in knowledge. As a critic, Chalmers regarded *Robinson Crusoe* as more of a poem than Defoe's actual rough-hewn verse: 'If we regard the adventures of Crusoe . . . as a poem, his moral, his incidents, and his language, must lift him high on the poet's scale.' Less conventionally, Chalmers was prepared to extend some critical sympathy to *Moll Flanders* as well:

■ The fortunes and misfortunes of *Moll Flanders* were made to gratify the world in 1721. De Foe was aware, that in relating a vicious life, it was necessary to make the best use of a bad story; and he artfully endeavours, that the reader shall be more pleased with the moral than the fable; with the application than the relation; with the end of the writer than the adventures of the person.[15] □

Not everyone would countenance such a defence of the novel, but it is interesting to see the possibility of positive evaluation opened up.

ROMANTICS AND THE EARLY NINETEENTH CENTURY

By 1810, Defoe was enough of a classic to merit a full-scale edition under the notional editorship of Sir Walter Scott (1771–1832). In his introductory essay, the most developed piece of criticism on Defoe there had been to date, Scott bypasses *Moll Flanders* and the other rogue novels, since though they show 'strong marks of genius', they make one feel slightly soiled, as a 'well-principled young man may do, when seduced [. . .] into scenes of debauchery, that, though he may be amused, he must be not a little ashamed of that which furnishes the entertainment'. The novels are not entirely 'fit for good society', however entertaining. They all are, however, marked by an extraordinary 'appearance of REALITY' throughout, and it is this that Scott sees as the essence of Defoe's narrative power, all other obvious sources (language, form, incident) having been ruled out.[16] The talent is wasted on the all too real *Moll Flanders*, but is perfect for *Robinson Crusoe*, which seems much more real than one could have expected. Defoe was artful enough to leave loose ends (Crusoe's brother and Xury are never heard of again, and for Scott this is more like the random caprices of life than stories usually permit themselves to be). On the island, Crusoe is 'an example of what the unassisted energies of an individual of the human race can perform; and the author has, with wonderful exactness, described him as acting and thinking precisely as such a man must have thought and acted in such an extraordinary situation'.

Scott speaks to the common experience of readers of Defoe's first novel:

■ the majority of readers will recollect it is among the first works which awakened and interested their youthful attention; and feel, even in advanced life, and in the maturity of their understanding, that there are still associated with *Robinson Crusoe*, the sentiments peculiar to that period, when all is new, all glittering in prospect, and when those visions are most bright, which the experience of afterlife tends only to darken and destroy. [. . .] It is read eagerly by young people; and there is hardly an elf so devoid of imagination as not to have supposed for himself a solitary island in which he could act *Robinson Crusoe*, were it but in the corner of the nursery.[17] □

The comments of Scott, made at a time when he was, in his own writing, moving from poetry to the novel, may be compared with those of Samuel Taylor Coleridge (1772–1834), a poet without aspirations to the writing of fiction. Coleridge is the kind of reader envisaged in Scott's account; he read the book early, and returned to re-read and annotate a copy of the book when he was sixty. By one account, he used as a child to 'fancy myself on Robinson Crusoe's island, finding a mountain of plum-cake [. . .] hunger and fancy!'[18] In 1818, during a lecture on the *Arabian Nights*, Coleridge remarked on the combination of the exotic and the normal in Crusoe's adventures:

■ The *Robinson Crusoe* is like the vision of a happy nightmare such as a denizen of Elysium might be supposed to have from a little excess of his nectar and ambrosia supper. Our imagination is kept in full play, excited to the highest, yet all the while we are touching or touched by a common flesh and blood. □

In his marginalia, written on re-reading the book at about the age Defoe was when he wrote it, Coleridge praises Defoe's accuracy (even in matters of geology), his defence of miracles, his presentation of prayer, the psychological acuteness in the delineation of Crusoe's guilt, and famously, irony: the passage in which Crusoe, while ransacking the wreck for anything useful, address a speech of denunciation to some useless money, and then takes it anyway 'upon second thoughts', Coleridge thinks this 'Worthy of Shakespeare'. Above all stands the sense of common humanity: Defoe is superior to Swift, in Coleridge's reading, because he makes him forget 'my specific class, character, and circumstances, raises me into the universal man. [. . .] You become a man while you read.' This is why Crusoe must not be a superman or even a specialist in any one art, for then he

■ would have ceased to be the universal representative, the person for whom every reader could substitute himself. But now nothing is done, thought, suffered, or desired, but what every man can imagine himself doing, thinking, feeling, or wishing for. Even so very easy a problem as that of finding a substitute for ink is with exquisite judgment made to baffle Crusoe's inventive faculties. And in what he does, he arrives at no excellence; [. . .] the carpentering, tailoring, pottery, &c., are all just what will answer his purposes, and those are confined to needs that all men have, and comforts that all men desire.[19] □

More sedately, Coleridge's erstwhile poetic partner William Wordsworth (1770–1850) expressed the view that Crusoe was as good a theological manual as any more strictly orthodox religious text.[20] Similarly, the Scottish poet William Drennan (1754–1820) saw in *Robinson Crusoe* a kind of godly manual of instruction:

■ Mark, in this book, th' inventive powers of man;
In worst extremes, what resolution can;
How the soul, kindling in the glorious strife,
Compels a good from every ill of life;
Outlives the storm, the sea-worn wreck explores,
Mans the rich raft, and gains the savage shores:
There builds, there plants, there stores the grain, the fruit,
Talks with the parrot, educates the brute:
Cheers the lone desert with the mimic voice,
And bids its wond'ring echoes cry, rejoice!

Thus, in the world, and in the wilderness,
Strong to create, and provident to bless,
Man finds, or makes, his share of happiness.
And thus, in Crusoe, has there been designed
A chart of life to serve for all his kind! □

The poem concludes with a comforting address to Napoleon (then in exile on the island of Elba) urging him to read and learn from Crusoe's example.[21]

Other writers picked up Scott's sense of Defoe's brilliant inventiveness, which does not look like literary art. In 1836 Edgar Allan Poe (1809–49) commented that *Robinson Crusoe*

■ is so good that people have no conception that art lies behind it. Men do not look upon it in the light of a literary performance. Defoe has none of their thoughts – Robinson all. The powers which have wrought the wonder have been thrown into obscurity by the very stupendousness of the wonder they have wrought! We read, and become perfect abstractions in the intensity of our interest; we close the book, and are quite satisfied that we could have written as well ourselves. All this is effected by the potent magic of verisimilitude. Indeed the author [. . .] must have possessed, above all other faculties, what has been termed the faculty of identification – that dominion exercised by volition over imagination, which enables the mind to lose its own in a fictitious individuality.[22] □

Comments such as these make Defoe an artist of the kind of intensity described and espoused by the Romantic poet John Keats (1795–1821).

One source for such remarks as Poe's might have been Coleridge's friend the essayist Charles Lamb (1775–1834), who was enthusiastic about all of Defoe's fiction. In 1822 he wrote to Walter Wilson, a historian of Protestant dissent then researching a biography of Defoe:

■ It is perfect illusion. The *author* never appears in these self-narratives [. . .] but the *narrator* chains us down to an implicit belief in everything he says. There is all the minute detail of a log-book in it. [. . .] It is like reading evidence given in a court of justice. [. . .] plain and *homely* Robinson Crusoe is delightful to all ranks and classes but it is easy to see that it is written in phraseology peculiarly adapted to the lower conditions of readers; hence it is an especial favourite with seafaring men, poor boys, servant-maids, etc. His novels are capital kitchen-reading, while they are worthy, from their deep interest, to find a shelf in the libraries of the wealthiest and the most learned. □

In a separate assessment, prepared in 1829, he argued that while it was right that 'all ages and descriptions of people have delighted over the *Adventures of Robinson Crusoe*, and shall continue to do so we trust while the world lasts', Defoe's other novels, *Moll Flanders* amongst them, were based on a similar premise (survival in a hostile environment) and deserved equal attention for their direct, vivid and 'homely' narration. Though Lamb recognises that 'Moll Flanders, both thief and harlot' and the other rogue heroes are unlikely to feature on 'the bill of fare of modern literary delicacies', he again argues that their moral soundness makes them 'excellent reading for the kitchen' – that is, for 'the servant-maid or sailor' – an observation on class nicely offset by his own evident enjoyment of the tales; the class anxieties of the very early responses to Defoe seem no longer to operate, and a moral lens has begun to function:

■ We would not hesitate to say, that in no other book of fiction, where the lives of such characters are described, is guilt and delinquency made less seductive, or the suffering made more closely to follow the commission, or the penitence more earnest or more bleeding, or the intervening flashes of religious visitation upon the rude and uninstructed soul, more meltingly and fearfully painted.[23] □

These observations were given wide currency in the three-volume *Memoirs of the Life and Times of Daniel De Foe* (1830) by Walter Wilson (1781–47). *Robinson Crusoe* is easy to praise for its natural succession of incidents and its inbuilt moral lessons: 'the attention is irresistibly riveted to them as an essential part of the narrative [. . .] The reader [. . .] is taught to be a religious, whilst he is an animal being.'[24] *Moll Flanders* caused more problems because of its subject matter, but with Lamb's advocacy behind him, Wilson makes an effort to see the narrative as a moral 'thief's progress', and in that sense morally pure. Yet it 'cannot be recommended for indiscriminate reading':

■ The scenes it unfolds are such as must be always unwelcome to a refined and well-cultivated mind; whilst with respect to others, it is to be feared that those who are pre-disposed to the oblique paths of vice and dishonesty, will be more alive to the facts of the story, than to the moral that is suspended to it.[25] □

Wilson's biography was reviewed by, among others, William Hazlitt (1778–1830), who took exception to Lamb's defence of *Moll Flanders*, and stonily remarked: 'Mr. Lamb admires *Moll Flanders*; would he marry Moll Flanders.' In the review, Hazlitt allowed some merit to *Robinson Crusoe*, in part because he felt that Defoe had his religious peculiarities under control in that novel. Otherwise,

■ Defoe was divided between God and the Devil – and hence we find in this style of writing nothing but an alternation of religious horrors and raptures [. . .] and the grossest scenes of vice and debauchery: we have either

saintly, spotless purity, or all is rotten to the core. [. . .] all Defoe's characters [. . .] are of the worst and lowest description – the refuse of the prisons
and the stews – thieves, prostitutes, vagabonds, and pirates – as if he
wanted to make himself amends for the restraint under which he had
laboured [. . .] as a moral and religious character, by acting over every
excess of grossness and profligacy by proxy! □

/all the fore end of his time

As for *Moll Flanders*, there could be no possible moral 'suspended' to it as
Wilson claimed, for virtue was made to look as repellent as vice. We have

■ only the pleasure of sinning, and the dread of punishment here or here-
after; – gross sensuality, and whining repentance. The morality is that of the
inmates of a house of correction; the piety, that of malefactors in the
condemned hole. [. . .] nothing is left of the common and mixed enjoyments
and pursuits of human life but the coarsest and criminal part.[26] □

In a later notice, indeed, Hazlitt reverted to the standard view of *Robinson
Crusoe* as a national treasure:

■ Next to the holy scriptures, it may safely be asserted that this delightful
romance has ever since it was written excited the first and most powerful
influence upon the juvenile mind of England, nor has its popularity been
much less among any of the nations of Christendom. At a period when few
of the productions of English genius had been transferred into any of the
languages of foreigners, this masterpiece of the homely, unaffected, unpre-
tending, but rich and masculine intellect [. . .] had already acquired, in every
cultivated tongue of Europe, the full privileges of a native work.[27] □

Defoe might well have been gratified to have become a national export
in this way.

VICTORIAN VIEWS

Defoe's canonical position (or perhaps Crusoe's) grew still stronger in the
Victorian age, with new biographies and multi-volume editions. A
remarkable number of male writers testified to the early influence of
Robinson Crusoe on their sentimental education. Bernard Barton
(1819–1900), a Quaker poet befriended by Lamb, wrote a long 'Poet's
Memorial of Robinson Crusoe' often printed with Victorian editions of
the book, which hails the 'classic of Boyhood's bright and balmy hour'
and relives the experience of reading the book fervently in bed.[28] The
art critic John Ruskin (1819–1900) remembers how he was brought up
on Scott and Homer during the week; 'on Sunday, their effect was
tempered by Robinson Crusoe and the Pilgrim's Progress; my mother

having it deeply in her heart to make an evangelical clergyman of me'. Ruskin explains that this plan was undermined by the presence of an even more evangelical aunt, whose severe cooking 'greatly diminished the influence of the Pilgrim's Progress; and the end of the matter was, that I got all the noble imaginative teaching of Defoe and Bunyan, and yet – am not an evangelical clergyman'. The philosopher John Stuart Mill (1806–73) stated that of his few books, 'Robinson Crusoe was pre-eminent, and continued to delight me through all my boyhood.' The historian Lord Macaulay (1800–59) commented on the nostalgic contrast between childhood and adult readings of *Robinson Crusoe*: adults perceive the hand of artistic mastery but miss the simple pleasures of just being the adventurous child. 'That awful solitude of a quarter of a century – the strange union of comfort, plenty, and security with the misery of loneliness – was my delight before I was five years old, and has been the delight of hundreds of thousands of boys.' He told educationalists: 'Give a boy Robinson Crusoe. That's worth all the grammars of rhetoric and logic in the world.'[29]

The most detailed account of such boyhood experiences is that of George Borrow (1803–81), in his perhaps unreliable autobiography *Lavengro* (1851). Borrow all but equates *Robinson Crusoe* with the origin of his intellectual life. A friend of the family left a parcel of books for him and his brother on the table one day, and to the child the parcel took on a mystical presence: 'All at once a strange sensation came over me, such as I had never experienced before – a singular blending of curiosity, awe, and pleasure, the remembrance of which, even at this distance of time, produces a remarkable effect upon my nervous system.' Although he had been given books before, to no great effect, 'yet something within told me that my fate was connected with the book which had been last brought'. As he opens the book, his eyes light upon a picture, a 'wild scene' with 'a heavy sea and rocky shore, with mountains in the background, above which the moon was peering'. In a boat there are two figures, one firing a gun at a sea monster. The child's curiosity is awakened, and he turns the pages until he finds another illustration, and 'a new source of wonder' and anguished sympathy, a shipwrecked mariner struggling to reach the shore. A third illustration shows a man clothed in goatskin on a beautiful lush beach, staring 'in an attitude of horror and surprise' at a human footprint upon the sand.

At this point in his narrative Borrow asks rhetorically whether it is necessary to name the book of which he has been speaking.

■ Scarcely, for it was a book which has exerted over the minds of Englishmen an influence certainly greater than any other of modern times, which has been in most people's hands, and with the contents of which even those who cannot read are to a certain extent acquainted; a book from which the most luxuriant and fertile of our modern prose writers have drunk inspiration; a book, moreover, to which, from the hardy deeds which it narrates, and the spirit of strange and romantic enterprise which it tends to awaken, England owes many of her astonishing discoveries both by sea and land, and no inconsiderable part of her naval glory. □

His 'raging curiosity' awakened, the child Borrow pores over the 'wondrous volume [. . .] my only study and principal source of amusement. [. . .] My progress, slow enough at first, became by degrees more rapid, till at last, under "a shoulder of mutton sail," I found myself cantering before a steady breeze over an ocean of enchantment, so well pleased with my voyage that I cared not how long it might be ere it reached its termination.'[30]

As we have seen, Borrow was not alone among Victorian writers in finding 'the paths of knowledge' opened by *Robinson Crusoe*. But he was much rarer in associating *Moll Flanders* with a significant turning point in his life. He comes up to London to try his fortune as a writer, and finds work compiling a series of criminal biographies for a publisher. By some tangential instinct, Borrow finds himself making the acquaintance of a poor apple-seller who keeps a stall on London Bridge. It transpires that her son has been transported for theft, and that she has some fairly unusual ideas about crime, which are in part down to her reading of the one book she possesses:

■ would the blessed woman in the book here have written her life as she has done, and given it to the world, if there had been any harm in faking? [thieving] She, too, was what they call a thief and a cut-purse; ay, and was transported for it, like my dear son; and do you think she would have told the world so, if there had been any harm in the thing? Oh, it is a comfort to me that the blessed woman was transported, and came back – for come back she did, and rich too – for it is an assurance to me that my dear son, who was transported too, will come back like her. □

Borrow looks at the book, 'a short, thick volume, at least a century old, bound with greasy black leather', and recognises at once 'the air, the style, the spirit of the writer of the book which first taught me to read'. It is *Moll Flanders*. He suggests to the apple-seller that the book was actually written 'to show the terrible consequences of crime: it contains a deep moral', to which her amicable reply is, 'A deep what, dear?' To the old woman, the book is a talisman which she will not sell to him for any price, though she allows him to buy her some tobacco in memory of Moll's plantations.

At a later encounter, Borrow finds the old woman traumatised by the theft of the book by some boys; she recovers it, joyfully kissing it despite the mud into which it has fallen, and wishes to see the boys hanged for the crime: 'what's stealing handkerchiefs, and that kind of thing, to do with taking my book; there's a wide difference – don't you see?' Borrow reads the book, with the apple-seller watching him intently, until his eyes hurt. Later still the old woman loses interest in the book, and tries to give it to him. It transpires that she has begun to hear warning voices declaiming against theft; it also appears that she has been involved, like Moll's 'Governess', in the trade of receiving stolen goods, which she now feels might have inclined her son to crime. She tells him that 'for a long time she supposed there was no harm in doing so, as her book was full of entertaining tales of stealing; but she now thought that the book was a bad book, and that learning to read was a bad thing'. Borrow struggles with what *Moll Flanders* has done: it makes him feel 'wiser and better', but the poor woman, in concentrating on 'the funny parts [. . .] all about taking things, and the manner it was done; as for the rest, I could not exactly make it out', is worse off than ever. As an educated man, he has no trouble identifying the 'high' moral line that Defoe's preface lays down; but the old woman is like a confused emanation of Moll herself, with a transported criminal son, whom Borrow resembles in her eyes. He takes the book, with a view to exchanging it for a bible for her, but immediately loses it; he buys her a bible anyway, and the book is later sold as a rare first edition for 5 guineas. As if by obscure consequence, Borrow catches a pickpocket; relinquishing him, he makes an acquaintance which leads him away from the criminal underworld of London, though not before he has completed his book on crime for the publisher. It is a hallucinatory sequence of suggestive and not quite logical substitutions, much less straightforward than his account of learning to read through imaginative sympathy with *Robinson Crusoe*.[31]

There is perhaps something of Borrow's magical reading behind the 'Crusoemancy' practised by the fictional character Betteredge, in *The Moonstone* (1868) by Wilkie Collins (1824–89):

■ I have tried that book for years [. . .] and I have found it my friend in need in all the necessities of this mortal life. When my spirits are bad – *Robinson Crusoe*. When I want advice – *Robinson Crusoe*. In past times, when my wife plagued me; in present times, when I have had a drop too much – *Robinson Crusoe*. I have worn out six stout *Robinson Crusoes* with hard work in my service. On my lady's last birthday she gave me a seventh. I took a drop too much on the strength of it; and *Robinson Crusoe* put me right again. Price four shillings and sixpence, bound in blue, with a picture into the bargain.[32] □

Betteredge uses the book much as Crusoe himself uses the Bible, as an infallible tool of divination in times of trouble; he judges people on the strength of their knowledge of it, and situations by comparison with the 'prophecies' in the book. It is comic, of course, but also not completely unrelated to the kinds of value found in the novel at this point in its history.

Robert Louis Stevenson (1850–94), who inherited something from Crusoe in *Treasure Island* (1883) and *Kidnapped* (1886), also has a fantasticated version of the hero's talismanic effect on the imagination:

■ A friend of mine, a Welsh blacksmith, was twenty-five years old and could neither read nor write, when he heard a chapter of Robinson read aloud in a farm kitchen. Up to that moment he had sat content, huddled in his ignorance, but he left that farm another man. There were day-dreams, it appeared, divine day-dreams, written and printed and bound, and to be bought for money and enjoyed at pleasure. Down he sat that day, painfully learned to read Welsh, and returned to borrow the book. It had been lost, nor could he find another copy but one that was in English. Down he sat once more, learned English, and at length, and with entire delight, read Robinson. It is like the story of a love-chase. □

Samuel Richardson (1689–1761) may be the greater novelist; but for Stevenson, Defoe wins on 'charm of circumstance' and liberating fantasy.[33]

These views have in common a nostalgic autobiographical thread, the making of the self in combination with the model provided by Crusoe. In the wider literary world, criticism was more mixed and outward-looking, not to mention occasionally hostile. Defoe, especially the Defoe of *Moll Flanders*, was not unassailable. John Forster (1812–76), later the biographer of Charles Dickens (1812–70), wrote an account of Defoe in which *Robinson Crusoe* features, normatively, as a 'romance of solitude and self-sustainment' which

■ could only so perfectly have been written by a man whose life had for the most part been passed in the independence of unaided thought, accustomed to great reverses, of inexhaustible resource in confronting calamities, leaning ever on his Bible in sober and satisfied belief, and not afraid at any time to find himself Alone, in communion with nature and with God. □

Forster also felt the need to defend the crime novels from the views of Hazlitt and others by reference to the state of the society in which they were written.[34] This kind of argument did not cut much ice with one reviewer, who claimed that Defoe 'put his hand to works that all serious men of his own religious views must have regarded with warm disapproval', for the motive of mere money. The review then goes on to mount a remarkable attack on Defoe's lack of high art:

■ All Defoe's novels [. . .] are but a string of separate anecdotes related of one person, but having no other connection with each other. In no one of them are there forces at work that necessitate the conclusion of the story at a certain point. One meets with no mystery, no denouement in them. They go on and on, usually at a brisk pace, with abundance of dramatic position, till it apparently strikes the author he has written a good bookful, and then he winds up with a page and a half of 'so he lived happily all the rest of his days'; intermixed with some awkward moralizing by way of apology for the looseness of the bulk of the work. □

The reviewer, however, agreed that *Robinson Crusoe* was the unforgettable book of childhood reading, a visionary opening onto a breathtaking world of imagination:

■ At whatever distance of time, the scene expands before us as clearly and distinctly as when we first beheld it; we still see the green savannahs and silent woods, which mortal footstep had never disturbed; its birds of strange wing, that had never heard the report of a gun; its goats browsing securely in the vale, or peeping over the heights, in alarm at the first sight of man. □

This childish adventuring (which may well have more to do with post-Romantic conceptions of landscape than with Defoe's own prose) gives way to adult moral reflection, for the book is in reality 'a great religious poem'.[35]

In 1856 the publisher Henry Bohn (1796–1884) put out yet another new edition of Defoe's novels, which was met with a very acute and thoughtful critique. Like Scott, the reviewer found *Moll Flanders* and the crime novels vividly done, remarkable pictures of the social life of Defoe's time and a completely different system of crime and punishment, if unsuitable for 'modern readers' because of their subject matter. They show, valuably, a kind of social flexibility not really available any more:

■ De Foe puts his characters in degraded enough positions, and plunges them deep enough in the meanest criminality; but he was able to show them not absolutely dislocated from the regular order of society; they wind in and out from it, and retain some points of contact. [. . .] They are the histories of criminals, who remind us at every page that they are human beings just like ourselves; that the forms of sin are often the result merely of circumstances; and that the aberration of the will, not the injury done to society, is the measure of a man's sinfulness. □

Like Scott, the reviewer cites 'their life-likeness' as part of the novels' success; whatever facts lie behind them are 'entirely dissolved and incorporated in a homogeneous work of imagination'. This is the more striking for Defoe's lack of other qualities normally associated with imagination: his is 'at once so vivid and so curiously limited'. Defoe 'abides in the concrete: he has no analytical perception whatever'.

■ Never was there a man to whom a yellow primrose was less of any thing more than a yellow primrose. [. . .] He never conceives abstract passions: his only idea of anger is a particular man in a passion. He has an enormous reconstructive and a very narrow creative imagination. He takes up things just as he finds them; and when he wants to create, he re-sorts them, or at most makes others exactly like them. □

Defoe lacks the art of distillation: where other novelists condense conversations into a few dramatic utterances, he 'gives you every word of it, traces it backwards and forwards through its repetitions, its half-utterances, its corrections, its misconceptions, its chance wanderings, its broken and re-united threads [. . .]'. This is actually how people talk.

We do not get inside the characters (who are all, in this reading, versions of Defoe himself). In Defoe, people are not bound by affection but by interest. Even the scene where Moll meets her long-lost son in Virginia, which the reviewer transcribes and calls 'one of the most moving passages that can be found in the range of English literature', is seen not as a description of affection, but as a preternatural imitation of maternal instincts, the kind of intense imaginative identification that Defoe was capable of but chose not to use for the purposes of evoking emotion. The characters, at best, are 'deeply self-engrossed' (Crusoe); at worst (Moll) they are 'selfish to the last extremes of baseness'. They are absolute individualists, clinging to others for interest's sake, but always 'with a reserved power of disengagement, as a limpet clings to a rock'; they never root. They are, in short, Defoe, vigorous and resilient in the way he was, 'pachydermatous, tough, and tenacious of life'.

Defoe is not really interested in Crusoe the man, but in his adventures: 'His name calls up the idea not of a man, but of a story' – the island, in fact. It is a work of genius, but of 'low' genius, suitable for boys. 'The boy revels in it. It furnishes him with food for his imagination in the very direction in which, of all others, it loves to occupy itself.' The boy does not care for Crusoe; he *is* Crusoe, performing the adventures and tasks in a corner of the playground. *Robinson Crusoe* is the remarkable product of the best hand at simple, unvarnished story-telling that the reviewer knows: that the chimney sweep and the aristocrat 'both understand and both find interesting'.[36]

Another anonymous reviewer acknowledged both Defoe's Puritan background (Crusoe's penitential agonies remind him of Bunyan) and his attendant influence on children: 'There is not a child who does not believe in the adventures of Crusoe as strongly as he believes in the history of Joseph.' But he felt that the greatest pleasure in the book stemmed from an unwitting admiration for 'the progressive triumph of man over matter [. . .] we see material nature, animals and savages, gradually succumbing to the coercive control of [. . .] contriving power [. . .]'.[37] In the Victorian period Crusoe's activities as a colonist attracted little censure. Perhaps the loudest complaint against Crusoe's imaginative dominance came from Karl Marx, who objected to the use of the story by classical economists like David Ricardo (1772–1823) and devoted a few acid pages of *Das Kapital* (1867) to the subject of the hero's economic prowess.

■ Moderate though he be, yet some few wants he has to satisfy, and must therefore do a little useful work of various sorts, such as making tools and furniture, taming goats, fishing and hunting. [. . .] In spite of the variety of his work, he knows that his labour, whatever its form, is but the activity of one and the same Robinson, and consequently, that it consists of nothing but different modes of human labour. Necessity itself compels him to apportion his time accurately between his different kinds of work. [. . .] he commences, like a true-born Briton, to keep a set of books. □

Marx goes on to imagine this, satirically, as a sort of stock ledger. But what really interests Marx is the possibility of imagining this self-sufficient version of labour transformed to a social institution. 'All the relations between Robinson and the objects that form this wealth of his own creation, are here [. . .] simple and clear. [. . .] And yet those relations contain all that is essential to the determination of value.' In contrast to medieval Europe, with its feudal property relations, Marx imagines a

■ community of free individuals, carrying on their work with the means of production in common. [. . .] All the characteristics of Robinson's labour are here repeated, but with this difference, that they are social, instead of individual. Everything produced by him was exclusively the result of his own personal labour, and therefore simply an object of use for himself. The total product of our community is a social product.[38] □

If Marx was a fairly lone voice in arguing about Crusoe's work in this way, there were signs in the later nineteenth century that Defoe's position was beginning to be challenged once more. Dickens, for example, remarked in conversation that *Robinson Crusoe* was 'the only instance of an universally popular book that could make no-one laugh and could make no-one cry'. He felt that Defoe was lacking in real human sympathy: 'there is not in literature a more surprising instance of an utter want of tenderness and sentiment, than the death of Friday' (in the *Farther Adventures*, which Dickens rated as 'perfectly contemptible'). Dickens complained that Crusoe's decades of experience on the island have made no 'visible effect [. . .] on his character'.[39]

Later, Victorian faith in Defoe the pious crusader was a little shaken by the research published in William Lee's three-volume *Daniel Defoe: His Life, and Recently Discovered Writings* (1869). Lee had discovered Defoe's work for the government through correspondence in the state archives, which gave some handle to charges of political trimming and treachery. Lee did not have much to say about the fiction, though he did make the interesting suggestion that *Moll Flanders* and *Colonel Jack* were written for the purpose of edifying those reprieved from execution and transported to the colonies, as a sort of optimistic promise that they too could achieve prosperity, given this new chance. In a review of the biography, *Robinson Crusoe* was once again given full marks for the expression of Defoe's characteristically 'intense imagination which at times leads him to the verge of poetry'. The other heroes are, like Crusoe, versions of Defoe, but the context demeans the fictions, dragging his general reputation down:

■ Yet the descent from the light and purity of the great romance to the oppressive and noxious atmosphere of the minor novels is great indeed. *Robinson Crusoe* stands out from its companions like a noble mountain amidst a range of stunted hillocks; it is a book so manly in tone, so feminine in sweetness, so Christian in feeling, that it deserves a place on the same shelf with the *Faery Queene* [1590–6, by Edmund Spenser (?1552–99)] and the *Pilgrim's Progress*. But on what shelf, and with what companions, shall we place [. . .] *Moll Flanders* [. . .]? [. . .] among books that display, with the fidelity of a photograph, human nature at its worst, vice in all its grossness, and the low aims of low people in all their vulgarity.[40] □

The Victorian period offered two further substantial accounts, which represent a kind of balancing out of these views of the two novels. William Minto's short book *Defoe* (1879) finds Defoe working out the Crusoe idea 'as an artist'; indeed, the novel had survived best by being essentially detachable from its own time, as if 'organized for separate existence'. All the rest of the hero/ines are essentially Complete English Tradesmen who have 'strayed into unlawful courses' and must help themselves out of it. *Moll Flanders*, Minto thought (with some originality), 'is in some respects superior as a novel. Moll is a much more complicated character than the simple, open minded, manly mariner of York; a strangely mixed compound of craft and impulse, selfishness and generosity – in short, a thoroughly bad woman, made bad by circumstances.' In analysing Moll's criminal career, Defoe 'has gone much more deeply into the springs of action and sketched a much richer page in the natural history of his species than in *Robinson Crusoe*. True, it is a more repulsive page,' but the real reason for its neglect is its lack of a 'central principle of life' (here Minto shows the influence of Victorian natural history). *Robinson Crusoe* grows from a 'vigorous germ', the simple idea of being completely alone and cast away; Moll, by contrast, 'is only a string of diverting incidents, the lowest type of book organism, very brilliant while it is fresh and new, but not qualified to survive competitors for the world's interest. There is no unique creative purpose in it to bind the whole together; it might be cut into pieces, each capable of wriggling amusingly by itself.' The interest in criminal negotiation and sharp practice is too close to Defoe's own interests in trade: 'he enters into their ingenious shifts and successes with a joyous sympathy that would have been impossible if their reckless adventurous living by their wits had not a strong charm for him'.[41]

The views of Sir Leslie Stephen (1832–1904), editor of the first *Dictionary of National Biography* and a commanding literary figure in the last two decades of the nineteenth century, sounds a still more cautious note. Stephen accepts the autobiographical element in *Robinson Crusoe* as part of its vivid strength. But like Dickens he finds it 'singularly wanting as a psychological study. Friday is no real savage, but a good English servant without plush.' The psychology is weak, and does not show what would really happen in such a situation, giving only 'a very inadequate picture of the mental torments to which his hero is exposed [. . .] His stay on the island produces the same state of mind as might be due to a dull Sunday in Scotland.' For this reason, the want of power in describing emotion as compared with the amazing power of describing facts, '*Robinson Crusoe* is a book for boys rather than men. [. . .] It falls short of any high intellectual interest.'

On the other hand, 'We have the romantic and adventurous incidents upon which the most unflinching realism can be set to work without danger of vulgarity.' On the island, Defoe's attention cannot wander. 'It is one of the exceptional cases in which the poetical aspect of a position is brought out best by the most prosaic accuracy of detail.' Defoe's imagination was very powerful but limited, very intense but unable to transcend what it saw: so he will not satisfy 'a grown-up man with a taste for high art'. *Moll Flanders*, by contrast, cannot 'fairly claim any higher interest than that which belongs to the ordinary police report, given with infinite fullness and vivacity of detail'. It is without true sentiment or passion and hence, for this late Victorian, not very interesting.[42]

MODERNIST READINGS

Robinson Crusoe attained a kind of talismanic place in world culture. We find the Dutch painter Vincent Van Gogh (1853–90), on the face of it an unlikely reader of realistic prose, writing to his brother to urge that we should all

■ retain something of the original character of a Robinson Crusoe. Make and remake everything oneself, make a 'supplementary gesture' toward each object, give another facet to the polished reflections, all of which are so many boons the imagination confers upon us by making us aware of the Houses's inner growth. To have an active day I keep saying to myself, 'Every morning I must give a thought to Saint Robinson'.[43] □

The Austrian novelist Franz Kafka (1883–1924) used Crusoe as a kind of signpost in his exile:'I am away from home, and must always write home, even if any home of mine has long since floated away into eternity. All this writing is nothing but Robinson' Crusoe's flag hoisted at the highest point of the island.' The French novelist and essayist Albert Camus (1913–60) quotes Defoe's allegorical claim for Robinson Crusoe ('all these reflections are just History of a State of forc'd Confinement, which in my real History is represented by a confin'd Retreat in an Island') as an epigraph to La Peste (1947; translated as The Plague, 1948). Another French writer, André Malraux (1901–76), cited Robinson Crusoe as one of the three books (the other two are Cervantes's Don Quixote, and The Idiot by Fyodor Dostoevsky (1821–81)) that retained their truth for those who had seen prisons and concentration camps.[44]

In Britain Defoe provoked some remarkable responses amongst modern novelists, which show an interesting shift in the relative balance between Robinson Crusoe and Moll Flanders. James Joyce (1882–1941) has Bloom, the hero of Ulysses (1918), sing from a popular song, 'O, poor Robinson Crusoe! / How could you possibly do so?'; his Molly Bloom bears traces of Moll Flanders, and is made to say during the famous concluding soliloquy:'I don't like books with a Molly in them like that one he brought me about the one from Flanders a whore always shoplifting anything she could cloth and stuff and yards of it'. Joyce himself called Robinson Crusoe 'the English Ulysses', according to Frank Budgen, who said that Joyce owned and had read Defoe's complete works.[45] In a lecture on Defoe, given in Italian, Joyce declared that Defoe was the first English writer to 'infuse into the creatures of his pen a truly national spirit'. Joyce contrasted Defoe's forceful realism with the 'studied ardour of indignation and protest which lacerates and caresses' of the modern European realist tradition.'You will find, if anything, beneath the rude exterior of his characters an instinct and a prophecy.'The prophecy comes from Moll as well as from Crusoe: 'His women have the indecency and the continence of beasts; his men are strong and silent as trees. English feminism and English imperialism already lurk in these souls.' Joyce (an Irishman in European exile) has some choice comments to make on the question of Empire:

■ The true symbol of the British conquest is Robinson Crusoe, who, cast away on a desert island, in his pocket a knife and a pipe, becomes an architect, a carpenter, a knife grinder, an astronomer, a baker, a ship-wright, a potter, a saddler, a farmer, a tailor, an umbrella-maker, and a cler-gyman. He is the true prototype of the British colonist, as Friday [. . .] is the symbol of the subject races. The whole Anglo-Saxon spirit is in Crusoe: the manly independence; the unconscious cruelty; the persistence; the slow yet efficient intelligence; the sexual apathy; the practical, well-balanced reli-giousness; the calculating taciturnity. Whoever rereads this simple, moving book in the light of subsequent history cannot help but fall under its prophetic spell.[46] □

Perhaps slightly less interested in Crusoe's imperial spell was Virginia Woolf, daughter of Leslie Stephen, whose views on Defoe we observed in the previous section. Woolf wrote two striking essays which explicitly defended Defoe's female as well as male protagonists.[47] The essay 'Defoe' was written in 1919 on the 200th anniversary of the publication of *Crusoe* and was included in her essay collection *The Common Reader* (1925). Woolf vividly re-creates the sense that the story had entered consciousness like a myth, before it was known as an actual book: it was like 'one of the anonymous productions of the race rather than the effort of a single mind'. Because 'we have all had *Robinson Crusoe* read to us as children', the story was like Stonehenge, a monument already there; Defoe the writer did not really exist as its creator. In a later essay, 'Robinson Crusoe', published in *The Second Common Reader* (1932), Woolf returned to the novel to try to set down its meaning to her as a practising novelist. Rejecting approaches through the literary context or the biography of the author, as foreign to its particular character, Woolf declared that our task with Defoe was to 'master his perspective', to analyse his way of ordering the world. She argues that Defoe's perspec-tive is very different from the mythic archetype we might imagine from a plot summary: we might dream pictures of 'some far land on the limits of the world; of the sun rising and the sun setting; of man, isolated from his kind, brooding alone upon the nature of society and the strange ways of men'. But this is Romantic, and Defoe 'thwarts us and flouts us at every turn'. 'There are no sunsets and no sunrises; there is no solitude and no soul. There is, on the contrary, staring us full in the face nothing but a large earthenware pot.' Only if we accept Crusoe's cautiousness, prac-ticality and shrewdness do we find ourselves 'at sea, in a storm; and, peer-ing out, everything is seen precisely as it appears to Robinson Crusoe'.

■ He is incapable of enthusiasm. He has a natural slight distaste for the sublimities of Nature. He suspects even Providence of exaggeration. [. . .] We are much more alarmed by the 'vast great creatures' that swim out in the night and surround his boat than he is. He at once takes his gun and fires at them, and off they swim – whether they are lions or not he really cannot say. [. . .] We are swallowing monsters that we should have jibbed at if they had been offered us by an imaginative and flamboyant traveller. But anything that this sturdy middle-class man notices can be taken for a fact. ☐

Though Defoe was no psychologist, Woolf argues that Crusoe's prosaic, under-emotional renderings of experience convey in small gestures an effect 'as deep as pages of analysis'. The ordinary is transfigured: 'To dig, to bake, to plant, to build – how serious these simple occupations are; hatchets, scissors, logs, axes – how beautiful these simple objects become.'

■ Thus Defoe, by reiterating that nothing but a plain earthenware pot stands in the foreground, persuades us to see remote islands and the solitudes of the human soul. By believing fixedly in the solidity of the pot and its earthiness, he has subdued every other element to his design; he has roped the whole universe into harmony. ☐

Woolf subtly remakes Crusoe/Defoe in the image of her own impressionism. The earlier essay on 'Defoe' had done something further: it had quietly diverted attention from the Crusoe anniversary towards the other novels, and especially towards *Moll Flanders*, on which novel she differs sharply from her father, as might be expected from the author of *A Room of One's Own* (1929). Woolf notes Defoe's own work on the education of women (in *An Essay upon Projects*, of 1697) as a reason for taking his female characters seriously. She protests against the omission of *Moll* from contemporary celebration: 'On any monument worthy of the name of monument the names of *Moll Flanders* and *Roxana*, at least, should be carved as deeply as the name of Defoe. They stand among the few English novels which we can call indisputably great.' Woolf's reasons for this judgement focus to begin with on his documentary knowledge. 'He had spent eighteen months in Newgate and talked with thieves, pirates, highwaymen, and coiners before he wrote the history of Moll Flanders.' But Woolf also wants to contest the view that Defoe is 'a mere journalist and literal recorder of facts', and finds in Moll's story an existential turn.

■ From the outset the burden of proving her right to exist is laid upon her. She has to depend entirely upon her own wits and judgement, and to deal with each emergency as it arises by a rule-of-thumb morality which she has forged in her own head. ☐

Woolf warms to Moll as a convincing and inspiring female character; she has courage, she stands her ground, and Defoe endows her with inner power even as he strips her of external fortune:

■ He makes us understand that Moll Flanders was a woman on her own account not only material for a succession of adventures. [. . .] Since she

makes no scruple of telling lies when they serve her purpose, there is something undeniable about her truth when she speaks it. [. . .] She has a spirit
that loves to breast the storm. She delights in the exercise of her own
powers. [. . .] Moreover, her ambition has that slight strain of imagination in
it which puts it in the category of the noble passions. □

Woolf is aware that the character is in some ways more vivid than the
book's stated moral purpose, which she sees as a general case for Defoe's
fiction:'his characters take shape and substance of their own accord, as if
in despite of the author and not altogether to his liking. [. . .] He seems
to have taken his characters so deeply into his mind that he lived them
without exactly knowing how; and, like all unconscious artists, he leaves
more gold in his work than his own generation was able to bring to the
surface.'

Woolf was not alone in refusing to give *Robinson Crusoe* precedence
over *Moll Flanders*. The American novelist William Faulkner (1897–1962)
is reported to have declared:'I remember Moll Flanders and all her teem-
ing and rich fecundity like a market-place where all that had survived up
to that time must bide and pass,' and to have named the book as one of
the three he would like to have written – the others being *Moby-Dick*
(1851), by Hermann Melville (1819–91), and, rather oddly, *When We Were
Very Young*, by A. A. Milne (1882–1956).[48] The novelist E. M. Forster,
when preparing his series of lectures later published as *Aspects of the Novel*
(1927), noted privately his disagreement with Woolf's 'dreary
Bloomsbury conclusion that the pot's perspective may be as satisfying as
the universe if the writer believes in a pot with sufficient intensity. I say
such a writer's a bore merely.' Crusoe was 'an English book, and only the
English could have accepted it as adult literature: comforted by the feeling that the life of adventure could be led by a man duller than themselves'. It reminded him of a 'Boy Scout manual'. *Moll Flanders*, by
contrast, he found 'a great novel of adventure'. In the lectures as
published, Forster concentrates on *Moll Flanders* as an example of the
novel's ability to portray character.

■ Moll is a character physically, with hard plump limbs that get into bed and
pick pockets. She lays no stress upon her appearance, yet she moves us
as having height and weight, as breathing and eating, and doing many of
the things that are usually missed out. [. . .] Whatever she does gives us a
slight shock – not the jolt of disillusionment, but the thrill that proceeds from
a living being. □

For Forster she also represents a test case for what novels do with character, 'our example of a novel in which a character is everything and is
given freest play'. Plot is merely perfunctory; Moll is all. But her reality

is a literary one: 'the odd thing is, that even though we take a character as natural and untheoretical as Moll, who would coincide with daily life in every detail, we should not find her there as a whole'. She is too perfectly revealed; 'she cannot be here because she belongs to a world where the secret life is visible, to a world that is not and cannot be ours', because in the real world the perfect knowledge of inner life that novels provide does not exist: everything is makeshift and imperfect. Novels compensate, and Forster suggests that the wholeness of Moll is a kind of therapeutic illusion that solaces readers for the disorders of actual human interaction.[49]

With Woolf and Forster, we are on the verge of a poetics of fiction, and the rise of academic criticism. These early readings of Defoe include more personal testimony about the reading experience than one would expect from modern criticism, but they do define, sometimes inadvertently, a number of themes: authenticity, experience, perspective; effects on readers; religious significance; moral status; form and structure; colony and empire; sexual politics; criminal behaviour. These questions have been much revisited by the formal literary criticism to which we now turn.

CHAPTER THREE

The Rise of Novel Criticism (1925–60)

DEFOE IN THE ACADEMY

By the time Joyce, Woolf and Forster were testifying to the influence of Defoe on the modernist novel, academic criticism of his fiction had already begun, in a modest way, and the first half of the twentieth century saw a large growth in studies of Defoe's technique in terms of point of view, narrative perspective, structure, verisimilitude, moral intent, and irony. Amongst the very earliest of these was a linguistic investigation into Defoe's characteristic use of certain verbal formulations, published in Sweden in 1910, which treated the book as an object of serious scientific inquiry. Lifted out of its role as a talismanic book of magic fantasy, *Robinson Crusoe* is a document in the history of the language, and looked at from this point of view, it shows some key features: very long sentences governed by a sense of continually growing thought and recollection rather than conventional grammatical ordering, vivid uses of tenses such as the historic present, free use of colloquial phrases: a prose designed to sound like an ordinary man relating his adventures, with a keen sense of the storyteller's voice.[1]

In another early book, *Studies in the Narrative Method of Defoe* (1924), Arthur Secord produced the first analysis of how Defoe's 'reality effect' actually worked. Secord's title presents the writer as a fully self-conscious artist, whose 'method' is not only conscious and full of intent but worthy of analysis. Secord concentrates on the male-centred novels, with only passing glances at *Moll Flanders*. The analysis focuses very distinctly on Defoe's use of sources, in particular his familiarity with travel literature. Secord disputes a received idea that Defoe's fictions were essentially projections of his private experience, or to be understood as extensions of his own previous writing; while acknowledging some strong resemblances with works like *The Storm* (1704), he draws attention to Defoe's reading. The most obvious source for Defoe was the experience of Alexander Selkirk, a mariner born in Fife in 1676, who in 1704 was set down, after a dispute, on the main island of the Juan

Fernández group, 400 miles off the coast of Chile. He was given a set of basic tools and, indeed, a bible. Four years later he was picked up by the leader of a privateering expedition, Woodes Rogers (died 1732), and eventually returned to England. An account of him by Edward Cooke, another sailor on Rogers's expedition, appeared in *A Voyage to the South Sea, and Round the World* (1712), and Rogers's own *A Cruising Voyage Round the World* (1712; 2nd edition, 1718) also recounted the story. Another version was written by Sir Richard Steele (1672–1729) in his periodical *The Englishman* (3 December 1713). The influence of this story on Defoe's novel had been highlighted in early criticism. Secord shows that Defoe also picked up motifs, ideas and details from several other travel narratives – in particular, storms, shipwrecks, and slavery. William Dampier (1672–1729), a mariner who had been present at the marooning and rescue of Selkirk, published a series of *Voyages* between 1697 and 1709 and colonial adventurers of this kind furnished Defoe (who had himself owned ships and whose brother-in-law was a ship-builder) with information about remote countries, and other materials which (like his own hero) he then refashioned and re-imagined. Dampier is rich in descriptions of the islands and peoples of the north-east coast of South America, the supposed area of Crusoe's island; he supplies details of parrots and other birds that Defoe imagines there. Several of the types of food and utensils that Crusoe finds or makes are present in Dampier.[2]

Secord considers a wide range of possible sources for the 'island' idea, disposing of most of them as simply too brief to have influenced Defoe much. He argues that Defoe's most useful source was Robert Knox's *Historical Relation of Ceylon* (1681), in which Captain Knox gave a detailed account of his 19 years as a captive on what is now Sri Lanka. There was also a manuscript of additional material which Defoe may have known. Knox was not alone, but was isolated all the same, and a good deal of Crusoe's sense of imprisonment, his gradual adaptation to his environment, and practical spirit, can be traced to the model of Knox. The making of planks and the taming of goats, for example, is in Knox but not in Selkirk, and Knox provides a source for some of the cultural observations on indigenous peoples and religious practices that feature in *Robinson Crusoe*. Knox was also an autobiographer of a kind familiar to us from the novel, whereas Selkirk did not write his own story, and Secord draws attention to the fact that Knox, like Crusoe, went to sea against his father's inclinations.

After Secord the most significant academic critics were James Sutherland and John Robert Moore. The latter is now forever associated with a somewhat over-enthusiastic attempt to revisit the canon of Defoe's writings and assign to him anything that could with any show of plausibility be thought to be his.[3] Moore's checklist was the culminating point of the bibliographical recoveries instituted by Chalmers in the eighteenth century and by Lee in the nineteenth, and the 550 items listed marked the high water mark of Defoe's literary empire. Since then, scepticism about the list has increased steadily, and the work of P. N. Furbank and W. R. Owens has in particular substantially refocused the Defoe canon.[4] Moore's work did, however, have the effect of raising the stakes in academic writing about Defoe, and he brought to the surface a large body of contextual and historical material that bore on Defoe's moments of writing. His biography of Defoe, published in 1958, was very detailed in such matters, though it had less to say about the fictions: we learn that *Robinson Crusoe* draws on Defoe's own experiences: swimming, boating, baking clay (in the brick and tile business), rivalry with his father, and so on. Moore also finds a lot of links with Defoe's earlier writings, such as the *Family Instructor*.[5]

Sutherland's work was more in the main tradition of criticism of Defoe, and has in many respects lasted better. In 1937 he published a well researched and still very readable critical biography which picked up a number of the threads of Victorian estimations of Defoe alongside more modern factual research.[6] Sutherland's views on the novels start from an appreciation of Defoe's realism, his embroidering on experience and fact rather than fantasy or invention. But he is also concerned to analyse the effects of the fiction on the reader: to read *Robinson Crusoe* 'is in some sense to retrace the history of the human race; it is certainly to look again with the unspoilt eyes of childhood on many things that one had long since ceased to notice at all'. We experience 'the human delight in making things – strongest in the child or the artist, but present in varying degrees in the minds of most normal adults. . . . The reader experiences another sort of delight in watching how Crusoe succeeds in "making things do".' We delight with Crusoe in his discoveries and share his pride in the built environment. The island presents a kind of child-friendly safe zone for the working out of the kind of darker emotions explored more directly in *Moll Flanders*:

■ Stealing on Crusoe's island is impossible, but the satisfactory emotions of successful theft are at least suggested by his looting of the wreck. There can be no cheating of one's fellows upon an island inhabited by one man; but that emotion, too, is gratified to some extent by Crusoe's getting the better of nature, his outwitting of the birds that are eating his corn, his taming of the goats, and all the little stratagems by which he overcame the hostility of natural forces.[7] □

Sutherland also sees *Moll Flanders* as a psychologically subtle case study, with finely-graded emotions, and the novel as a kind of imitative investigative journalism with unpredictable moral results: Moll has a professional path to follow, and Defoe interests himself in her careful market negoti-ations. He argues that Defoe approves intellectually of rogues who live by their wits even if he disapproves of them morally. Moreover, 'the disarm-ing frankness of Moll Flanders disinfects her doings of all obscenity'. Defoe, in short, 'has proved his humanity. He has shown beyond all possi-ble doubt the kindliness and tolerance that lay behind the stiff front of his nonconformity. [. . .] He took a quite un-puritanical delight in expe-rience for its own sake.'[8]

Sutherland followed his critical biography with a very short but very lively overview of Defoe for the British Council. Sutherland draws atten-tion to Defoe's ability to give us scenes of middle-class domesticity and gentility normally associated with the later fictions of Samuel Richardson: 'Defoe is not always given enough credit for his close obser-vation of contemporary manners and his lively interest in human behav-iour.' Sutherland gives us perhaps the best statement of the classic praise of Crusoe as a character:

■ The hero is matching his wits and his resolution with the forces of nature; and the energy which in a Moll Flanders is purely destructive, or at best acquisitive, is here applied to constructive ends, and to producing order and a primitive culture out of the wasteful and unprofitable profusion of nature. In the process Crusoe is building up some sort of good life, and developing all that is best in his character. Crusoe's success is due to the sturdy qual-ities in his character, to his own unaided efforts, to his courage and patience, to his practical skill and his intelligent persistence.[9] □

In a later, book-length revision of his earlier work, Sutherland confirms his sense of the pleasures of reading *Robinson Crusoe*: 'One of the strongest impressions made upon the reader [. . .] is the sense of diffi-culty and frustration encountered by Crusoe in his attempts to create order out of disorder and comfort out of privation.' But we are also responding to a kind of make-believe, like a child's game, even to the extent of Crusoe's 'naïve and playful delight' in his own 'kingdom'. This return to basics is, however, a serious, elemental matter: Defoe has 'got down to the roots of human experience', to 'the permanent feelings and essential interests of the human race'. Sutherland also contends that *Robinson Crusoe* is Defoe's most emotional book: 'the intensity with which Defoe realizes the loneliness and anguish of his hero, is compati-ble with some kind of self-involvement on the part of the author in the vicissitudes and sufferings that he describes'.[10]

Moll Flanders seems to Sutherland an example of Defoe's 'unusually liberal ideas about women', and he shows how Defoe treated the economic and social position of women in his *Review* and other writings. It might

■ be considered as our first sociological novel. Defoe is interested not only in marriage and extra-matrimonial relationships, but in the effects of education or the lack of it, in the problems presented by illegitimate children, in the habits of the criminal class and the way in which one form of delinquency leads to another. He touches the life of the day at many of its sore points, and he clearly intends to draw the attention of the reader to various social problems and abuses.[11] □

This does not turn the novel into propaganda, however, for Sutherland thinks that Defoe was largely able to say what he wanted to without compromising the personality of his heroine. The inconsistency and suspect penitence that some critics discerned in the characterisation of Moll, Sutherland finds to be within reasonable psychological limits: 'a certain amount of moralizing on the sins of her sprightly youth and unregenerate middle age is in order'. Inconsistency is part of her character (which, at this point in literary history, need not be coherent in the Dickensian or modern sense). He defends her vacillations about sexual mores, parenthood, and the farming out of children to nurses, as plausible psychologically in context (Moll is in trouble, but parts with her children only reluctantly) while also allowing Defoe to 'ventilate' social problems about family life: how is a woman in this situation supposed to survive? Moreover, Sutherland follows Woolf's sense that Moll gets 'the better of her creator':

■ However little Defoe may approve of Moll's activities, his natural preference for intelligent women and his admiration of efficiency clearly affect his attitude to his errant and erring heroine, and he ends, however reluctantly, by being the first of her admirers. □

Like many other critics, Sutherland tends to speak of the central character as if she were an actual person, and a rather seductive one at that.[12]

ART OR NATURE

Sutherland's later views were expressed partly in response to a critical debate that had been taking place since his first study in 1937. *Moll Flanders* (both novel and character) had been subject to particular attack in the 1950s. Mark Schorer saw Defoe's much-lauded realism as a naïve reflection of Defoe's own experience and interests as a dissenting tradesman who had seen the inside of Newgate prison. Defoe 'is not telling us about Moll Flanders, he *is* Moll Flanders'; the novel constituted an unintended 'revelation of the mercantile mind'. Both character and author were morally impoverished; the ethical element was pious humbug, less than skin-deep. The novel had some value as an indication of the small range of options available to women of Defoe's time, but if it were stripped 'of its bland loquacity, its comic excess, its excitement' then we would have only 'the revelation of a savage life, a life that is motivated solely by economic need'.[13]

Dorothy van Ghent responded to Schorer's challenge by affirming that Defoe's novel went beyond spatial–temporal realism, which gives us a novel in which a heroine is conditioned for material living and is 'astonishingly without spiritual dimension', and that it displayed a consistent use of certain devices to create a certain kind of world, one as symbolic as Bunyan's. While material things, especially moveable goods, connote wealth and 'reality' in the novel, these are not actually vivid in texture: things are 'good' or 'fine' but not 'red' or 'small'. It is a selective, not a photographic technique; the emphasis is on status and price. Moll herself is a 'lusty, full-bodied, lively-sensed creature' but her descriptions (of sexual activity as of theft) are completely desensualised; sensuality stands in ironic contrast to the conversion of sexual acts to cash value. This kind of irony has a structural function: 'a complex system of ironies or counterstresses holds the book together as a coherent and significant work of art'; Moll's sexuality acts as a counterstress to her financial obsessions, and this defines the world of the novel. *Moll Flanders* is 'not a case history; it is a hypothesis of personality development in an acquisitive world'. Moll is (paradoxically) superbly adapted to her world even as she exhibits 'violent abnormality as a representative of the species called human' – that is, in the matter of her children, she only thinks of economic consequences. She is eminently sane in her adaptation to circumstance, but her 'subjective life is sunken nearly to a zero'. She does this also with spiritual life, turning virtue into stock. This must be irony, whichever way it is looked at, but the question of how intentional the irony is remains. Van Ghent analyses passages where Moll moralises about her crimes, as, for instance, when she muses that taking the necklace from the child will teach the parents a lesson; this is a 'burlesque of morality' to us. The fact that we continue to read the book with pleasure and wonder, rather than abhorrence, suggests that it must be a coherently ironic and artful novel, that Defoe must intend and embody an ironic distance from his heroine and her fake morality.[14]

Brian Fitzgerald argued that *Moll Flanders* is more complex and subtle than *Robinson Crusoe*, and treated its heroine to a full-scale and rather devoted character analysis:

■ Moll [. . .] so human and lovable, is a much more complicated character than the simple, open-mouthed, manly mariner of York. She is the victim both of heredity and of environment, a magnificently alive common girl, caught in the meshes of her too responsive temperament, her seducer's egoism, and the monster, the lumpish monster, of capitalist society that makes her an outcast. She is both the victim and the product of the society which disowns her. In tracing her fortunes and misfortunes Defoe delves much more deeply into the springs of human behaviour than he does in *Robinson Crusoe*, and the outcome is perhaps the most remarkable example of pure realism in literature. □

But Defoe himself was not really aware of this, because his protagonists constitute fantasy identities for Defoe's own explorations of self, free imaginings of adventure and travel: they are 'attractive, energetic persons who live by their wits, their main purpose in life being the making of a fortune, or at least the wherewithal to exist. [. . .] One and all, they are so many Daniel Defoes.'[15] There is therefore no case to answer on the question of irony.

The emotional component of the novels was defended by Benjamin Boyce. In his reading, passionate encounters in *Moll Flanders* are a little underplayed and anti-climactic by later standards; Moll's discovery that she is half-sister to one of her husbands is met with a practical question: what to do (the husband himself is actually more disturbed than Moll). She is not defeated by emotional problems. But Boyce argues that there is always present some anxiety or insecurity which is the real focus of energy and interest: all security is vulnerable to sudden disaster; the fear of Newgate, for example, comes across as real in the way that we expect emotion in novels to be real. Similarly, while agreeing with Woolf that Crusoe does not have any sunrises to react to, that he 'is not interested in the aesthetic aspects of his exotic surroundings' at all, Boyce stresses the degree of terror that Crusoe feels: his horrors may not be as developed as those of Kafka but 'they are unmistakably present'. Crusoe is always alluding in the early stages of the story to emotions that were too extreme to bear the light of recollection. The second shipwreck, the footprint, the two haunted years following that, are all 'loaded with fear'.[16]

Other articles on *Robinson Crusoe* looked for large meaning from small detail. Edwin Benjamin interpreted the geography of the island in moral terms using the typological techniques of Bible criticism, and Eric Berne produced the first Freudian reading of Crusoe's environment.[17] Berne sees Crusoe's explorations and measurements as a key to the sense of self, beginning with the immediate surroundings and moving out gradually to convert the whole island to Crusoe's vision of it. Exploration is (in this reading) a type of sublimation of primal urges ('every child is an explorer'), in this case an oral drive, though 'anal and phallic drives also come into play in proper sequence'. Crusoe's 'insular fear and anxiety' relating to cannibals and the devil are projections of guilt about exploration and exploitation: if you eat, you are likely to be eaten. Crusoe is a case history, exhibiting 'familiar clinical variations', though in this case 'the anal and phallic elements are minimal, highly obscure, and indecisively expressed'. Crusoe, in short, is diagnosed: 'because of his oral fixation and the accompanying intense anxiety, [he] never did explore the whole extent of his island effectively'. The challenge of this reading of the book was not immediately taken up.

THE NOVEL RISES

In the late 1950s three books appeared which placed Defoe's fictions in the context of a history of the novel. E. M. W. Tillyard defended *Robinson Crusoe* as a novel of richly suggestive character, plotting and incident; it was the best constructed and deepest of Defoe's fictions, offering a 'steady seriousness' and intensity which linked Crusoe with the high virtues of literary epic.[18] A. D. McKillop claimed Defoe for one of the 'early masters of English fiction', even though he found him lacking in the psychological richness of later writers. McKillop's account of *Robinson Crusoe* finds the island situation actually slightly abnormal for Defoe's method:

■ The way of life on the island establishes a dominant pattern seldom to be found in Defoe. The situation makes Defoe substitute a tighter analysis of a situation for the loose travel and adventure formula, enables him to attain the range and variety of adventure within the compass of the strictly relevant. □

McKillop finds *Moll Flanders* more typical, or more successful as literature, for here,

■ Defoe combines his conception of character as brought out by immediate practical problems, his sense of social and economic reality, his selective and vivid presentation of detail significant for action, his application of a bourgeois success philosophy in a dangerous hinterland beyond the limits of respectability. Moll is a victim of society, showing the workings of economic and social compulsion; an unfortunate adventuress, showing the workings of chance and random circumstance; a cool exponent of self-interest, systematically trying to figure profit and loss in business, love, and crime. □

Moll Flanders represents

■ Defoe's closest approach to deliberate realism according to a program, and it is this anticipation of the hard-boiled novelist of later times that gives the story its present high position. The reduction of the entire record to acquisition and calculation and the spiritual impoverishment implied in the practical and moral warnings that echo through the story operate on us with the effect of a marvellously constructed piece of art – no one could be so monolithic by accident.[19] □

This was written in 1956, a year before the much more iconoclastic readings of Ian Watt's *The Rise of the Novel*, which to some extent over-shadowed McKillop's literary approach. Watt had opened the scoring in 1951 with a substantial article on the mythic resonances of *Robinson Crusoe*. Watt starts from Woolf's position that *Robinson Crusoe* seems less like a novel in the modern sense than a foundational cultural myth, along the lines of the Faust legend, Don Quixote or Don Juan. He finds that it has been adopted culturally as the exemplar of three idealistic trends: 'Back to Nature', 'The Dignity of Labour', and 'Economic Man'.[20] Rousseau is cited as the advocate of Crusoe as a primitivist return to nature, a pre-economic state which involves the stripping away of all socially learned prejudice and the relearning of basic self-sufficiency. To read the book in this way necessitates some large blinkers, since Crusoe regards the idyll as a disaster that he cannot wait to escape, and only comes to terms with it by viewing it 'with the calculating gaze of a colonial capitalist [. . .] he glows [. . .] not with noble savagery, but purposive possession'. The jungle cannot be left as it is: it 'must succumb to the irresistible teleology of capitalism'. What Émile will read is not actually Defoe's novel but a kind of purified adaptation of it.

Watt's second category, dignity of labour, which he sees as 'the central creed of the religion of capitalism', found its apotheosis in Victorian sanctification of self-help. Crusoe's story can be read as a prescription for 'the therapy of work'; man is redeemable only through 'untiring labour'. Work is life, on the island; the arrival of Friday does not lessen labour but increases production. To regard Crusoe in this light as some sort of heroic Everyman is, however, once again to read very partially, since Crusoe's real identity is that of capitalist: he owns the means of production, in the shape of the toolkit rescued from the wreck (a detail sometimes omitted from nineteenth-century adaptations in order to enhance the purity of Crusoe's heroism). He is not reduced to a 'state of nature' at all, but handed a freehold island from which all economic competitors have been conveniently banished. What Crusoe really likes to do is make money out of other people, as in the Brazil plantation which just goes on earning in his absence – an absence caused by his desire to get slaves to increase production without his own labour.

The third category, 'economic man', starts from Marx's demolition of the use of Crusoe by classical economists as the foundation of an economic theory of individual labour, and goes on to link Crusoe with other aspects of Marxist theory, notably the 'process of alienation by which capitalism tends to convert man's relationships with his fellows, and even with his own self, into commodities to be manipulated'. It is as if Defoe had unwittingly provided a subversive element of detraction to the hero of modern capitalism. Watt points out that Crusoe treats Xury and Friday more or less purely in terms of the cash nexus, that he has little sense of family loyalty and apparently no feeling for women at all, getting himself married and widowed in the space of half a sentence. In the *Farther Adventures*, wives are provided, in 'a parcel', for his colonists, who are wise if they choose partners according to their ability to work, and stupid if they don't. Crusoe's essay on 'solitude' in the *Serious Reflections* is for Watt a kind of confession of the fully alienated (or 'islanded') capitalist man.

Watt returned to these themes, with a much richer historical context and a wider range of fiction, in *The Rise of the Novel* (1957), perhaps one of the most influential interpretations of the place of the early eighteenth-century novel in literary history. Despite the great many differences between the fictions of the three main protagonists, and the absence of clear definitions at the time, Watt argued that 'the novel' does emerge as a clear formal category between (though not before) 1719, the date of *Robinson Crusoe*, and 1749, the date of Fielding's *Tom Jones*. Moreover, the arrival of three major novelists within a generation is seen by Watt as no accident but rather the product of cultural and social shifts. In the first place, Watt argues that the novel is defined by its commitment to 'realism', as against the free adventuring of aristocratic romance or the low humour of the picaresque. Realism is a vexed category, and Watt tries to provide a kind of poetics of novelistic realism in terms less of the class or type of experience portrayed by the novel than of its manner of delivery.

In his first chapter, Watt links the realism of the early novel to changes in philosophical method, in particular the new scientific commitment to the test of empirical experience: nothing is taken on trust, everything is subjected to sceptical, rational questioning. The novel broke with conventional literary plots by refusing to adapt experience to traditional prejudice or practice, and by privileging the unique subjective experience of an individual. The test of truth is the individual's direct knowledge. The novel's formal looseness (compared with epic, or ode) is a price paid for this nuanced, evolving truth. Defoe is the first major writer who does not take his plots from available mythology or legend and does not impose an obvious structure on them: events flow in accordance with the unfolding circumstances of a life, not from a preconceived doctrine.

Watt links the primacy of individual consciousness with further philosophical debate and questioning about the nature of selfhood, as exemplified in the work of empiricist philosophers in Britain such as John Locke. Consciousness became the main subject of philosophy. Fiction gave its protagonists proper, realistic names for the first time: 'Robinson Crusoe' is more individually 'realistic' than the type-names of contemporary comedy: Belmour, Horner, Blunt. The Lockean sense that personal identity was essentially a matter of consciousness and memory extended through time promoted autobiographical narrative as a model of selfhood. The philosophy of Locke, and the physics of Sir Isaac

Newton (1642–1727), also required dimensions of particularised, minutely measured space and time, which the novel, in Defoe's hands, now provided, in contradistinction to the idealised or non-existent landscapes and vague time-schemes of romance. Because selfhood is a matter of accretion and accumulation, there is a sense that events are causally associated, like links in an explanatory chain, which again fits Defoe's model of succession rather than the a-historical and coincidence-led reversals of romance. Defoe's characters are strongly associated with particular locations and physical surroundings, both indoors and out, and the presentation of specific physical objects through the sense of touch is a further 'realistic' hold on character and setting. Watt also sees Defoe's language as relatively plain and non-figurative: consciously anti-literary, a medium rather than part of what is being presented. This is in accordance with Lockean requirements also; immediacy and directness of experience are privileged over 'style'.

Watt's second chapter is devoted to the social changes, especially in the reading public, which lie behind these intellectual movements. Having established that literacy was not greatly extended at the bottom of the social scale, and that opportunities for private reading were at that level very limited, Watt provides some evidence that a new middle-class readership, consisting of professionals, administrators, shopkeepers and merchants, together with their wives, apprentices and servants, emerged to a significant degree in the period leading up to Defoe's novels and began to have an effect on the kind of literature that was published. Literacy was quite simply a pre-requisite for business but not for manual labour. Aristocratic forms in poetry and romance, partly sponsored in the seventeenth century by direct patronage from the court or nobility, gave way to more straightforwardly commercial kinds of publication, in particular realistic, practical, secular fiction, accessible to an audience without university education or classical background. This class was also able to afford books, a relatively expensive commodity; *Robinson Crusoe* cost five shillings on first publication, perhaps half of a labourer's weekly wage. Additionally, there appears to have been more leisure for reading among middle- and upper-class women, and novels were (according to several anxious observers of the time) more to their taste than epic poetry.

Defoe, and to a lesser extent Richardson, fitted this new market very well. They were both businessmen first and novelists second; they were capable of writing very copious prose relatively quickly; they were suspicious of elite literary forms and aristocratic values; neither attended university. Defoe is absolutely Watt's key case, however, partly because of a further shift in taste, from religious to secular reading, though this was masked by the continuing enormous output of theological work and the complex relation to religion within commercial classes. Watt argues that 'the outlook of the trading class [. . .] was much influenced by the economic individualism and somewhat secularized puritanism which finds expression in the novels of Defoe'.[21] Watt works out this formulation in much greater detail in his chapter on *Robinson Crusoe*, where two linked principles predominate: the rise of economic individualism, based on industrial specialisation, and the spread of Puritan versions of Protestantism.

Watt sees the emergence of the middle classes as stimulating a much greater emphasis on the autonomy of the individual at the expense of rigid social hierarchies and fixed identities within them. Locke, in his political guise, also founds the social order on the indefeasible nature of individual rights, including the property in one's own labour; this matches the psychological individualism upon which Locke founds consciousness and selfhood. Crusoe, like all Defoe's heroes, is for Watt a virtually pure embodiment of economic individualism, pursuing personal profit methodically and single-mindedly. Adventure and circumstance are ordered by a book-keeping mentality of profit and loss. Relationships between people tend to be contractual and establish hierarchies of power rather than community (as when Crusoe's island is colonised). The primacy of economic motives depresses the value of other modes of feeling, associated with family, social group, village or nation: Crusoe makes himself utterly free of all such arrangements, rendering himself an 'island man' in every possible way. He does little that does not contribute directly to his personal prosperity: the island is simply the mythic embodiment of total economic self-absorption, unrestrained by law, taxation or contract. Women feature as part of the economic structure of his colony, and otherwise not at all. Crusoe is lonely, but his real needs are met by Friday, in effect a devoted labourer without hire and without 'romance'. Friday replaces Xury, whom Crusoe has more or less arbitrarily sold, and whom he misses only when he needs extra labour on the island.

Watt deals with the problem that Crusoe is effectively removed from the normal avenues of commercial exchange by seeing his travel and exile as mythic encapsulations of the normal tendencies of economic society. He also sees Crusoe's island economy as crucial for a particular and profound effect on the reader that we have already noted. Because of the economic specialisation (the 'division of labour') and system of exchange, which renders complex products such as novels possible, readers lack direct experience of making everything themselves. There is therefore something satisfying and redemptive in watching Crusoe go back to basics and produce everything through a one-man industrial process. Not only does he really own everything, through straightforward exercise of labour, like Midas turning everything if not to gold then at least into commodity; he touches everything, and provides vicarious experiences of the craftsmanship we have lost. 'Defoe sets back the economic clock, and takes his hero to a primitive environment, where labour can be presented as varied and inspiring, and where [. . .] there is an absolute equivalence between individual effort and individual reward.'[22]

The secular emphasis of this commercial reading is complicated, of course, by the presence of a strong religious vein to his narrative: Crusoe is never free of the providential surveillance of God. But Watt argues that Crusoe's 'Original Sin' in disobeying his father (a substitute for God, importing biblical echoes of the Garden of Eden and the parable of the prodigal son) does him no harm in the end because he becomes hugely wealthy as a result; in any case, it constitutes 'the dynamic tendency of capitalism itself, whose aim is never merely to maintain the status quo, but to transform it incessantly'.[23] The gospel of work, or 'work ethic', is strongly associated with some forms of religion; individualism itself, moreover, can come from that essentially Puritan or Calvinistic form of self-examination associated with the Protestant Reformation, of the type familiar to Defoe, himself a dissenter, in the Puritan tradition, from Bunyan's spiritual autobiography *Grace Abounding* (1666). All Defoe's narratives are presented as confessional autobiographies, with self-examination and psychological scrutiny as their core. Crusoe is particularly given to examine events for their allegorical significance and underpins much of his interpretation with biblical quotation; his 'spiritual book-keeping' aligns him with God rather than family. At the same time, this model of self-examination is easily adaptable to wholly secular purposes. Watt does not see the relationship between economic and spiritual individualism as simply complementary and settled. Of the two sequels Defoe wrote, one, the *Farther Adventures*, is more or less wholly secular; the other, *Serious Reflections*, is all but completely spiritual. It can go either way, and Watt senses considerable tension between religious and economic drives in the book. Crusoe's religion is nothing like so straightforwardly identifiable as Bunyan's, and Watt points out how Crusoe not only tolerates all forms of worship on his island, but also happily passes for a Catholic when needful. He does not adhere very strongly to religious form. In the end, the secular economic drive is dominant; and Defoe in this pivotal novel begins to suspend the structures of control (social, religious, political) which bound the individual in all previous literature. (His later novels would develop the process.) Crusoe's isolation ignores the actual psychological effects of solitary living reported by travellers whom Defoe had read (loss of speech, recrudescence of animal instincts, derangement) and indeed he turns it into a kind of golden opportunity for self-development. Modern readers tend to view Crusoe in terms of alienation and 'anomie' – 'a monitory image of the ultimate consequences of absolute individualism'.[24] More positively, Watt sees the novel's demolition of all existing structures of social connection as a kind of necessary prelude for the return of those things in more analytical, less unexamined ways, amongst social philosophers – and novelists.

Having established his scheme with the breakthrough novel *Robinson Crusoe*, Watt then sees *Moll Flanders* as something more like a modern, rounded novel with developed social relations. Moll is, like Crusoe, an economic individualist, whose criminality is another version of the assumption that personal prosperity is the highest or most essential form of value. She has the same energy, the same 'inarticulate stoicism', the same survival instinct, the same Teflon-coated lack of rootedness: everything happens to her but 'nothing leaves scars'. Some of her husbands are not even named, just given a number; children are farmed out, abandoned, forgotten; 'the criminal individualism which Moll pursues in her later days tends to minimize the importance of personal relationships', in the same way that Crusoe's pursuit of economic dominance does, though Moll is very much more 'in' society than Crusoe is. She pursues economic success in difficult circumstances, substituting the availability of her body for Crusoe's manual labour, and graduating to straightforward theft when marriage and mistressing no longer present themselves as options.[25] She is representative of a historical type, a developed criminal class or underworld attendant on the unequal distribution of prosperity in London, of a kind Defoe dealt with in his social journalism, and the state dealt with through capital punishment and transportation – the latter a very obvious conversion of criminal impulse into economic property since the transported criminals worked on colonial plantations.

The 'reality effect' of detail and object is as convincing as in *Robinson Crusoe*, but *Moll Flanders* is the more troubling novel in Watt's reading, and he devotes considerable time to close scrutiny of particular passages. There are plot inconsistencies and a surprising number of loose ends; Defoe paid 'little attention to the internal consistency of his story'. He appears to have worked rapidly, without revision, and without much of an overall scheme, though Watt does block out the main sections of the narrative, and allows that it does fall into a crude architectural form with 'a fairly neat conclusion'. It has, in fact, 'a degree of structural coherence which makes it unique among Defoe's novels', though nothing like the expertly conscious design that Woolf finds in his fiction. Nonetheless, even where narrative closure is easy and obvious, Defoe seems to prefer to leave things hanging, or to remind readers of the presence of the inconsequential or confusing detail. 'Defoe flouts the orderliness of literature to demonstrate his total devotion to the disorderliness of life.'[26] But Watt finds that Defoe does not handle different modes of presentation well: the episodes are starkly real, the moral reflections rather flat. Language is plain, in accordance with the movement against figurative language sponsored by philosophers such as Locke, and its repetitions, tangents, parentheses and occasional lack of grammatical connection do suggest a mind recalling a past event vividly but from the perspective of a reformed old age. But the inconsistencies of detail, and even more, of narrative perspective, pose considerable problems of moral judgement for the attentive reader. There is no external voice through which to gain any perspective on Moll's self-analysis, beyond the edgy and ambivalent preface (which itself establishes the story as an 'edited' version of Moll's original papers, but does not specify what form the editing has taken). We cannot determine whether some of her inconsistencies of utterance are conscious indications on Defoe's part that her narrative is to be viewed sceptically, or simply authorial forgetfulness. Her version of Crusoe's dominance is the apparent devotion everyone around her feels. 'Everyone seems to exist only for her, and no one seems to resent it': is this delusion on her part, or simply a sign of her inner worth?[27] How does Moll remain so completely untainted by her criminal milieu?

'Defoe does not so much portray his heroine's character as assume its reality in every action.' Watt thinks that Moll is only superficially feminine and that in fact she is really very similar to that bustling entrepreneur and apologist, Daniel Defoe. In her obsession with her 'stock' and with middle-class respectability, in her 'restless, amoral, and strenuous individualism', she resembles both Crusoe and Defoe himself.[28] Essentially, Defoe falls victim to the trap of first-person narration: his 'identification with Moll Flanders was so complete that, despite a few feminine traits, he created a personality that was in essence his own'. As a consequence, he 'cannot bear to let Moll Flanders come on evil days'; she must win out, like a fantasy businesswoman. Above all, this places some big question marks against her repentance. Forster had struggled with this in *Aspects of the Novel*, wondering in his notes how it was that Defoe/Moll seemed to manage to be 'ribald and pious with equal sincerity'. In the published lecture he asserted firmly that 'Her penitence is sincere, and only a superficial judge will condemn her as a hypocrite,' but most modern readers have found troubling the fact that Moll gets away with more or less everything in the end and does not really repent until under sentence of death.[29] Watt states the case clearly: 'Moll's penitent prosperity [. . .] is based on her criminal career, and the sincerity of her reformation is never put to the acid test of sacrificing material for moral good. The plot, in fact, flatly contradicts Defoe's purported moral theme.' There is no 'real psychological change' and penitential Moll reads very much like criminal Moll, only more economically successful.[30]

Because only Moll tells the story, she has to be both central actor, reformed narrator, and editorial mouthpiece, and (Watt argues) there was no available narrative technique for accomplishing this mixture successfully. We often cannot tell whether a moral reflection is supposed to have been made at the time of the act (whether theft or bigamy), or whether it is being made 'now' as part of the retrospective narration, or whether it is being imposed covertly by Defoe. The didactic element is radically unstable. Since formal realism is 'ethically neutral', Defoe is left with the problem of 'how to impose a coherent moral structure on narrative without detracting from its air of literal authenticity'. The problem is not solved by adducing the concept of irony, that is, a defined and visible distance between Moll and Defoe; for Watt, Defoe is more or less incapable of retaining that kind of control. The famous 'money' moment from *Robinson Crusoe*, which Coleridge cites as a great example of Shakespearian irony, Watt sees as probably just accidental in the first place, and compounded by some tidier editorial punctuation in the edition Coleridge read.[31] There is dramatic irony, as when Moll has to listen to the tale of her own incestuous marriage from the mouth of someone who does not know who she is, and there is self-deprecatory irony, as when Moll relates how, as a child, she wished to be a gentlewoman without knowing what that meant. But there is no sceptical irony, for the reader to use against Moll's assertions; Defoe simply does not see the problem. When Moll kisses the ground her son has walked on, but gets up as soon as she is reminded that it is 'damp and dangerous', the 'lack of insulation between incongruous attitudes' is not meant comically as a critique of her emotions: Defoe simply has to get his heroine moving again and does not much care how he does it. When Moll steals the child's necklace and then diverts the blame onto the parents who let her out wearing it, the episode is psychologically perfectly understandable, since most criminals blame their victims, but it is not ironic: Defoe means the criticism of the parents and does not see the moral duplicity of his heroine that inevitably results. The fact that money always comforts Moll in her emotional distress seems, to modern readers guilty about such things, ironic; but Watt doubts it would seem so to Defoe: 'for Defoe and his heroine generous sentiments are good, and concealed cash reserves are good too, perhaps better; but there is no feeling that they conflict, or that one attitude undermines the other'.[32] We are to believe her penitence and her prosperity without any sense that they conflict.

In the end, the problem is historical, and what seems ironic is actually the natural product of secularisation: 'one group of apparent ironies [. . .] can be explained as products of an unresolved and largely unconscious conflict in Defoe's own outlook, a conflict which is typical of the late Puritan disengagement of economic matters from religious and moral sanctions'.[33] If there are ironies, they come from the way in which the novel was produced:

■ they are better regarded not as the achievements of an ironist, but as accidents produced by the random application of narrative authenticity to conflicts in Defoe's social and moral and religious world, accidents which unwittingly reveal to us the serious discrepancies in his system of values.[34] □

Defoe was the master of the brilliantly-imagined episode, but not of a total design which would incorporate lifelikeness with internal coherence: that had to wait for Richardson. *Moll Flanders* is 'not so much a great novel as Defoe's richest anthology'.[35]

Watt's thesis, and his particular readings, have been extremely fruitful over the last half-century of Defoe criticism. Like all grand and general theories, it is beset by problems, not least in the teleology implicit in the suggestion of the (irresistible) *rise* of the novel (that is, leading to the grand fictions of the nineteenth century). Master narratives of this kind have a tendency to play down writers who do not fit the model or who actively subvert or counter it; Watt writes as if no woman novelist had ever existed, a defect much remedied in recent years. There was a huge variety of forms available to Defoe, who could have found plenty of circumstantial, realistic detail in the picaresque tradition. Not everyone is happy with historical and sociological explanations of literary history, essentially a simplified version of Marxist literary theory.[36] Diana Spearman questioned the whole idea of the 'middle-class novel'; she pointed out that it would be unwise to set a story about economics on a desert island where there is no mechanism for exchange, and tried to reassert that *Robinson Crusoe* was fundamentally 'a story of man against nature'.[37] Some historians place the rise of the middle class much earlier; some doubt that it existed at all before the industrial revolution broke the dominance of agricultural production in the nineteenth century. 'Class' may not be necessarily a useful or accurate term for Defoe's society – though the opening pages of *Robinson Crusoe* do certainly point to a notion of professional status on some sort of scale and Defoe did analyse class structures elsewhere. In 1967 Watt responded to some of these charges in an article.[38] Scholars have continued to contest and revisit these issues in a number of ways, and we will look again at the 'rise' of fiction in Chapter 6. The response to Watt's thesis among Defoe scholars, however, was in the main a reaffirmation of the author as a conscious artist, in touch with many literary forms and modes of thought. As the next chapter will show, the 1960s and 1970s saw a great outpouring of this kind of reconstructive effort, with Watt often featuring as a negative case to be answered.

CHAPTER FOUR

The Art of Fiction (1960–75)

IRONY

Watt's main thesis and critical observations on *Robinson Crusoe* and *Moll Flanders* provided a large set of arguments to adopt, disagree with, or modify, though of course there was more to the Defoe industry of the 1960s than simply a response to Watt. One notable feature was a renewed rash of articles on *Moll Flanders*, for the most part, though not exclusively, defending it against Watt's account (and earlier critiques). There were many attempts to establish Defoe's artistry as on the level of Richardson or Fielding, rather than on the historically contingent level assigned him by Watt. Terence Martin defended the thematic unity and artistic structure of the novel. Alongside Moll's own developing psychology, Martin contended that there is a 'significant episodic pattern' which constitutes a genuine artistic structure (over which, birth in Newgate and the threat of death there hovers like an arch). The second part of the novel appears as a mirror of the sexual/economic security of the first: Moll turns to thieving when sexuality no longer produces marriage, and many of her thefts involve items to do with children: linen and other articles for babies, household items, the small girl's necklace; dressing as and lying, undetected, with a male criminal associate suggests a symbolic reversal of earlier bedroom scenes. Martin finds symmetries in the journeys to and from America, and symbols in the thefts – such as the stolen watch which she gives her recovered son, in a transforming gesture towards what she was 'really' trying to steal (lost time, gentility, and motherhood). Theft becomes 'a supplemental way of characterizing Moll's deepest motives'.[1]

Dennis Donoghue returns us to the matter of the kind of life that is represented rather than the means of representation, finding the title character and the novel as a whole short on complex feeling. 'Moll has to set aside many feelings and attitudes which she cannot afford. [. . .] Moll lives a life crowded with event and absolutely bare of feeling.' It is not that this is wrong, so much as insufficient: 'What Defoe says about life, in *Moll Flanders*, is true, as far as it goes, but the book is based upon a set of terms which ignores two-thirds of human existence; these terms cancel all aspects of human consciousness to which the analogies of trade are irrelevant. . . . As a result, the book cannot conceive of human action as genial, charitable, or selfless.'[2] It is, however, possible to defend the novel as a complex moral structure, as Howard Koonce did by reverting to the concept of ironic distance between author and creature. According to this argument, Moll is both conscious of the significance of her life and powerless to change it; she cannot live up to the honesty of her own narration. Inconsistencies in the story that is told are a realistic part of Moll's moral muddle. Koonce sees this as deliberately created, through ironic perspective.

■ On the one hand, we have a character compelled towards self-realization and able to act in a series of situations where real spiritual and moral awareness would be paralyzing. And on the other, we have that character's compulsion towards a moral and spiritual respectability which needs that awareness to be valid. It is the juxtaposition of these two forces that creates the real and sustaining conflict of the piece.[3] □

Similarly, Robert Columbus argues for the 'conscious artistry' of the book as a 'deliberate attempt and conscious attempt to unriddle the soul of Moll Flanders' by making her relish for her criminal past show through a pose of disapproval and regret.[4] Arnold Kettle finds real depth to the character and the writing that realises her. 'Moll is immoral, shallow, hypocritical, heartless, a bad woman: yet Moll is marvellous. Moll's splendour – her resilience and courage and generosity – is inseparable from her badness.' Defoe is writing the first major plebeian heroine as a kind of sociological experiment, and doing it with skill and accuracy.[5] Robert Donovan solves the problem of irony by teasing out the 'double vision' of the story, a 'consistent principle of organisation' in the handling of the heroine as both subject and object of the narration. This results not so much in a frame of irony as in a 'continuous and simultaneous awareness' of the present (telling) and retrospective (experiencing) aspects of Moll.[6] M. A. Goldberg revisits the debate on Moll's ethics by seeing the novel as a new kind of allegory, under the influence of the social theory of the philosopher Thomas Hobbes (1588–1679), by which evil is identified not with the material world, but with poverty: 'virtue does not bring about wealth; money is what opens the way to virtue'.[7]

MONEY

In 1967 Watt surveyed the 'recent critical fortunes' of the novel in the wake of his own work, in which he wove a sort of compromise position, while remaining suspicious of attempts to project modern critical values onto that of Defoe. He comments:

■ Defoe's genius as an observer, together with a narrative technique that did not force him to prejudge his material, may well have produced a masterpiece which is, unintentionally but enduringly, a comprehensive image of the ambiguous and dehumanizing conflicts into which modern civilization plunges its unhappy natives.[8] □

For Watt, the novel remains riven by 'pressing and yet finally unresolved conflicts [. . .] between spirit and matter, between salvation and ill-gotten gains, between love and egoism, between feeling and reason'. As well as the critics already mentioned above, Watt was responding to Maximillian E. Novak, one of the most prolific of all Defoe scholars. In the 1960s Novak produced a series of articles on various aspects of Defoe's fiction, including the question of irony in *Moll Flanders*. Novak's view was that irony develops in the novel once Moll can be seen to be continuing to use law-of-necessity arguments to defend her thieving when she is no longer in real need. 'When Moll blames herself for her crimes she judges herself from a standpoint of divine law and excuses herself on grounds of natural law.' Novak based his argument in part on Defoe's journalism, where he quite obviously does use irony.[9] Novak also compiled from various sources and statements a kind of set of rules for fiction by which Defoe might have been operating: while Defoe had no consistent theory in the modern sense, his position was that fiction could, if used with sufficient gravity, be a vehicle for moral ends, and for Novak this has to be taken seriously. Novak sees Defoe writing in the context of a new social myth of exploration, voyaging and opportunity, but coupling this with a basic allegorical awareness derived from biblical criticism. Rendered in journalistic detail, the fictions produce 'a sense of the social, religious, economic, political and moral implications of events which had no parallel in fiction until the nineteenth century'.[10]

Novak's most substantial contribution to the debate was, in the first instance, a major monograph designed in part to look sceptically at Watt's views on Crusoe as a capitalist by setting the novels in the context of the economic theories of Defoe's time. Thus parts of the novels, in Novak's view, 'read like fictionalized economic tracts'.[11] But Defoe was by no means the precursor of the laissez-faire theories of the economist Adam Smith (1723–90) that proponents of the capitalist Crusoe take him to be; he was much closer to the fading theory of mercantilism, a form of state direction and regulation of trading interests, including colonial exploitation, which protected the wealth of the mercantile middle classes on the grounds that this was in the national interest. Defoe, while not always maintaining a consistent position, was in favour of national management of economic concerns as the best defence against the chaotic energies of human self-interest. His culture heroes were joint-stock merchants (and, to a later and lesser extent, shopkeepers); the villains of his thinking were 'stockjobbers', people who played the money markets without produc-ing or transferring an actual product, and companies like the East India Company, whose importation of foreign cloths resulted in the export of bullion and the depression of the home textile industry. Defoe wrote a vitriolic pamphlet on these issues in 1719, the year *Crusoe* was published.

Looked at from this perspective, Crusoe is not the embodiment of free economic individualism, but rather a critique of capitalist self-advance-ment. The 'personal characteristics' with which Defoe endows him render him, certainly, a 'complex and fully developed personality', but by no means a model capitalist; he cannot hold to a steady profession, prefers pointless wandering, is economically imprudent and fails to look after his colony.[12] He works; he has ingenuity and invention; he takes control; but every time he has the makings of a regular business he abandons it. His father's warning has the 'operative power of a curse', in that Crusoe refuses the steady bourgeois life that Defoe espouses elsewhere in his writing. His 'original sin', the rejection of 'the calling' sanctioned by reli-gious as well as social theory, only relates to economic individualism in the sense that it attacks it. In Defoe's world, people really should mind their own business. The island is not a utopia of economic self-promo-tion: Crusoe is punished by having to work manually, like the original Adam (another aspect of his father's curse), and spends the majority of his time trying pathetically to re-create the gentlemanly plantation lifestyle he has abandoned for no good economic reason. 'Crusoe is continually running from his world'; he defies his family not 'in the name of free enterprise or economic freedom, but for a strangely adventurous, roman-tic, and unprofitable desire to see foreign lands'.[13]

Defoe equips his hero with three necessities: a favourable climate, a set of tools, and an inventive turn of mind. Only this combination produces results, and to that extent Crusoe is a special being, given to hard work and ingenuity, emphatically not a simple 'everyman'. John Locke in *Two Treatises on Civil Government* (1690) had argued that value was not an inherent quality in objects, that value was always produced by labour. Defoe takes things back to value as determined by labour, but also by usefulness; the famous passage about money is perfectly in keeping with the utility theory of value, since there is no exchange mechanism on the island, but also reminds us of the mercantilist system that Crusoe comes from. Crusoe does not fully articulate the connection and cannot actu-ally rid himself of would-be gentlemanly ways.

One of Locke's examples was the many different forms of labour that went into the making of a single commodity, bread. Defoe reverses economic specialisation as a kind of experiment and reminder of this labour theory. Crusoe shows how many divided and different labours lie behind familiar commodities like bread – 'the strange multitude of little Things necessary in the Providing, Producing, Curing, Dressing, Making and Finishing this one Article of Bread', from the making of a plough onwards. Yet Crusoe's labour does not fully entitle him to ownership in the way it might do under Lockean political theory, for he grants himself ownership of the island before he has expended any labour on it, as if by right of seizure; and he maintains his right when other 'subjects' arrive and a system begins to evolve. He sees himself as lord, king, governor, overseer, monarch; he demands submission and obedience by contract; he converts those he has conquered into economic subjects by leasing the island to his colonists. Crusoe's island is placed in the area where Defoe's hero Sir Walter Ralegh (1554–1618) once searched for El Dorado, and where Defoe was agitating to develop modern colonies. But as the sequel shows, Crusoe also lets it languish: 'Crusoe's failure, caused by his unwillingness to lead a productive life as the patriarch of his people, might have been intended as a reflection on England's unwillingness to treat her colonies with kindness and respect'.[14] Novak points out that most of the lands where Crusoe wanders come into Defoe's consideration elsewhere as zones for colonisation.

Novak also related *Moll Flanders*, as Defoe's first 'social issue' novel, to these questions, by discussing the novel alongside Defoe's writings on prostitution, poverty, and crime. Defoe turns the dispossessed hero common to picaresque fiction into a more rounded personality whose success or failure is connected with social systems that might be altered. He recognises the poor as a social and economic problem in other writings, against the run of mercantilist thinking, which regarded the poor as lazy and expendable. The state needs to take care of early education, as Moll declaims in one of the more obviously issue-led sections on the first page of the novel. Moll is situated in Colchester, which Defoe elsewhere praised for its ability to find work for child labourers. Novak studies Moll's career with the Colchester family in the light of Defoe's didactic work on servants, and sees the failure of her liaison with the elder brother (who will inherit the estate) as an economic problem, a kind of failure of trade. It is also a social comment on the dowry system, and the potential disasters of marrying for money and position. *Moll Flanders* also has much to say about the punitive bankruptcy laws: Defoe takes the opportunity to deliver some heartfelt views about business insecurity and imprisonment for debt. Moll and her husband are driven into fraud by the impossible conditions placed on those in economic trouble: necessity generates crime because the property is moved to the Mint, an area safe from debt collectors, before the creditors get wind of Moll's husband's financial difficulties.

The discovery that Moll has married her brother ruins a promising business venture in Virginia. Moll saves and invests what she can from the mistress episode, and learns to hang on to money: the fraudulent marriage to Jemy, where both parties are under the impression that the other is rich, constitutes a new economic failure, but she retains a portion of her money whereas he shares all he has. Her bank clerk husband seems secure but fails and dies through bankruptcy. Moll's flotation of herself as mistress or prostitute is for Defoe a matter of pure economics, rather than inherent vice: he endorses survival at whatever cost, even if it means cheating or thieving. As a thief, Moll needs a network, and has to be trained in what can be pawned and what cannot. The 'Governess', with her multiple roles, shadows Moll as a kind of possible semi-legitimate or at least stable version of a businesswoman, managing her at each stage of her profession. That Defoe can salute with sympathy the courage and ingenuity, even in illegal forms, that ensure survival rather than despair indicates that these things are matters of economic/social concern; Defoe sees that the line between pirate and privateer is often very blurred. Out of the wreckage of thieving come renewed possibilities for economic advantage in the New World, in the penal colony of Virginia. Here indeed Moll and her husband (who initially prefers the economic prospects of Ireland) do well enough to retire in the manner of colonial landowners, because they apply themselves with diligence and acumen – and because Moll arrives with money and tools, a kind of secularised forethought in answer to Crusoe's desperate salvage job. Unlike Crusoe, they add to England's prosperity as well as their own, for colonies created new markets, employed the poor, and improved the navy; Novak argues that this is more heroic in Defoe's eyes than Crusoe's elemental self-rescue.

The other aspect of Defoe's work which Novak explored in the early 1960s was 'natural law'. In an article published in 1961, Novak saw *Robinson Crusoe* as a kind of thought experiment about pre-civil society. Crusoe is 'always afraid, always cautious'; fear is the 'dominant passion of a man in Crusoe's condition'.[15] In another monograph, *Defoe and the Nature of Man* (1963), Novak revisited this state as a reflection of problems and dilemmas in contemporary philosophy and social theory, especially the codification of natural law by seventeenth-century lawyers and thinkers such as Hugo Grotius (1583–1645) and Samuel von Pufendorf (1632–94) into 'a complete code of behaviour, a code based on a universal reason with its origins in human nature and God'. Novak contends that questions relating to the moral nature of Defoe's protagonists need to be referred to the standards of natural law, which upheld 'the individual's rights of self-defence and self-preservation', making it 'an explosive political and moral doctrine'.[16]

Crusoe's island shows what man might be like when stripped of the normal securities of civilisation. Society was contracted for mutual defence, because the alternative was the Hobbesian nightmare state of perpetual brutish warfare. Crusoe's crude early reactions (fear, despair, hunger, thirst, fatigue), his subsequent doubts and his pervasive obsession with self-defence are in exact keeping with the state of natural man as described by Pufendorf and other theorists. This is why the tools are crucial: without them, Crusoe could do nothing except tear and scratch; with them, he can attempt to re-create civilisation around him. Isolation was not regarded as a panacea for ills of all kinds but a curse, liable to degrade the human into the savage. The coming of Friday returns Crusoe to a model of social interaction – albeit one based on dominance. Similarly, Novak argues that while Defoe occasionally used the innocence of non-western societies as a satiric stick with which to beat morally corrupt Europeans, he had very little time for the sentimental ideal of the noble savage, which was already becoming familiar from the writings of the playwright and novelist Aphra Behn (1640–89). 'Unlike Crusoe, Friday has almost all the virtues: gratitude, honesty, and courage. He is the perfect natural man. But he abandons the state of nature for the advantages of civilisation.'[17]

Novak sees Defoe as holding to a natural principle of self-preservation beyond all social forms. Defoe 'did not believe that anyone could resist using all his efforts to save his own life', whatever the consequences. Cannibalism was a violation of the laws of nature for the savages, since it does not correspond with hunger; but it could be conceived as a natural act in cases of extreme necessity. Similarly, theft is never justified but it is understandable in cases of dire need, a theme Defoe shared with several seventeenth-century commentators; so too was prostitution, and here Defoe was unusually broad-minded. Moll's thievery gets out of hand, since it persists beyond the immediate occasion of need; but her whoredom is always a bit half-hearted and secondary to the business of securing a stable economic partnership. Moll's marriages are often adulterous or bigamous, because positive law does not allow for the situations in which she finds herself; natural law suggests that couples can dissolve and remake their unions in accordance with need. Moll is an affectionate enough mother when not in need; when in need, she preserves herself first, in accordance with natural law. Defoe's novels offer a critique of a society which 'failed to provide for the poor, drove them to crime, and then hanged them'. What they are punished for are 'breaches of morality' only, not 'crimes committed in accordance with the laws of nature.'[18]

RELIGIOUS CALLINGS

Novak's work analysed Defoe's novels as explorations of social matters. He was less concerned with the religious aspects of the fiction, as foregrounded, sceptically, by Watt. Other commentators rose to this challenge. William Halewood argued that Crusoe's incessant religious reflections are a marker of how imperfect his religious life actually is, an ongoing 'Puritan drama of the soul', full of shortcomings and backslidings, but as a piece of fictional characterisation 'certainly the deliberate achievement of a novelist who knew what he was about'. Crusoe emerges from biblical myths like the story of Jonah to find himself 'divided between earth and heaven, between accumulation and renunciation, action and contemplation'. He is aware of the disparities between his theology and his secular behaviour, and this is shown by such gestures as the quiet pocketing of money immediately after denouncing it as useless.[19]

George Starr sought a unifying principle in the artistry of the novels as a whole, not just in the brilliance of particular episodes, and he finds this in the modelling of selfhood on the autobiographical model of English Protestantism. This stressed the individual's relation with God, the necessity of self-examination for signs of grace or of providential warning, and life structured as a series of events leading to conversion. The best known example of specifically dissenting spiritual autobiography is John Bunyan's *Grace Abounding to the Chief of Sinners* (1666); and its fictional offspring, *Pilgrim's Progress* (1678) and *The Life and Death of Mr Badman* (1680), have often been linked to the development of the novel form. But Starr's investigations delve much deeper into the theological framework of conversion narratives, and show how widespread the practice of 'spiritual book-keeping', in diaries and published narratives, had become. Regular self-scrutiny, often in the form of diary-keeping or journals, influences the novel form because it offers a sense of overall strategy and meaning to life. Narratives were published to encourage others in their struggles for spiritual advancement, 'the didactic growing out of the autodidactic'. The business of everyday life became not a random series of unrelated events but an unfolding pattern; material objects signified a spiritual message. These narratives often involve 'a climax of physical or mental agony and an overpowering sense of helplessness or abandonment immediately before conversion', because ultimately conversion is God's gift of grace, not the work of human endeavour alone. They also lend themselves to metaphor, since metaphor elevates the common object or experience to something transcendent and significant; Starr notes that shipwreck was in some ways the default metaphor for being 'cast away' by God, with obvious implications for *Robinson Crusoe*. Starr also provides a chapter, 'The Transition to Fiction', which gives an account of a book from 1708 called *An Account of Some Remarkable Passages in the Life of a Private Gentleman*, which may or may not be fictional, and may or may not have been a source for Defoe: the point is that it represents 'an intermediate stage' in the transition from obviously genuine memoirs to obviously fictional ones. Counterparts for Crusoe's sense of sin, his mental torments, his identification as the 'prodigal son', his afflicted life as a mariner, his journal and his self-questioning, can all be found in this earlier text. Starr contends that 'the hero's vicissitudes, highly individual and complex as they appear to be, actually follow a conventional and regular pattern of spiritual evolution. [. . .] By leading his hero through a series of conventionally meaningful actions, [Defoe] fuses a great deal of interpretation and comment into the narrative itself.'[20]

Crusoe labels his running away to sea, against the express wishes of his father, as his 'original sin' and the narrative is overtly concerned with the placing of moral issues on a theological scale. Crusoe represents unregenerate 'natural' man, his rebelliousness a sign of resistance to God, his 'prodigal' rejection of his father's domestic line an example of 'radical perversity and impiety'. The sin is aggravated by repetition; storms warn him to go home, other father figures (fellow mariners) repeat the warning; every new voyage offers him further chances to repent and go home, and he rejects them all. His bodily journeying is 'a graphic representation of erring spiritually'.[21] His spiritual condition is represented in concrete and realistic terms, but the events are founded on essentially biblical metaphors and parables (such as the story of the prodigal son); this is less a story of individual psychology than a template for the universal narrative of sin and redemption. God saves Crusoe from the final shipwreck partly to show him yet again that he is chosen, and partly to corner him, to force him to reflect on the meaning of his life. He cannot run from the island. Various events – notably the accidental/providential crop of barley, and the terrifying earthquake – offer themselves for both secular and spiritual interpretation. Crusoe must learn to see the events of his life in terms of providence's plan for him. Crusoe notes dates and seasons in a secular, practical way; only after his conversion does he decode the 'strange concurrence' of significant dates in his story.

The conversion is aligned, as often in straightforward spiritual narratives, with acute illness, the nadir of his resistance to God. The warning dream is a communication, psychologically plausible but also unanswerably direct. 'Crusoe's malady is another striking instance of Defoe's ability to exploit fully the narrative possibilities of commonplace events, and at the same time to avail himself of their conventional spiritual significance.'[22] In his weakness, Crusoe acknowledges God's power, and thus makes himself available for divine relief. Rummaging for tobacco, he finds a copy of the Bible, and opens it at the words 'Call upon me in the day of trouble, and I will deliver thee, and thou shalt glorify me' (from Psalm 50). Further divinations of this kind follow, and Crusoe progresses through a discipline of prayerful thanks, to reap the rewards promised by God. It is not instantaneous; practical living remains to be done; hazards remain, and spiritual conviction does not render him immune from fear. But Crusoe feels himself strengthened by God in all future encounters, an exemplary lesson in fortitude. Work is conditioned by prayer, not rebellious will. He learns to listen to inner promptings and mysterious voices, which several times keep him out of trouble, especially once other people are found on the island. He becomes the agent of providence in the reclamation of other souls, not least Friday, whom he instructs in 'true' religion, at the same time teaching himself more than he knew.

Thus, for Starr, the apparently secular and psychological aspects of the book are all subordinated to a divine order, which clears away many of the accidental ironies and contradictions noted by Watt. Crusoe's conversion can be simply summarised thus: 'In seeking to be a law unto himself, he had lost the power that was properly his; in surrendering to the sovereignty of Providence, he gains extraordinary powers.' 'Sinful independence' brings enslavement, literal and metaphorical; 'virtuous dependence' produces self-mastery, which has its effective counterpart in the political mastery over Friday, his tribal relatives, and the European colonists to whom he is the 'governor'.[23]

Starr also reads *Moll Flanders* in the light of these models of religious introspection and spiritual self-scrutiny, finding that apparent ironies and contradictions can be explained by reference to 'a traditional conception of the sinner's progress, which Moll's portrayal largely embodies'.[24] Spiritual autobiography looks for a higher coherence within the contingencies of everyday life. The novel as it developed after Defoe would look for shape and structure in plot alone, but Defoe was still using an inherited pattern which privileged the stages of spiritual development over the loose ends of outward action. In *Moll Flanders*, 'the chronological sequence of events is halting and abrupt'; but, Starr proposes, there is an 'underlying continuity' in the way the events contribute to a pattern of increasing sin and eventual conversion. Inside the outer narrative, or 'administrative' business of plotting, there lies a core of increasing significance. Moll's economy, so prominent on the page, is in one sense a mere decoy, for the real interest lies in the state of her soul. There is no real discontinuity between her sexual adventures and her criminal forays: it is just that the guilt takes on a more legal form. Like Crusoe, she allows herself some serious reflections on her conduct, and some miniature and ineffectual repentances, which Starr sees as part of the demonstrative process of hardening in sin. Her moral scruples about her transgressions are really a sign of inner habituation to crime, for they demonstrate consciousness of her sin. Her reliance on her own reason always leads to defeat and a worsening of her situation: it is a kind of self-confidence that denies the superior power of God.

Moll's eventual repentance, in the condemned hold at Newgate prison, has been a matter of much scepticism amongst critics. The death sentence, like Crusoe's serious illness, has obvious psychological plausibility as an agent of repentance, which of course results in the commutation of the sentence. But Starr argues that the 'real' repentance, through an external agent, a clergyman, who extracts her first proper confession of sin, is conspicuously contrasted with the several inadequate or incomplete repentances displayed elsewhere in the book, which come from Moll's own imperfect reason. Rescuing Moll from the gallows becomes the equivalent of saving her from damnation, and her conversion conforms 'to the classic pattern of spiritual rebirth'. Starr is emphatic that the conversion is authentic, though he admits that subsequently 'the completeness of her regeneration is called into question'.[25] *Moll Flanders* differs from *Robinson Crusoe* in that in the earlier novel, many of the events had traditional typology attached – the seed, the cross, shipwreck itself, the Jonah myth; in the later fiction the applications need to be spelled out, and there is competition from other discourses which have nothing to do with spiritual autobiography: commerce, crime, women's position within marriage and society, and straightforward narrative detail.

Starr's groundbreaking work was almost immediately supplemented by a further book on a similar theme, this time completely confined to *Robinson Crusoe*. J. Paul Hunter also focused on seventeenth-century Puritan thinking and its relation to eighteenth-century fiction but had, in his concern for the conscious artistic form and technique of fiction, a different sense of how that relation works.[26] The first half of the book is devoted to a study of the intellectual context of Defoe's fiction. Hunter disputes the importance of economic contexts, such as renewed interest in the colonisation of the area around the Orinoco, as a secular prompt for the novel, and does not find anything especially convincing in accounts of *Robinson Crusoe* which see it as a fictional travelogue. He doubts the centrality of the Selkirk source in Defoe's mind, pointing out that many other stories of the same kind were current – often recounted in narratives of miraculous preservation, told for the glory of God. The basic pattern of *Robinson Crusoe* is the Christian one of 'disobedience–punishment–repentance–deliverance'. Crusoe 'sees each event of his life in terms of the conflict between man's sinful natural propensity, which leads him into one difficulty after another, and a watchful providence, which ultimately delivers man from himself'.[27]

Hunter sets out several forms of sub-literary writing associated with the Protestant dissent in which Defoe was educated. The 'Guide' tradition offered handbooks of religious guidance based on exhortation to observe the will of God in all aspects of everyday life as a preservative against contemporary moral laxity. One such guide was written, appositely enough, by Timothy Cruso, who had been at the same school as Defoe, and who had gone on, as Defoe had not, to become a clergyman. These handbooks place strong emphasis on 'preserving the social order through loyalty to one's calling', with parents acting as a sometimes ambiguous surrogate for God. Defoe himself contributed to the tradition in books like *The Family Instructor*, which includes a narrative concerned with a son's resistance to his father's control. *Robinson Crusoe* does not borrow particular incidents from the genre, but 'concretizes in dramatic, symbolic particulars the saga of life as seen by the Puritan mind'.[28]

Hunter's second category, the 'Providence' tradition, shows that dissenters of Defoe's class were inclined to argue that God interested himself directly in the small details and events of everyone's life; dissenters were, indeed, often criticised for claiming this level of importance for their own lives. In literary terms, narratives of miraculous rescue were put forward in especially vivid detail as examples to follow and rejoice in: Selkirk's survival on Juan Fernández was celebrated in this manner in a pamphlet called *Providence Displayed* (1712). 'Sea-providences', involving critical life-and-death situations and deliverance from impossible circumstances, were particularly popular as evidence of God's protection for individuals. Again, Hunter is arguing less for the use of such narratives as source material for Crusoe than for the establishment of a context in which the strange and miraculous elements of life were interpreted according to a theological model. Defoe contributed to this kind of understanding in *The Storm*, his account of the great hurricane which swept England in 1703.

Hunter has a chapter on 'Spiritual Biography', differentiating his account from Starr's by focusing on lives that were published and thus had particular rhetorical effects embedded in them, as opposed to auto-biographies, which were more often handed about in manuscript among the faithful. (Defoe's supposed contribution here, *Memoirs of the Life [. . .] of [. . .] Daniel Williams* (1718), is one of many works once ascribed to Defoe that may actually be by someone else.) Hunter sees three dominant metaphors in Puritan writing about life in the world: spiritual warfare; the journey; and the wilderness. The two last of these are more important for *Robinson Crusoe* than the first. Puritan writers emphasise the uncertain, wandering progress of life, often comparing it to a sea voyage without control; sins and temptations are likened to rocks; irrational desires to tempests and storms. The wilderness metaphor, deriving from the exile of the Israelites from their promised land, fruitfully linked biblical history with the common trials and vexations of spirit experienced by contemporaries, deepening their significance.

When put together as a comprehensive system, these forms of writing and thinking produced allegory, a connected way of describing the randomness of life in a theological frame. Contemporary events became 'emblems of concepts, and the contemporary world itself became emblematic of the spiritual or conceptual world which was the ultimate referent for all creation, the ultimate reality'. Puritans were, however, very suspicious of anything so distracting and secular as fiction, and a good deal of theorizing went into such fictional templates as Bunyan's *Pilgrim's Progress*. Timothy Cruso argued, for instance, that Christ's stories often do not clearly demarcate themselves as either factual histories or illustrative parables. In this context, Defoe seems to have taken a small but decisive step further than Bunyan, 'by the particularizing of typical experiences in a specific time and place'; Hunter argues that his prefaces to *Robinson Crusoe* show an increasing confidence in the use of fictional case histories for religious instruction. Defoe produces the first 'symbolic novel', in which ordinary secular activity has a divine significance.[29]

In the second half of his book, Hunter studies *Robinson Crusoe* directly, seeking to define what the story adds to the context he has established. Crusoe's struggle to survive is seen against the backdrop of well-known metaphors for spiritual exile; his primitive conflicts have a cosmic and spiritual significance. The book is both individual and general: 'it [. . .] portrays, through the struggles of one man, the rebellion and punishment, repentance and deliverance, of all men, as they sojourn in a hostile world'.[30] The island section dominates this reading, for here Crusoe is forced to look inwards for meaning, rather than running away; he is also punished by the abrupt blockage of his 'original Sin', the wandering temperament. Travel stops being flight and becomes pilgrimage. Everything before the island establishes Crusoe as a weak and fallen sinner, resisting his allotted place in the world and ignorant of God's providence. He resembles Adam (restlessly uncomfortable in his protected space), Jonah (in his refusal of God's will and exemplary sea-deliverance) and the prodigal son (one of the most popular stories of repentance and conversion).

It is less a matter of introspection than retrospection, a double perspective in the narrative, which allows us to see Crusoe's blindness (as he experienced events) and insight (as he recalls them). It takes time for conversion, which alone can give Crusoe self-mastery, to work.

■ Once he has established Crusoe's pattern of perception, Defoe counts on the reader's memory of the before-and-after contrast and usually allows Crusoe to describe events in his uncomprehending state. But Defoe chooses these events with great care so that they bear an intrinsic significance which the reader may perceive even when Crusoe does not.[31] □

Thus the accident with the seeds, the storms, and the earthquake are all 'obvious' to the reader, whether Crusoe understands them or not.

Finally, God intervenes directly in the fiery vision. After the illness, in which he finally understands that his physical distress is a symbol of his spiritual malaise, Crusoe becomes contemplative, looking properly for an understanding of how God has structured his life; in this mood he is allowed to retrieve from the seaman's chest (emblem of his former life) the magical text of the Bible. Defoe dramatises Crusoe's mental development through his heightened awareness of language, for words which

Crusoe had previously used carelessly ('soul', 'deliverance', 'saved') now become meaningful to him. Defoe keeps Crusoe on the island for a further 27 years to validate his conversion – whatever one may think of Moll Flanders' repentance, Crusoe's conversion is not merely a deathbed one. He makes some immediate changes to his routine; he begins to keep the Sabbath and to pray regularly; he becomes aware of the concurrence of crucial dates and he makes regular divisions of time and seasons. He comforts himself in his allotted place and is aware that he is happier than in his previous life of sin. The island becomes more beautiful and Edenic to him; his kingship more like Adam's. He still has to work, however, to convert this Eden to its full usefulness; but agricultural method brings him manna in the wilderness. 'Emblematically, Crusoe has beaten the sword of his vision into the ploughshare of his experience.'[32]

Progress is erratic and full of backsliding; Hunter sees this as a normal part of the structure of religious deliverance, not as mercurial and inconsistent. Crusoe is not an instant saint, but a representative of the salvation available to every ordinary person. He is still learning by trial and error, as he does in his experimental labours, which include the disastrously immoveable canoe. This is in line with *Pilgrim's Progress*: you do not get to the Celestial City on a magic carpet, even after conversion. Hunter thinks there is gradual progress, even so. The footprint is a major stumbling block, instantly demolishing the spiritual labours of years. However, this too turns to triumph as Crusoe learns to convert Friday, the personal embodiment of the footprint, thus making his religion social as well as individual. His genocidal reaction to the band of cannibals also requires God's approval before it can be partially enacted; he does not simply act on his own authority. Friday, as a transformed victim of human sacrifice, also represents a kind of resurrected Xury, whom Crusoe sold for sixty pieces of eight; Friday is a 'convert who can help "deliver" Crusoe on both levels of the book's concern'.[33]

Hunter treats the 'adventure' element of the book as another sign of spiritual concerns over the life of man in a dangerous and threatening world. Crusoe is spiritually adrift, in bondage to sin, spiritually shipwrecked, as symbolised by his wandering, his enslavement, his physical shipwreck. Small details (such as the bread, raisins and water Crusoe gives Friday, which distantly connote a priestly communion) are emblems of larger patterns. Hunter defends the often-denigrated last section of the book, with the attack of the wolves, in connection with these themes. The prospect of arrival in Languedoc parallels Moses's vision of the promised land; threatened with armies of wolves, Crusoe must deliver his people to their allotted destiny, which he now does like an assured biblical leader (Joshua). 'Crusoe's final victory over bestiality culminates a pattern which had begun early in his life with encounters against a lion, a leopard, and a nameless beast on the coast of Africa'.[34]

In *Defoe and Casuistry* (1971), Starr revisited *Moll Flanders* from a different, if allied, perspective. Casuistry deals with ethical problems about which general rules (derived from theology, or statute law) either have nothing to say or appear to conflict and which therefore need to be dealt with as individual cases. This was a common part of theological debate in the late seventeenth century. A periodical produced by the bookseller and writer John Dunton (1659–1733), *The Athenian Mercury*, from 1690 to 1697, devoted its column inches to similar queries (supposedly) sent in by the public. As a Protestant dissenter, and a man very thoroughly involved in the day-to-day business of the world, Defoe had every reason to reflect on complex moral issues not specifically covered by state or church law; his own periodical, *The Review*, occasionally dealt with such matters, as did his family conduct manuals, *The Family Instructor* (1715–18) and *Religious Courtship* (1722), which had short narrative sections exploring similar problems. Starr argues:

■ Many scenes are not only based upon traditional cases of conscience, but organized internally in ways that reflect the casuistical method of posing and resolving moral dilemmas. There is a constant marshalling of motives and sanctions, choices and circumstances, precedents and hypothetical analogues; although this procedure can jeopardize any larger pattern or design a book may have, it can also supply a kind of minimal consistency between episodes, and can give them a fullness and complexity lacking in earlier fiction.[35] □

Common themes included the circumstances in which theft might be morally justified and the extent to which a wife may intervene when her husband's extravagances threaten family stability – matters of obvious concern to the plot of *Moll Flanders*. Moreover, a lot of 'cases of conscience' deal with marriages which turn out to be technically invalid for some reason: consanguinity discovered too late, unwitting incest, or the return of a former husband supposed dead. Similarly, the rights of women to remarry once abandoned with no hope of redress also feature among the cases. Moll would find herself in many of these situations. Almost all her 'marriages' are technically illegal, invalid, or at least immoral, but the focus on casuistry allows Starr to revisit these lapses and contradictions without drawing the exact moral lines popular amongst some critics. She suffers from the 'husband and no husband' paradox, just as some of her partners have a wife, and no wife (because of adultery or madness). Starr's initial point is that casuistry tends to dissolve the structure of imaginative fiction into 'a series of discrete episodes'. Life for Defoe works as a series of local crises, between which connection may not be structural: just one situation to deal with after another. Defoe avoids tightly constructed plots: 'Whatever larger thematic coherence his

books may have, individual episodes tend to be connected chronologi-
cally, not causally, and far from helping to organize them into a sustained
narrative, casuistry appears to be one of the factors responsible for their
disjointedness.'[36]

Starr now sees the structure of *Moll Flanders* as 'paratactic', allowing for
a series of cases which do not imply subordination of each other to a
dogmatic moral plan. Beyond that, however, the casuistical reflection on
choice does impart a certain consistency of character, and this is partly
achieved through effects on the reader's sympathy. So Moll, having
discovered that she is incestuously married, appears unable either to go
or to stay; but Defoe manages to arrange the options so that each is, to
an extent, realised, in a sequence which also appeals 'to our indulgence'.
Helping her friend to deceive a fortune hunter is not a digression but
preparation for Moll's own careful self-presentation within the marriage
market; it also complicates original responsibility for this kind of technique. Additionally, it allows Starr to propose a rational ordering to the
paradox that our human sympathies may be with Moll even if our moral
judgements are against her. We can separate the crime from the criminal,
or judge the crime differently according to the circumstances of the
'case'. Law is not absolute, and right and wrong may change according
to the 'total context of a given act'. Moll's narrative often works these
contexts to her advantage, and Starr contends that we are never in fact
able to hold a consistently ironic detachment from the figure Defoe
presents. Moll often represents herself as swayed by the sophistry of other
characters (especially her first seducer, who palms her off in marriage to
his younger brother after much ingenious persuasion), but Starr sees
these manoeuvres as a sort of projection of Moll's inner calculations,
embodying disagreeable arguments which she cannot directly acknowledge but acts on nonetheless. More simply, she confesses to us. She
displays a perplexity in dealing with circumstance which is essentially
'tactical, not ethical – a matter of maintaining advantage, not adhering to
a prior principle; but her economy with the truth is concentrated
towards other characters in the novel, not towards the reader'. Starr does
admit, however, that Moll's 'biggest problem with rhetoric (as with
shoplifting) is not knowing when to stop'; that is, sometimes the
manoeuvrings undo the effect of sympathy.[37] Moll tends to argue cumulatively, always adding caveats and qualifications, so that what seems to be
leading towards a coherent conclusion often actually renders the account
more ambiguous and undecided, leaving the reader unable quite to reject
the criminality of her behaviour.

Other critics have continued to refine these positions on the religious
content of (especially) *Robinson Crusoe*. Robert Ayers, for example, studies the novel broadly in terms of Crusoe's growth in spiritual knowledge
and increasing ability, or determination, to establish analogies between

details of life on the island and grand religious narratives (Crusoe's father as God, caves and grapes as symbols, Xury as a type of Christ). Robert Bell takes the religious structure of conversion narratives as a kind of foil to what Moll sees herself as doing: 'For all her immersion in the flux of real life, Moll is not yet ready to assert that quotidian experience is inherently meaningful. So she drifts into imitating the literary form which had always exonerated and given coherence to life-stories.'[38]

Some critics have found a quasi-religious construction submerged in the very texture of the novels, ready to be decoded by the patient reader. Douglas Brooks sees the structure of *Moll Flanders* as built up of echoes and repetitions, especially the incest motif in various manifestations, and the two important voyages to Virginia. Using numerological analysis in search of formal symmetries, Brooks considers *Robinson Crusoe* as a series of structural repetitions and echoes around the central image of the solitary footprint, which occurs halfway through the story and is linked to other median points (noon, halfway between locations). This suggests a hidden divine order to what may seem a shapeless text. He also notes that Crusoe's shipwreck and conversion are nine months apart, a suggestive piece of dating to say the least.[39]

SECULAR VOICES

Secular readings were also put into play, however. Michael Shinagel links the fiction with Defoe's biographical urges to graduate from merchant to gentleman, and with his many sociological writings on the subject of class.[40] The promise of gentlemanly affluence, and the miserably anxious realities of bankruptcy and debt, act as twin poles of the human condition for Defoe's heroes. The characters themselves come from more than one walk of life: middling in Crusoe's case, the very bottom in Moll's. But they share ambitions to rise in the social hierarchy through effort and invention rather than through inherited position, laying stress on character and circumstance, not rank. Shinagel broadly endorses Watt's position on economic factors, situating Crusoe's conflict with his father at the point of transition between an older Puritan sense of social stability and a newer and more aggressive spirit of capitalist venturing. Shinagel finds nothing at all ironic in Crusoe's rescue of the useless money from the wreck, pointing out that he keeps on referring to it and 'reassuring' his middle-class readers that the money is still safe and will be reclaimed at the end of the island exile. Crusoe's assumption of lordship over the island and his building of a country house are, similarly, not really whimsical but representative of proper social aspiration. Colonisation is less about exploitation and empire than about self-improvement: here were areas ripe for development and investment, and the shipwrecked could make a fresh economic start. 'Defoe faithfully presented his readers with pictures of life with which they could identify, as well as into which he himself could project his own middle-class ambitions and values.'[41]

In Moll's case, the desire to be a 'gentlewoman' is at first comically misunderstood, but the comedy is gradually replaced by a sense of valid aspiration to secure social position. Moll, in effect a foundling, marries into a gentry family, and this represents not merely a Cinderella fantasy but a fully-realised and rationalised career possibility, 'appropriate to the audience for whom Defoe writes because it panders to the dreams and aspirations of the middle- and lower-class readers'. Her situation varies and dips as economic forces take over (the extravagance and bankruptcy of the second husband come from Defoe's direct experience and are paralleled in his writings on trade habits). But even in hard times, both as a potential wife and as a criminal, Moll's disguises often represent social aspiration (rich widow, woman of quality). In Virginia, where convicts were transported to work on plantations, Moll notices 'in astonishment that a new class of gentry has grown up there, a gentry that owes its beginnings largely to Newgate prison'. Nonetheless, this is not morally straightforward, for the point about Moll's way of living is that it is never quite simply a matter of necessity: 'Moll must live "handsomely" or she feels she is not really living at all.'[42] She carries on thieving when she has enough to eat; the 'necessity' argument for crime is very relative in Moll's case. Desire for gentility can be over-reaching: Moll cannot resist the 'trappings of gentility' and falls in love with Jemy, who has cheated her, because he was at least bred a gentleman – among her last pleasures is dressing him in exactly that manner. At this point in the argument, however, Shinagel sees Defoe as aligning Moll with his own aspirations and having her pay for her mistakes through the Puritan scheme of repentance.

In a subsequent article, Shinagel was scathing about the moral hypocrisy of Moll's mothering, ascribing the union with the long-lost son to material motives and the gestures surrounding it as largely sham and hypocritical: 'During her stay on Humphry's plantation Moll's behaviour is so consistently selfish, calculating, and businesslike that her emotional displays cannot be seen as sincere and natural.'[43] Indeed, the moral and aesthetic status of *Moll Flanders* continued to be a vexed matter, with critics such as William Piper discerning amid the chaos of autobiography a loose but convincing 'structure of topics', and others, such as Lee Edwards, objecting to the effect of 'wobble' (as opposed to the more deliberate and literary 'irony') generated by the separation of moral reflection from criminal act.[44] There were 'literal' readings of the novel, studies of the symbolic nature of Moll's disguises and cross-dressing, defences of the novel's unity from the perspective of picaresque fiction.[45] Ralph Rader argues that Moll is the last of the 'true stories' type of fiction, rather than the first of the self-consciously artistic 'pseudo-factual' type, with Defoe effectively off the screen, and no consistent moral perspective possible – we just accept the character Moll and her narrative without question. Pat Rogers discusses the foregrounded inexactness of style and calculated vagueness in Moll's manner of telling.[46]

In *The Created Self* (1970), John Preston is interested in the kinds of reader that novels project and invent in order to make their fictional worlds function. He concentrates, in Defoe's case, on *Moll Flanders*, which he takes to promote a particular kind of reader-response. The novel has of course a preface identifying, somewhat ambiguously, its target readership: 'the Work is chiefly recommended to those who know how to read it'; but Preston contends that 'the story is overall an oblique criticism of a presumed reader'. Defoe wants 'to re-route our thinking about social principles and motives. Irony is for him more than a literary mode, it is a way of life and a way of living to some effect.' The books 'work' in the mind, they extend into 'praxis'. Moll herself is given to a curious kind of doublethink.

■ Moll is honest about her own dishonesty, but without any quickening of conscience. In fact she has equal facility with truth and falsehood. [. . .] The book deals with the need for honesty and also the need for deceit. It is a study of the double standards society seems to expect, in the form principally of an examination of the way people speak.[47] □

Preston sees these interactions not as a test of character ('Defoe [. . .] has no interest in character, nor even in the absence of character') but as a kind of geometric, situational display of the limits and possibilities of language use. Moll learns to use appropriate kinds of language, analyses situations in which different levels of truth and honesty conflict, and takes responsibility for the 'double-talk' which necessarily results. Thus there is 'really no question of her reforming. Her usefulness is that it is in her nature to be both truthful and dishonest.' Her life is a kind of demonstrative irony in action: effectively, a form of social satire. Moll discovers 'the social usefulness of hypocrisy': social behaviour has a kind of dark mirror in criminal business practices. Because we are in on the secret, because Moll 'compels us to accept her as a habitual liar' without making excuses, we face unusual conflicts in our own responses. 'We are, or are meant to be, uncomfortable in her presence.'[48] Like the rogues of picaresque narrative, Moll confronts us with low social estimations of our own behaviour. 'It is not that she is morally confused, but that she establishes herself in that area of confusion which society finds it expedient to tolerate [. . .] she does not allow us to evade our own confusion.' Preston quotes a line from Defoe's *Serious Reflections of Robinson Crusoe*: 'You say, you are an honest man, how do you know it?' and contends that in the end, judgement of Moll is handed over: 'It is not a story that has come to an end. It is concluded in the conscience of the listener, or reader.'[49]

As a protagonist, Crusoe has tended to present less troubling issues, at least at the level of personality. Nonetheless, the means of creating and maintaining subjectivity also came in for much scrutiny at this point in Defoe research. Homer Brown's 'The Displaced Self in the Novels of Daniel Defoe' (1971) picked up Watt's point about the non-romance names of Defoe's characters, but sees them as less a matter of realism than one of invention: all his characters tell their stories under assumed or false identities, except for Robinson Crusoe, and even his name is originally Kreutznaer. Brown sees these assumptions of false public identities partly as a strategy for dealing with fear of exposure and partly as an example of 'the way the self becomes somebody else in conversion'. The novels are 'based on a notion of radical egocentricity'. On his estate in Brazil, Crusoe is already living 'like a man cast away upon some desolate island that had nobody there but himself', and the novel makes this condition literal, just as it gives material circumstance to the overarching allegory of spiritual autobiography. But the island is not really solitary: it is peopled by fear, by signs of a threatening 'other'. Defoe does not dwell on relationships which involve a struggle between equally-matched wills: the hero is against *everyone*, subordinates and overcomes everyone, but is still paralysed by obsessive, castle-building fear (of being devoured, buried, overwhelmed). At the same time, the island is full of dark spaces, never explored, which confront Crusoe with suppressed versions of himself: footprints, the dying goat, the parrot's voice. Crusoe fears the devil but also resists God, as if submission would mean extinction; the sickness and conversion represent a symbolic death of an older, incomplete self and the rebirth of a new, authentic being – though this sacrifice and rebirth has to be repeated in an endless cycle. Brown considers, further, that the fictions themselves represent a false front for Defoe, and suggests that the splitting of self and acting of disparate identities, autonomous and not controlled or centred by an overmastering myth or symbolic process, prefigure modern theories of subjectivity.[50]

Another way of looking at subjectivity in Defoe came from George Starr, who returned to the matter of the 'realism' of Defoe's prose and found that it was not quite as outward-directed as Watt believed. Rather, it is a means for the construction of subjectivity in perception. Defoe's characters 'tell us directly rather little about themselves or their external world, but they create an illusion of both by projecting themselves upon their world in the act of perceiving it'. Character is displayed through response to the external phenomenon, whatever that is; and the phenomenon is described less 'as it is in itself' than 'as it is perceived by the narrator'. Thus the description of Friday is not an impartial, scientific analysis

as of a laboratory specimen, but a suggestively ethnocentric interpretation of Friday as an exotic being graced by European virtues; at the same
time it represents Crusoe finding a fellow human where he had expected
to find a monster. The prose is not factual or referential in the style associated with the Royal Society's experimental observations, but actively
interpretative. The world of things is rendered through a prose invested
with psychological, moral and aesthetic significance; everything is mediated rather than immediate. Ultimately (as in Brown's argument), what
the heroes seek is control. Starr speculates that Freudian criticism might
celebrate *Robinson Crusoe* as exemplifying the process of finding psychological order: 'initially torn between the anarchical demands of a powerful id and the constraints of superego, Crusoe eventually pieces together
not only an economic utopia, not only a spiritual salvation, but an ego'.
According to Starr, this order is achieved through a kind of Adamic
verbal power. Externally, wild animals are domesticated, the wilderness is
enclosed, Friday is Europeanized, and so on; internally, the hero's own
chaotic, wasteful and sinful impulses are sublimated, disciplined, or
converted into methodical, productive and virtuous industry. It is all
done, as it were, through prose style, for Crusoe and for Moll, 'the act of
recounting their lives, no less than the struggles they narrate, represents
an effort to achieve control over experience' – a precarious mastery, Starr
suggests, which involves 'insulation and repression rather than openness
and liberation', an imposition of order rather than neutral acceptance of
what is out there.[51]

Narrative voice was another aspect of work on Defoe's deployment of
subjectivity, especially insofar as the monologic autobiography might
disclose troubling 'other' voices. E. Anthony James analysed from a
rhetorical point of view Crusoe's uncertainties of description, his
agonised qualifications and corrections, his ever-lengthening sentences.
Crusoe is a habitual splitter of verbal hairs, never quite able to get beyond
descriptions that seem accurate but are actually quite fuzzy. There are
uncertainties over the status of the island as kingdom or prison and
Crusoe's condition as monarch or slave; he uses the self-confirmatory
language of authority in both political and religious forms as a means of
countering the disparities of his experience. Moll shows similar inconsistencies between action and reflection, and between the voices of
conscience and of personal expediency.[52] For some critics, the effects of
these fractured constructions are deliberately destabilising. Leo Braudy
suggests that Defoe's novels are designed to introduce an element of
uncertainty into the telling of stories in the first person. Unlike spiritual
autobiography and criminal biography, which told the life under the
guise of extinguishing it by system (conversion, or death), 'Defoe's first-
person novels may make us uneasy because the panoply of didactic same-
ness coexists with definite personalization' – there is an excess of

selfhood, beyond what is required by the form. 'Defoe's novels engage the uniqueness of human identity outside the rhythmic repetitions of public history and the causal control of a verifiable past.' There are, in addition, limitations to what the first-person narrative can tell us, as the debate on irony shows. Reaching for the comfort of recognisable form, Defoe discovers 'darker potentialities' which destabilise given patterns of living, stressing uniqueness and eccentricity. All the narrators tell their stories under some threat – of capture, extinction, discovery, incorporation by family – and they combine self-assertion with disguise and doubt. Especially after *Robinson Crusoe*, Defoe seeks out selves looking to elude control; Moll always withholds something from the most intimate companion, and we never learn her true name. 'Defoe [. . .] seems to define personal identity simultaneously as a structuring and merchandising of the self in a public form [. . .] and a final reticence about the depths of the private self. [. . .] His works deal basically with the difficulty of knowing and being yourself, amid the bankruptcy of previous psychological and autobiographical forms.'[53]

Subjectivity was thus becoming one of the major themes of work on Defoe, whether conceived as a matter of language, of novelistic form and perspective, or of psychological analysis. Two very substantial monographs, which might be said to take up these challenges, were published in 1975, and it will be appropriate to begin a new chapter with the syntheses and advances they offer.

CHAPTER FIVE

Traditions and Innovations (1975–85)

SELFHOOD

Two major accounts of the theme of selfhood in Defoe appeared in 1975. One was more concerned with psychological and aesthetic order, including the order of deliberate irony, and the other with the vicissitudes of selfhood in the world, represented in fictions which care rather less about formal matters. Both books, in fact, share a good deal of territory in terms of the placing of selfhood.[1] Everett Zimmerman's *Defoe and the Novel* looked at Defoe's long career as a manipulator of men and ideas, arguing that he was an experienced writer, who largely knew what he was doing, whose techniques got more self-conscious and confident as he went along. Zimmerman also sought to situate Defoe's appropriation of various existing literary forms, including satire as well as criminal biography and spiritual autobiography, in relation to questions of selfhood as formulated by such influential philosophers as Locke. The autobiographical format allows his characters 'to try out many explanations of their lives, using the book as their final organizing device'.[2] Locke's sense of the problem of personal identity – that we are mysteriously conscious of continuity despite bodily change – is mirrored in the desperation of Defoe's characters to maintain a stable core of identity in the face of radically threatening circumstances. Locke solves the initial problem by using memory as the seat of identity, but (as later philosophers like David Hume (1711–76) pointed out) this does not take account of the fact that memory is not continuous, and it does not completely solve the problem of personal agency and responsibility. Defoe's own life was a continued miracle of shifting allegiance and position, as many of his critics stressed. In the novels, Zimmerman contends, he seeks to contain the waywardness of self within an ethical scheme.

Zimmerman sees Crusoe as a figure driven by 'destructive impulses' which have to be curbed, obscured and mastered by reconfiguring the material world: through writing (obsessive lists, journals, contracts, in defiance of the absence of ink), and most obviously through the elaborated fortifications and other defensive habitations: 'Crusoe fortifies to restore his psychic equilibrium; whenever he has brought his defenses to seeming perfection, he is again disturbed.'[3] This is a psychic and internal problem rather than a mere 'fact' of the situation, akin to his ravening and irrational need to gut the ruined ship. Nothing can be wasted, not even obviously useless things: not merely the famous 'drug' of money, but animal skins, bottles, beeswax and people (Xury) are converted as they emerge into things of use. Gradually the world is reconfigured in order to provide protection for Crusoe; nothing escapes the process. Crusoe is always at the centre of a barricaded space, outside which is projected chaos and fear. The most directly expressed of Crusoe's emotions are his fear of being devoured and his hatred of the wild men and beasts who devour. There is for him a fate worse than death – subsequently being eaten up: the body is his last barricade. The cannibals who visit the island produce extravagances of fear and hatred in him – intensities of emotion that are sustained for years. Nor is this fear confined to the 'realistic' visits of the cannibals, visits which seem in a sense conjured by Crusoe's pervasive terror: the fear of being devoured is present as soon as Crusoe escapes from the Moors (he hears savage howlings at night and imagines cannibals everywhere), it hits him as soon as he comes ashore on his island (he sleeps up a tree to avoid animals which turn out not to exist), and it persists in the journey across civilised Europe (bears, wolves). The ubiquitous references to being devoured point to a generalized fear: of being dematerialised – the reversal of the desire to accumulate. It is an anxiety shared by author and character; 'being devoured is a way of conceiving diverse fears'. The sea 'swallows' and 'buries' people.

While acknowledging that spiritual autobiography is one of the forms to which Crusoe's experiences are tailored, Zimmerman contends that the form does not adequately harness the energies of its central figure. Crusoe's fear 'is finally of the rage within'; his structures and defences 'all serve as self-protective psychic diversions' from his inner aggression.[4] Zimmerman is able to show that Crusoe's destructive impulses are given still more persistent amplification in *Farther Adventures*, which appears to revisit the island and other kinds of adventure in order to tidy up loose narrative ends and extend colonial dominion, but instead fuels the cycle of violence. While *Serious Reflections* reasserts the organising principle and hidden design of providence, Zimmerman doubts that Defoe saw providence quite so straightforwardly as the determining force of all narrative or life events. 'Providence often seems to be a method of interpretation, a theory rather than a force. And on several occasions, events suggest that it may be Crusoe's "fancy",' a projection of need.[5] This is still more obviously the case in *Farther Adventures*, just as original sin becomes psychological as much as theological. The ordering power of providential thinking, only partially sufficient in the first novel (as witnessed in the awkward and sometimes contradictory double narrative of the journal etc.), breaks down altogether in the sequel. Crusoe

■ attempts to organize everything external as part of himself. But by his doing so, his enemy becomes both internal and external. He must attack any forces threatening the order that he uses to control his own feared impulses. What he desires is related to what he fears: the external is his defence and his enemy. He encloses himself in masses of material, and is afraid of being devoured.[6] □

Crusoe's condition, which he does not really acknowledge, is solipsism; he teaches the parrot to say his name, and is woken in terror when he hears the words. And this is not irony: much of the conflict mirrors Defoe's own fears (of being 'devoured' by creditors): the novel becomes a kind of substitute psychic defence, a sympathetic analysis of his own condition.

With Moll, Zimmerman initially seeks more of an ironic focus. Defoe 'attempts to measure the impercipience of his narrator', that is, there is intermittently available to us a perspective which is neither reflective narrator Moll nor agent Moll. The preface carefully prepares us not to take Moll's voice ('edited' and offset by her later character) on trust. Zimmerman argues that Defoe combines the older, hardened Moll's voice with 'her passionate younger self' to distance the reader into a morally evaluative position. The older woman sees only tactical errors in her series of marriages, but Defoe's writing allows us to see what Moll does not: the personality she might have been if not so early corrupted by the failure of love. Using Defoe's writings on the family for context, Zimmerman sees sexual feeling as 'a constant dangerous pressure' for his heroine, especially in her state of social vulnerability. Moll sacrifices her natural sexual feelings to expediency (the first marriage) and in doing so opens the door to all kinds of raw deviance, most notably incest. The sequence of episodes is strictly 'organized to illustrate the loosening of Moll's moral inhibitions and social ties'. Every new marriage or liaison erodes one more moral scruple. The career of thieving carries on the work of disintegration: 'her disguises multiply, and she loses her sense of her own coherence', becoming merely 'an inchoate self'.[7] The chaos and disorder of Newgate (at once the end of all pretence and a psychological projection of her inner state) completes the destruction of coherent selfhood, but then 'brings Moll to herself'. When all is lost, Moll can 'generate a new identity' as caring Mother and loving Wife in the New World, but once again social expediency entails for this character a mere parody of respectability, with something always hidden or occluded. The act of narrating offers Moll the chance to purge guilt, but also to 'savour her past as she severs herself from it'; she can draw on her past life in whatever partial way will afford most stability.[8] Confession is necessary, indeed her only relief, though she often lacks the appropriate confessor (even the beloved Jemy cannot be told everything). Even we as readers do not know her real name.

As with Crusoe, external material here figures as a kind of projection of inner insecurity – most notably in the obsessive equation of everything (love, life, sanity) with money. Like Crusoe, Moll accumulates more than she needs; she goes on thieving when the promptings of poverty are past. The process is never under control, and the search for a place beyond threat never complete: she keeps trying to start again, but she 'lives so many lives that she does not know which is hers'.[9] Threatened with the madhouse herself, she sees the people around her go off the rails, become ill, commit suicide. For Zimmerman, 'hard-headed practicality', usually associated with Moll, is actually centred in her 'governess', who does the real business of managing Moll's by-products (children, stolen property, punishment); it is a quality that Moll aspires to without success. Moll never really understands the orders (family structures, social respectability, marital legitimacy) that she tries to join, and is condemned to a self-defeating mimicry of them. Zimmerman argues that at times Moll's decline is registered by a perspective that is not her own, that is, narrative irony; but that in addition the moral chaos she generates is too much for Defoe's own powers: 'a carefully defined ironic perspective succumbs to the formlessness of Moll's mind'. When Moll's pretences and parodies finally collapse, there is nothing left: Defoe 'fails to define any moral world that exists outside her consciousness', leaving only the ordering of repentance, asserted less through belief than through fear of the disorder that would otherwise prevail.[10]

John J. Richetti's *Defoe's Narratives* covers some of the same psychological territory, but is less concerned with matters of formal order, and more inclined to celebrate the selves which the protagonists generate. Richetti sees in the self-assertion of the central figures a coherence which, he argues forcefully, liberates them from the confines of ordinary experience; but the deepest level of coherence is well below the surface of authorial intention. Richetti seeks to move beyond accounts of Defoe's fiction which (as in Novak and Starr) effectively look to reconstruct a consistent body of thought or ideology (in relation to economics, or social theory, or religion) which the novels may be said to reflect or dramatise. Novels are more relational and dynamic than the static theses they are sometimes taken to illustrate. Disputing also the naïve claim of autobiographical fiction to unmediated experience of selfhood, Richetti argues that all experience of selfhood is relational, directed towards an outer world, and that it necessarily fluctuates and wavers. The novel's 'energy as a form is essentially a matter of revealing that fluctuation and of preserving or asserting the authority over that fluctuation of the self that writes and, by extension, of the self that reads'. Inconsistency is not so much a matter of artistic blemish or a problem to be resolved by signing Defoe up to one side or another of theoretical debate, but a sign of a 'process of confrontation and mediation'. A necessarily relational self, in reciprocal and dynamic conflict with the world, somehow manages to produce the category of a 'primary and irreproachable self'. The narratives present a quest for autonomy, thwarted by 'unruly realities, the limiting reciprocity involved in those personal, social, natural, and historical determinants which threaten the autonomy and even the physical survival of the self'.[11] The novels are not 'naïve celebrations of individual possibility' but dramatisations of an individualist problem:

■ They communicate by their arrangements and strategies an implicit grasp of the tangled relationships between the free self and the social and ideological realities which that self seems to require. What they show us [. . .] is character carefully separating itself from that unsatisfactory tangle of private and public, personal and social, and establishing an unimpeachable selfhood, at least in the privileged space of the narrative.[12] □

Crusoe represents the effort of an eighteenth-century self to rise above the competing ideologies of an expansive capitalist ethos and the conservative religious tradition which should be its opposite. Events gradually accommodate themselves to the emerging self as its power to deal with those events increases. Survival is 'a form of autonomy'; self does not dominate the world but manages to produce 'a version of the world which is perfectly aligned with itself and its desires'.[13] The brutalist aspects of Crusoe's will to power (the annihilation of the father and domination of the 'other') are banished to an island where they can work themselves out in benign freedom from guilt, under the cloak of survival. Crusoe's motives are, to begin with, not simple or pure, but multiple to the point of confusion; he acts without a sense of full responsibility; he begins in ignorance of his selfhood (signalled as ignorance of his chosen route, the sea, and later of the many skills he must learn). 'Crusoe is [. . .] required to be ignorant that we may experience his acquisition of wisdom'. But this does not mean that Crusoe is a blank 'everyman'. The story 'is out to establish a pattern whereby the self can gradually discover outside itself that which it carries within'. The narrative does not develop a new self so much as offer 'discovery or establishment of an environment where the self can emerge without blame as a response to reality rather than as the creator of it'.[14]

Slavery and imprisonment paradoxically free Crusoe from responsibility for his inner urge to dominate, by providing an unimpeachable motive: survival in the face of an alienated other. The Moors, the island, the cannibals form a 'circle of compulsion' which converts Crusoe's self-aggrandisement into an acceptable desire. Everything which looks like a disaster or obstacle is actually an opportunity for self-display. The journal is a further act of ordering and self-mastery, since it separates self from circumstance and subjugates in analysis the chaotic aspects of his nature.

Crusoe tames goats in replication of the process by which his own unruly nature has been tamed. Learning the tides, which can liberate or annihilate him, maps his power onto the world. Finding order and regularity in the surface appearances of nature is linked to finding God's meaning in tiny details and accidents: both confirm a sense of inner control. Crusoe is finally able to think 'in coherent autobiographical terms', looking backwards and forwards with a full sense of order. He reckons up the chaotic disasters that might have been his fate, as a means of understanding the fullness of his own surviving consciousness.

New challenges emerge to recapitulate the pattern: at the point where mastery of self gives way to mastery of the island, he discovers the footprint and realises that 'his possession and rule of the island are in some sense illusory. [. . .] The free individual discovers that he is threatened by other individuals whose claim to freedom is as total as his own.' Worse, as cannibals, these others are 'full-fledged embodiments of the anti-type of himself that haunts Crusoe's imagination and sustains him in his drive for order and towards civilisation'. When he watches the coastline for cannibals he is also watching 'his own shifting desires and fantasies'. Crusoe rescues Friday, as he was himself rescued, and becomes godlike, 'suddenly visible, powerful, and obviously mysterious in that power'. Friday is Crusoe's 'heretofore menacing anti-type now completely domesticated, and Crusoe is now literally the master in acquiring an actual slave'.[15] Richetti traces the sequence of Crusoe's gradual rise through ever higher stages of mastery – over himself, nature, animals, native inhabitants, Europeans.

Richetti argues that 'the real movement of Defoe's novels is not simply towards the determinants of character but rather towards the depiction of a dialectic between self and other which has as its end a covert but triumphant assertion of the self'. All Defoe's narratives 'challenge the notion of simple or stable identity. His characters record nothing less than the fluid and dynamic nature of personality, a matter of changing roles, responding to circumstances, and discovering new possibilities of self-expression.' Moll is 'an instinctively free spirit, one not bound by inner compulsions like Robinson Crusoe [. . .] but aggressively eager to be independent of circumstances from the start'. Even while engaging with the seemingly limiting power of circumstances, Moll conceives of a selfhood which lies beyond them; she controls the impositions of fate by appearing to submit to them. Moll only seems to be determined by the circumstances of her birth and early upbringing, for the incidents she tells us of, from that period, 'are as much illustrations of her independence and somehow instinctive sense of strong isolation as they are examples of social determinism', as when she secretes herself from the gypsies who have taken her. Similarly, seduction by the elder brother at Colchester, is less to do with ignorance than with Moll's 'sense of freedom [. . .] the first step in the dialectic process which converts spontaneous desire into capable self-possession'. Self-knowledge is won for the purpose of retaining and reserving the self. Moll 'is most fully herself when she keeps something of herself (or her substance, frequently and literally her capital) aside and ready for future possibilities'. She is thus not a 'personality' in the normal sense but essentially a player of roles whose 'essence' is always withheld.[16]

Thus *Moll Flanders* is not really a documentary novel: while it 'is about eighteenth-century social and economic realities', it is also about the 'superior reality of a self which moves through them, mastering them with a powerful dialectic rhythm and never succumbing to their full implications as cumulatively limiting realities'. The Mint, for example, is 'distilled social compulsion', but Moll converts it into a version of freedom. Moll 'learns to be more horrified by disorder than by evil', because only order can provide freedom for a character. Questions of irony and moral perspective do not really arise in this reading. Richetti also thinks Moll's dynamic survival is not plausible in normative psychological terms: the discovery of incest produces a rapid shift from 'the rhetoric of desolation to the tactical joys of analysis and self-preservation' which has little to do with realistic characterisation. Moll's winning secret here is the rarely-spoken knowledge that 'the personal depends upon the legal and the financial for its existence'. By realising the full negative force of social forms, Moll gains a kind of positive wisdom and 'affirms a new kind of self' – hence her self-command, in contrast to her brother's suicidal melancholy.[17]

The sequence of marriages and liaisons consistently enhances Moll's power in relation to marriage, which becomes more knowing and calculating with each new partner. Again, this is a matter not of psychological or sociological plausibility but of function: Moll represents 'an extraordinary assertion of control' in her assumption of mastery of sexual economics. Her pattern tends towards 'free action in the context of compelling circumstances', and she does not so much 'grow' in the manner expected of novelistic characters but repeat and amplify certain structural patterns which, as with Crusoe, demonstrate the conversion of destructive natural appetite into 'profitable self-assertion'.[18] Crime is the 'ultimate test for the self because it requires at one and the same time utter dependence on circumstances and absolute freedom from them'. Moll is placed in a world of 'movement and opportunity in which she survives by observation of that movement and the taking of opportunity'. She avoids violent or direct crime and instead moves into the flow of circumstance, as if the world adapts itself to her needs, transforming itself 'from a collection of compulsive circumstances into a field of opportunities and relationships'. By 'observant self-reservation' she converts the bustle of the London street to her personal profit. Moreover, crime 'demands total secrecy and [. . .] thereby accumulates large amounts of selfhood, perhaps something like the total selfhood the novel aspires to portray'.[19]

The last and greatest test of her 'extraordinary freedom' is the death sentence:

■ What matters about Newgate is not its concrete existence as a wretched habitation but its power to suppress and transform the self. [. . .] The prison is a concrete embodiment of social restriction, unlike anything Moll has so far had to deal with in its effective concreteness, its real and effective exemplification of the control that society aspires to exercise over the self.[20] □

Moll recovers by confining her misery to a private space (the cell she has paid for), unseen by anyone but her confessor, and by maintaining outward calm while everyone else loses their heads, refusing to become part of the indiscriminate noise around her. Exposed by circumstance, she will not reveal herself. Moll reserves herself partially even from Jemy and the Governess, plays repositories of money and knowledge against each other, and conspires with her own son in a less than completely honest manner. 'To the absolute end, Moll survives by being secret,' Richetti notes, and he is much less troubled than Zimmerman by the absence of a higher order, whether of art or morality:

■ Her attractiveness stems from her function: to assert and enact the possibility of survival and prosperity in the face of impossibly limiting and even destructive circumstances. We respond as readers to her story because she enacts the delightful autonomy of the self without seeming to violate the equally autonomous facts of nature and society. She is an instrument for our delight in human survival, and towards that end she has to be more than human.[21] □

TIME

Defoe's fiction had thus become a matter of the generation, deployment, and representation of individual selfhood, however critics might argue about the precise degree of artistic consciousness that could be ascribed to Defoe. Subsequent work tended initially to argue for quite complex forms of art beneath an artless surface. One of the most unusual contributions to the debate was Paul Alkon's work on Defoe's construction of time in the novels. Arguing that 'criticism should account for the role of those temporal structures that narratives call into being' in the reader's mind, Alkon studies the novels in terms of the experiential structures of reading, that is, in terms of reader–response, rather than in terms of form as it is normally understood.[22] Memory, as it facilitates comparison of events and a sense of speed or 'tempo', is a crucial aspect for readers of Defoe's fiction. Alkon argues that settings, chronologies, and comparisons of dates need to be looked at consciously, as do the temporal allusions that lie at the periphery of a reader's consciousness. So *Robinson Crusoe* is set in relation to historical time, with a birth year specified, but is also structured as a study of the interaction of 'personal time and eternity': hence the calendars, the journal, and the obsessive building up of the 28 years of exile. Conversely, there is only one date in *Moll Flanders*, and that is at the very end: 'Written in the Year 1683'. This reference is problematic because Moll appears to refer to things that happened after 1683, and Alkon finds other anachronistic customs and details in the book. Additionally, Moll seems to have no interest in the very obvious historical events of her age, such as the English Civil War (1642–51), the Great Plague of London (1665–6), the Great Fire of London (1666), and the dynastic struggles of the Stuart reigns.[23] Alkon suggests that this is part of a process whereby Moll's time and the reader's time 'imaginatively fuse', with the final date deliberately setting us back into retrospective mode. The Moll who has seemed so vibrantly alive is removed into death by reminding the reader, at the very last moment, that the narrative was written down some forty years earlier. Alkon speculates that this encourages readers to suspend their moral judgements on Moll and think more in terms of eternal emotional verities such as the pity and terror of tragedy.

Moll's private time-scheme is easier to follow, for it foregrounds an economic curve of female productivity, from her first earnings and liaisons, through the menopause: at 48 Moll is too old to bear children. At 50 she turns thief after two years of terrified imagining which seem to signal some inner mental collapse at the point where her specifically feminine resource is compromised. Crimes, however, are not structured in any 'valid relationship to either present or future time', suggesting their morally skewed status. Her moral regress is emphasised by her entry into old age: by contrast with Crusoe, whose vigour is undiminished, Moll's allusions to age 'contribute to serious doubts about the protagonist's final state'.

Defoe is almost as keen on large tracts of time as he is on large amounts of money: Moll's 'vitious and abominable Life for 24 Years past', or Crusoe's famous 28-year stint on the island. He opts for the prodigious rather than precise. Defoe does not stick to temporal verisimilitude; Crusoe is born in 1632, shipwrecked on 30 September 1659, rescued on 19 December 1686; but like Moll he displays absolutely no curiosity about historical events. Instead Defoe frequently uses a system of time which overtly marks a journey away from calendar time towards 'the encounter with private and sacred time on his island', followed by return.[24] Time is frequently used in symbolic ways – especially in

Robinson Crusoe, where calendar time is marked by cutting notches on a great cross and thus underscoring a spiritual pattern. On the fever-ridden evening when he prays for the first time, Crusoe loses a day's reckoning on his calendar time, as if in symbolic limbo.

But time is also the element in which the reader experiences the unfolding of events. Defoe's plots are disjointed, not elaborately sequenced. Defoe relies on the reader's memory to imply connection. The books use double perspectives and retrospectives: 'What has often looked to twentieth-century critics like ethical incoherence in Defoe's novels may have seemed necessary for didactic purposes in narratives partly intended to show the hazards of making a judgment too quickly.'[25] The autobiographical stance cannot be sufficient authority because it does not include death; hence the external prefaces, outside the time of self-narration. The hastening and slowing of narrative tempo encourages the reader to think across and outside the first-person narration. Alkon takes issue with Watt's dismissal of the structural organisation of the novel by looking at a specific example, the multiple encounters between the Elder Brother and Moll that lead to her seduction. He shows that readers are directed (by Defoe) to compare and superimpose these scenes carefully, in a way which is closer to the suspenseful unfolding of actual experience than to the supposed authority of autobiographical retrospection, but which also suggests the composition of a repeated moral pattern. Memory takes the place of chapter structure and acts as the key to dramatic irony; it is we who note that Moll keeps doing the same thing. Consolidation devices, such as repetition and suspense, thicken the narrative texture; 'By these and similar invitations to remember Defoe often makes linear narrative sequences achieve many of the effects associated with spatial form' – that is, the unity built up in poetic and other forms by patterns of interconnected motifs.[26]

Alkon does, however, also argue that there are in addition elements of spatial form in *Moll Flanders*: the birth and imprisonment in Newgate, the repeated visits to Colchester and Virginia. Read carefully, Defoe's novels exhibit a commitment to over-arching design. *Robinson Crusoe* also signals its shape through repetition and doubling: storms, shipwrecks, voyages, different forms of captivity, the resurrection of Xury in Friday. Spatial form constitutes part of Defoe's 'emblematic method', in alliance with memory, for Crusoe is able eventually to compare the situation of (for example) mutineers' victims with his own remembered state. He runs over 'the whole History of My Life in Miniature, or by Abridgment [. . .]'. Crusoe keeps revisiting his own narration from slightly different personal perspectives. Alkon takes the example of the discrepant accounts of Crusoe's first night on the island; we have to ask what actually happened, in what order, and what the significance of the order might be; in doing so we notice that we are duplicating the Puritan practice of retrospective examination. Something similar obtains in all Defoe's narratives; discrepancies and repetitions make us engage in the process of verification and checking, and for Alkon this enhances verisimilitude and moral sympathy for his characters.[27]

PATTERNS OF EXPERIENCE

In a monograph published in the same year as Alkon's, David Blewett also contends that Defoe is more than a naïve or confused reader of his own accidental masterpieces.[28] Blewett's method is to locate a central 'vision of the human experience' in Defoe's non-fiction writings on social issues and then to search for corresponding material in the novels. Defoe's own attitude to fiction itself is found to become more positive, focused and artistic as these issues take more complex and assured form. The 'editorial' comments in his prefaces show a shift from stress on the authenticity of the story itself to more obviously fictional presentation and performance; gradually Defoe settles down to becoming a novelist. But this increasing confidence in art is mirrored by a decreasing confidence in human nature.

Blewett follows Watt in assigning a kind of realism to Defoe's avoidance of the aristocratic setting and 'intrigue' plot of most contemporary fiction. The autobiographical form allows him to imagine himself into situations, as well as to avoid simply writing 'fiction', about which he shared the anxieties of much of his age. Blewett thinks Defoe became more pessimistic about the tendency of people to ignore their own best interests or to degenerate completely, as he continued to write these imaginary life stories. Life for most of his pirates and explorers is a series of cheats and expedients, with advancement coming through cunning and disguise. Defoe is fascinated by such disguises, and his interest in those who successfully project a front for themselves or stage-manage situations also increases through novels; his names move from realistic to increasingly deceptive social labels, more obviously 'fictional' identities, as his pessimism about the world intensified. Characters fail to see what is going to happen; and they cannot trust each other: 'The intense loneliness of all Defoe's leading characters reflects his own sense of the essential isolation of human beings in a world where they can see little and trust few'.[29]

Unlike commentators who regard Defoe's fiction as essentially shapeless, Blewett is concerned to show that the fictions have the form appropriate to their theme. In the case of *Robinson Crusoe*, Blewett argues that the novel displays 'a rhythm of imprisonment and deliverance which can be felt throughout the novel and which establishes the basic alternation of the world and the island'.[30] This corresponds to thematic oppositions:

providence/human limitations, reason/fancy, temptation/resistance. The analysis picks out Defoe's use of repeated phrases, images, and events to show that Defoe's novel is not a random accumulation of accidents but a carefully planned didactic structure. Blewett comments that the pattern of disaster and deliverance begins before Crusoe's arrival on the island and continues after it. Crusoe's inner struggle with worldly desire is shown in contrasting ways: in isolation on the island, and in the thick of temptation off it. Like Alkon, Blewett thinks the book works partly by subtly prefiguring and recalling motifs: the series of storms, the sequence of wrecks, the coincidences of dates, the substitution of Friday for Xury. Crusoe is made to experience disaster and release as part of a pattern, a master-plan. Conversion awakens him to the structure of his experience, though his frequent backsliding into doubt and fear shows that the play of oppositional forces does not simply stop but carries on its educative effects.

Defoe keeps beginning new sequences. The footprint on the shore leads to a gradual journey back to the world: a few cannibals become many cannibals, the cannibals become individualised in Friday, who assists in the rescue of his father and Crusoe's fellow Europeans. Crusoe, himself now delivered, becomes the deliverer of others, and must now repeat the victory over his own irrationality in a new, social context, before returning to the full world of human society. Crusoe's previous emotional conflicts get played out once again in the contest between the restraining captain and the impulsive mutineers. Crusoe's self-conversion is mirrored and expanded in his conversion of Friday, whose filial piety is a reverse mirror-image of Crusoe's 'original sin' in defying his father. Like Hunter, Blewett defends the final journey through the Pyrenees as 'the final and appropriate demonstration of Crusoe's control in the face of the terrors and dangers of the world'.[31] The animals in the story act, in Blewett's reading, as one of the markers of form superficially they are just part of the 'realism', but taken together they accumulate into a pattern, from the wild howlings that so terrify Crusoe on the African shore, through the horrific beasts of his imagining on the island, to the domestication of cats and goats and his appearance in the skin of animals; the dog is a kind of intermediate figure, belonging neither to the island nor to the world, but forming a link to the wolves of the final journey. The wolves, described as 'three hundred Devils', and to a lesser extent the bear, mark the potential return of terror and destruction, but this time Crusoe is much more in control of himself and the situation. Human savagery (of cannibals but also of priests) is often suggested by this underlying presence of the animal. Blewett notices various other 'supporting motifs', such as the repeated imagery of imprisonment, which quietly emphasise the themes. Clothing crops up in significant ways throughout the book; so does money. Both motifs can be tracked to show Crusoe's changing attitudes to the world.

Blewett contends that *Moll Flanders* represents a darkening vision of the human condition: 'Crusoe's cheerful confidence and honest industry give place to Moll's cynical dishonesty and energetic exploitation of deception.' Crusoe works out that destiny has a pattern; Moll regards life as a cheat more or less from the beginning. Crusoe seeks an explanation in the deep structures of providence; Moll in the dog-eat-dog deceptions of the world. Moll is a supreme actress, most at home in the world of appearances; only when the pure reality of death impinges at the end does her world crumble. Her name becomes more famous as her identity is more and more hidden. Disguise is there right from the start; she meets the elder brother in special costume early on. 'What begins as a mode of deception is to become a mode of existence.'[32] In fact this reminds us of the presence of patterns. Moll, named after cloth, and forever in carefully-chosen dress, has an ironic association with lace from childhood onwards: making it, reporting on contraband, stealing it. Her identity is bound up with cloth; mercers and other dealers in textiles are often a threat to her. She repeats her mother's pattern of cloth theft and transportation after a death sentence. In terms of relationships, everything seems to promote a kind of family resemblance. The Governess becomes a 'mother'; her mother-in-law is actually her mother; marriage becomes incest because she has already started the pattern by marrying the younger brother in a kind of incestuous disguise of her liaison with the elder brother. Moll abandons children, as she herself has been abandoned; she steals from children and mothers.

Blewett compares Moll's views on marriage to Defoe's discussion of the issue of the mutual obligations and rights of parents and children in *Religious Courtship* (1722). He argues that it is possible to ascertain Defoe's 'real' concerns with marriage and the rights and responsibilities of parents and children from the tract, and thinks that the fact that Moll's views represent a partial distortion of them means that Defoe holds an ironic distance from his heroine. The gradual increase in levels of deception and disguise accompanies a catalogue of disasters – bankruptcy, incest, madness, adultery. Moll is condemned to follow the pattern of her mother. Even the marriage to Jemy recalls the marriage to a brother (in the motif of the deceiver deceived). Similarly, Blewett contends that the novel mirrors Defoe's concern with crime (on which he wrote several pamphlets in the 1720s). Moll's second theft (taking the necklace from the child), with its suggestion of murder, links the crime forward and backward: memories of Moll's own childhood and children, questions about her possible eventual fate. The shapeshifting takes on a criminal element, with the Governess who had suggested aborting a child now working as a pawnbroker and fence. Disguises that were put on to enhance marriageability now work for the black economy. Hence it is crucial that Newgate prison is the place of the destined return to origin, precipitating 'the discovery of her identity, the place where the other thieves finally, and triumphantly, call her Mary Flanders'.[33] Defoe pulls Moll's shapeshifting out of the fire, and redeems the criminal marriages by patching up the Lancashire husband on the Virginia estates, clothing him (substantiating him) as the gentleman he once pretended to be, backing up Moll's own primordial desire for gentility with the money that the role requires. It is a final and hard-won act of regeneration, closer to the optimism of *Robinson Crusoe* than to the dark days of *Roxana*.

Robinson Crusoe, meanwhile, was in 1979 the subject of a substantial introductory monograph by Pat Rogers, covering in reliable detail the book's publication history, sources and background, and the main social, religious and economic themes, style and critical history.[34] Rogers includes some acute stylistic commentary on Defoe's sentence structure and syntax, in part taking up the work of E. Anthony James and George Starr. Mary E. Butler supplements these studies with an account of Defoe's stylistic habit of writing descriptions which are repeatedly qualified or offered in slightly alternative versions using locutions such as 'or rather' and 'at least'. Because the narrative is always adjusting itself, we have the illusion that it is somehow being improved as we read, and 'thus makes its claim to perpetual self-creation independent of its narrator and of its author'. The text appears to acquire 'an unusual density, as if its abstract existence in our apprehension might consequently tend, if ever so slightly, toward substantiation' – like a kind of magical materialisation. *Robinson Crusoe* sounds more authentic because the narrator is always worrying about accuracy; by not being omniscient, the narrator appears honest and reliable. It is a story about making, and making do, so we come away with the sense that what is being attempted is somehow real.[35] Illusions of the real, or performance of it, is also the theme of James H. Maddox's article on Crusoe's performances of power: deprived of traditional structures of authority, he acts as director and playwright of a scene which helps the marooned captain to regain power over his rebellious crew, and confirms Crusoe himself as the island's governor.[36]

Leopold Damrosch revisits the traditions of Puritan plot-making from Milton and Bunyan onwards, to find Crusoe not so much analysing the self as asserting it against all opposition – whether or not this was what Defoe originally intended.

■ Defoe sets out to dramatize the conversion of the Puritan self, and he ends by celebrating a solitude that exalts autonomy instead of submission. He undertakes to show the dividedness of a sinner, and ends by projecting a hero so massively self-enclosed that almost nothing of his inner life is revealed.[37] □

The natural consequence of Puritan inwardness is really the kind of self-centredness of the essay 'Of Solitude' in the *Serious Reflections*. Everything is externalised. Solitude is no longer about self-examination for repentance, but 'the normal condition of all selves as they confront the world in which they have to survive'. Following Starr's 1974 article, mentioned in Chapter 4, Damrosch argues that in *Robinson Crusoe* the ego protects itself by rendering all objects of perception emotional figures of subjective apprehension. Defoe's characters avoid introspection, which heralds confusion and chaos, and instead set their faces towards and against challenges they can overcome. We do not see inside; experience is a sequence of responses to external objects. Damrosch describes analytically what Victorian readers thought of nostalgically: the book is a fantasy of retreat into a world innocent of sex, a vision of solitary power and self-creation in which the self fills everything – which is why it has been such a favourite with children. Crusoe rejoices in the absence of the savage, threatening 'other'. The island represents a kind of punishment fantasy that can be converted to an acceptable fate as the force of punishment diminishes; the mysterious impulse to resist the father finds a happy culmination in the freedom of solitude. Damrosch goes on to note that Crusoe's period of exile coincides with the restoration of the Stuart kings – and lasts as long as the first 28 years of Defoe's own life – thus indicating that the 'punishment' of exile appears to be also a reminder, even an assertion, of the authority that maintains power in the background, like the covert 'truth' of Puritanism under the Stuarts.

PARTICIPATION IN HISTORY

Ten years after the Zimmerman and Richetti volumes with which we began this chapter came another small glut of significant monographs on Defoe. In 1984 Laura Curtis published *The Elusive Daniel Defoe*, which circumvented the question of ironic frame by reading the fiction through two personae (plain dealer and sophisticated trickster) developed as a means of dealing with complex contemporary issues in Defoe's long-running journal of commentary, the *Review*. Crusoe represents the ideal self of 'order and rational control' that Defoe aspires to: he conquers his island, the cannibals, his loneliness, and his despair.[38] Yet Defoe was aware that the plain-dealing, straightforward, orderly Crusoe was also at something of a loss in the real world of political bargaining, and Defoe's 'other' self, his 'real' self, personified by the hoaxer and trickster who accommodates himself to the world as it is, gives us Moll, the outsider determined to survive and enjoy what the world has to offer.

Crusoe's emphasis is upon 'order, directness, clarity, simplicity, repression of emotion, and slow and patient work'. His defensive circles constitute a successful attempt to manage his fear of others; his consciousness strives for control of the world. Coming upon a bird he does not recognise on his island, he is momentarily aware of the otherness of this place, its absence from history, its non–human scheme of things: he shoots the bird, analyses it, and throws it away. The footprint reminds him of the possible presence of otherness in surroundings 'he was certain he had domesticated'.[39] Crusoe is thus an ambiguous figure, haunted by irrational desire, the quest for adventure, resistance to the staid, humdrum career which society (in the shape of his father) lays down for a man in his position. The main narrative is 'the account of how a single man gradually masters his own compulsions and extends his control over a huge, indifferent, even potentially hostile environment, learning to harness its inhuman forces and to put them to use for his own benefit', essentially a process of 'rationalizing the unknown'. But Crusoe's restlessness and his 'rambling Thoughts' constitute a standing threat to this orderliness. The island is both prison and realm, safe refuge and cannibal feasting ground, and Crusoe switches back and forth between these rival identifications, at once building up fortifications and thinking about destroying them. Curtis argues that Crusoe is made eventually to see himself as 'securely included' in his surroundings rather than separated from them, willing to 'allow himself to become merged with his environment', and that this represents a final success for that part of Defoe that 'longed for an ideal world of peace, harmony, clarity, order, and simplicity'.[40] Yet she also points out that the return of restlessness is flagged up at the close of the narrative, and returns in the sequel.

It returns with a vengeance in Moll, the representative of the hoaxing and masking motifs of 'Mr. Review'. Curtis claims that the spirit of anarchic desire mastered (imperfectly) in *Robinson Crusoe* 'finds its outlet in aggression against society and against the reader' in *Moll Flanders*. Crusoe's fear of others becomes a way of life for Moll, who never tells anyone the complete truth about herself (in contrast to Crusoe, who repeatedly tells his story to anyone who will listen). Moll lives in the 'other' world described in the *Review*, where truth is hard to find and judge, where effective action can only be accomplished through manipulation, disguise and deception. Curtis reopens the question of how far irony in the book is a structural feature of characterisation, and how far it is merely local and occasional. She argues that the book is 'an unstable equilibrium of picaresque narrative, criminal biography and spiritual autobiography', held together not by stable irony but by the comic spirit of the hoax.[41] Moll, of course, hoaxes everyone – plain–dealers and tricksters alike, from her first marriage to her last – but the book itself is Defoe's guilty and amused attack on readers who accept Moll's duplicity and moral failings because of their own self-deceptions. Readers are in effect implicated in a hoax perpetrated by Defoe. Because Moll's vitality is inextricably linked with her quintessentially human hypocrisy, we are powerless to break her spell over us. This paradox of reluctant acceptance belongs to the welcoming realm of comedy, not the repudiating realm of irony. Moll embodies Defoe's comic spirit, an explosive and anarchic force capable of shaking up the social order; the book is a kind of comic social satire, directed against class conventions, rather than an individual psychological study.

Curtis further observes that the solitariness of Defoe's heroes often occurs alongside 'patterns of character pairs' such as Crusoe's Friday and Moll's Governess. Isolation and power are childhood fantasies, bringing with them a characterisation of people who intrude on the purity of the fantasy as either threatening (cannibals) or servile. Friday is a docile help-meet, wholly under the control of Crusoe. But Moll's companion takes the form of an evil counsellor, perpetually reinventing herself as midwife, landlady, receiver of stolen goods, tutor in crime, business agent – whatever Moll needs in order to carry on her plot. Curtis thinks that this doubling of agency is an indication that Defoe found it difficult to conceive of individuals who embodied both instinctive and rational control, thus causing him to split certain aspects of his imagined person-alities into two. Defoe never manages to integrate these tensions, and it is hard to pin down intentionality in a personality driven by an unac-knowledged desire 'to have things two ways at once'.

While Curtis drew heavily on one relatively restricted element of Defoe's non-fiction writing, others were concerned to situate him in relation to an ever wider literary context. Paula Backscheider's 1984 study of Defoe alongside Bunyan and Swift takes Defoe as essentially the modern author, with the novels emerging from seventeenth-century modes and moralities to engage with newer materialist concerns. Backscheider followed this analysis with a monograph on Defoe which saw him as profoundly and learnedly engaged with the cultures and subcultures of his time, creatively at war with the established classicising structures of the literary profession.[42] Ian Bell situated the fiction in rela-tion to a (largely presumed) reading audience, which did not have very 'firm distinctions between art and artlessness, fiction and fact, or distor-tion and verisimilitude'; Defoe was never part of any 'great tradition' at all.[43] All the fictions were poised between security and jeopardy, much as Defoe's life was: Bell argues that this was what interested the reading public. Defoe's Puritan dourness was secure; his *Shortest Way with Dissenters*, the ironically vehement attack on his own kind which landed him in the pillory, was typical of his showy riskiness. But Bell sees the fictions as reflecting broadly shared life experiences rather than as personal allegory: it was history from below, from the margin. We partic-ipate in adventure; the mobility of the hero gives a reassuring sense that our own mobility is possible. It offers a fantasy of fulfilment; it is not about moral admonition so much as the illusion of escape. That is why Defoe's writing of fiction was as accessible as his writing on trade.

Bell's Defoe was the very type of modern author, involved in everything, learning it as he went along, with little received wisdom. Gradually he withdrew from the sharp end of political and social debate into a more ruminative position with space for fictional explorations. For Defoe and his readership, which he can thus address obliquely, the fictions offer comforting models of escape and mobility, in 'very stylised versions of the audience's experience, in the form of adventure and peril'. The chief point, for Bell, is that Defoe's fiction is 'popular fiction. It is escapist, diverting and enthralling, seeking to satisfy its audience more than to disturb them.'[44] Working partly from John Richetti's earlier book on the main genres of popular fiction that precede what we now think of as 'the novel' (pirate stories, roguery, travel, scandal, the erotic, and the pious), Bell argues that popular fiction appears in genres with fairly clear 'supervisory' boundaries, such as criminal biography or travel writing: the audience knows what to expect.[45] What such fiction lacks is the expectation of organic wholeness imposed by a coherent figure of authorship. Popular fiction presents life more as a flux, 'without eventual purpose'; it is not teleological, not pursuing an architectonic line of thought, as 'high' literature might. The depiction of central characters is less a matter of individual traits than of categories of clear understanding: soldier, sailor, whore, thief.

Bell does not argue that Defoe's fiction simply replicates categories from this storehouse, because 'there is also an attempt to break out of this referential framework, and to produce more independent books' – perhaps another version for Defoe of safety and risk, 'letting his imagination take the risks in a fairly safe market'.[46] Crusoe is a travel tale, with added irony; Moll a criminal biography with surprising levels of comedy. Nonetheless, Bell's reading of the particular books (of which he considers the most developed to be *Roxana*) strongly stresses Defoe's allegiances to popular genres, against the 'high art' readings of many critics. In particular, Bell thinks the providentialist readings of Starr and Hunter place far too much stress on the structural properties of the spiritual autobiography. For Bell, the handling of providence in Crusoe is muddled and often 'perfunctory', even to the point of working against some audience expectations. Bell shares some of Watt's scepticism about Crusoe's conversion. *Robinson Crusoe* is essentially an adventure or voyage tale, with pirates and storms keeping the business going; the psychology of 'original sin' overloads what is essentially a narrative device (somehow, Defoe must get his hero on board ship) with spurious significance. The real core of the story is the alternation of safety and danger, the world of volatile uncertainty in which the hero must survive. Defoe draws inclusively on many other genres, among them popular pious exhortation, but does not allow the providentialist element drawn from such sources more than a passing, opportunist display – heaven comes in handy as an explanation for changes of direction in the narrative. Key narrative moments, such as the disposal of Xury, or the rescue of the useless money, or the springing up of barley seedlings, on which so much critical acumen has been displayed, are regarded similarly as superficial, rather than as deep signs of structure or pervasive irony: narrative must just keep going, regardless of moral interpretation. There is only one real animating subject: Crusoe's control of his fate, and destiny's control over him; the 'continuousness' of this struggle, the thin line between success and failure, is what interests readers. The goat in the cave is not the devil after all; neither is the footprint; neither is the parrot who calls Crusoe's name. Providence is invoked and immediately forgotten – and this is not a prompt for ironic reading of Crusoe's failings, which are purely part of the narrative sequence, not a 'theme' as such. Irony is present locally, not structurally. Conversion happens to Crusoe as shipwreck happens to him: he is not 'changed' as an individual, and the cohesion provided by a spiritual reading is at best based on highly selective attention to a merely 'vestigial' element of the telling. Essentially, this is a linear sequence, drawing on travel narratives and on spiritual autobiography without simply being either of them. Psychological subtlety is not required, for the book shows a 'mixed, see-saw understanding of life', like that of its readers, and unlike that of a philosopher or satirist.

Bell sees *Moll Flanders* as dependent on audience recognition of a familiar world, a figure prone to disaster, read about by those who had avoided such disaster and might aspire to such success. Behind it lie criminal biography, illicit romance, confessional memoir, jestbook. Again, the story is one of varied adventure:

> ■ In Defoe's fiction, the principle of accumulation or compendiousness overrules the aesthetic niceties of unity, and his narrative invites reading as sequence rather than as a purposive development. Variety is not only the most immediate feature of Moll's life, it is also the first principle of Defoe's fiction.[47] □

To try to translate the ups and downs of Moll's fortunes into an architectural or moral plan is to impose the principles of sonata form on free improvisation. That Moll draws even-handedly on criminal biography and pious memoir makes it unlikely that any real cohesion will result. As with Crusoe, there is one dominating narrative drive: Moll's life will end up in gentility or in Newgate. Or, of course, both. Relationships are to Moll what weather is to Crusoe: a force which might help you or sink you. Bell does not deny that there are ironic moments, where Moll's reflections are at odds with the audience's estimation of her, but these represent 'another piece of rhetorical opportunism on Defoe's part, cheerfully adding irony to the various zestful delights of the criminal tale'.[48] Bell does allow for more 'individuation' of character here than in *Robinson Crusoe*, expressed in part through slightly bizarre emotional outbursts (which liken her to the heroines of Aphra Behn, in this reading). There is more guilt, more plausible misery. But characterisation is still sporadic, not consistent: it is not a case study. Moll's viewpoints are not stable and coherent, though they are involving; the book is more like a collection of anecdotes told by a slightly unstable teller; it is 'too eclectic to be understood as consistently ironic or consistently mimetic'. Bell points out that most critics who argue for full artistic coherence in the book have little to say about the incest motif, which for him 'thwarts any reading of the book as a single linear enterprise' – it does not fit tidily into any scheme, of character, psychology, repentance, or anything else.[49] It is just another kind of shipwreck. In conclusion, Bell reckons that Crusoe's life 'is just one damn thing after another, with only the most perfunctory and unsustained attempts to connect them' – a sort of 'and then' principle; Moll's is more 'and so', moving towards the greater connectivity and purpose of *Roxana*.[50]

SURVIVAL OF THE FITTEST

If Bell could be taken to be on the Wattian side of Defoe criticism, at least so far as the novels we are considering are concerned, the other major book on Defoe published in 1985 aligns itself more clearly with those who think of Defoe's fiction as promulgating a consistently thought-out world view. Virginia Birdsall notes that all Defoe's protagonists focus obsessively on 'personal survival in the midst of chaos'.[51] Acknowledging the presence of both the economic (Novak) and spiritual (Starr; Hunter) templates for selfhood, Birdsall argues that the apparent opposition between them disappears if the stories are looked at according to a 'Hobbesian' scheme of things whereby human nature seeks survival as the only valid form of transcendence. The political philosopher Hobbes is seen as promoting a world view where 'every man is Enemy of every man' and the best one can do is look for advantage within that permanent war. Spiritual credit or money in the bank are just two different forms of the same accumulated power. Dress, possessions, self-promotion, self-centredness, and other ways of interacting with the world which would, for commentators such as Swift, invite scathing moral denunciation are, for Defoe, aspects of an understandable, even admirable, drive to survive. Society simply does not offer sufficient protection or structure against the predatory chaos of the world. Moreover, life is permanently offset against the even greater threat of death: Defoe's characters 'will, in the last analysis, settle for anything that seems to work in providing an escape from, or at least a hedge against, the terror of their own mortality'. Psychologically, they are driven by this alone: 'Always the Defoe protagonist is waging a battle against an enemy from whom there can be no escape [. . .] the fear of obliteration is always to be felt. That fear rules their lives, dictating every move they make and every word they utter.'[52]

Crusoe must always attempt to subdue anything wild or chaotic to his own rational mastery. From his first moments on the island he is subject to the terrifying fear of death, of being eaten by wild animals, or by cannibals. His gun gives him an apparently impregnable sense of power over the environment and every human in it. His conversion is about reducing the formlessness and accident of his life to a schedule of meaning, one which allays the fear of destruction. Exploration, a key element of the Crusoe mythology, is always about allaying the fear of the unknown with the control of knowledge. Friday must be converted, forcibly, psychologically, to servitude, must be ordered to clean up the mess left from the defeat of the savages. And this is less about colonisation than about personal psychological subjugation of any environmental threat; Crusoe must eat, or be eaten; the structure of his island must be modified to protect rather than destroy him. Yet all protection is merely temporary; there is always some new threat. Having constructed a 'complete enclosure' in his cave, Crusoe flees during an earthquake, and Birdsall sees this as a recurring emblem, recapitulating the original loss of secure (paternal) environment through the agency of a deep subterranean urging that he does not understand. He never knows whether the protective structures he constructs (in all senses) will in fact collapse and envelop him. The bigger he makes his zone of protection, the more likely it is to fall in. However much he seems to assume power and exert control, the threat is never neutralised, just held in check. Other people are always pirates, savages, mutineers, figures projected by Crusoe's paranoia. The colonists dispute amongst themselves, because that is the natural state of Defoe's world; storms continue to rage, however well the trade routes are mapped. There is no secure closure: the *Farther Adventures* carry on, the *Serious Reflections* persist in trying to assign an always fugitive meaning to experience.

Fear is the dominant emotion for Moll Flanders, too, adrift and shipwrecked on the streets of London, perpetually in motion from one insecure hiding place or marriage to the next. She sees herself as either in pursuit of some prey (a marriageable man, or a bundle of linen) or pursued (by a fortune-hunter, or thief-taker). Like Crusoe 'she fears for her own physical survival with an intensity that rises many times to something close to animal terror'.[53] The aspiration to be a gentlewoman is not so much an ironic misunderstanding by the young girl as the first manifestation of a desperate need to be free from servitude. At every stage, even in prison or en route to transportation, Moll needs to differentiate herself, buy a better cabin, find means to be above others. Like Crusoe she must have servants as indices of her own free power. She is not merely a thief but the *best* thief, the most skilled, the least stupid. Artfulness, money, 'wit' or intelligence, narrative ability, are all signs of power and dominion, equivalent to Crusoe's gun and governorship; the police are her wild animals; coins are her fortifications against a devouring chaos. Money replaces children (she steals from children, and steals things associated with children, as a sign of this substitution or conversion), for Moll is less interested in propagation and descent than in protective accumulation, the continual, almost ritualised telling-out of her bag of guineas. Money brings control and deliverance. And yet, like Crusoe, Moll is never safe, and persistently laments the need for 'friends', helpers, mother figures, anyone to offset the sense of abandonment and helplessness; those who notionally help her (fellow thieves, husbands) are also those who can most damage her, who leave her having to start all over again. Narrative disclosure is carefully modulated to avoid danger; none of the other characters in the book hears Moll's full story, and her real name is withheld even from the reader. There is no irony in the book for there is no deep distinction between Moll's moral reflections on her activities and the activities themselves, both of which are projects for survival; morality helps her deal with her history and with the prospect of death. We are looking at mental agility, not moral repentance; we cannot speak of her internal or natural moral qualities, for she has only the unalloyed instinct of self-preservation, an instinct rendered sympathetic by the vulnerability to which it is allied.

The decade from 1975 to 1985 thus saw a number of carefully elaborated attempts to find a central coherence to Defoe's fiction: in literary form, in the presentation of selfhood, in the methods of addressing and involving the reader. All, in one way or another, pay tribute to Defoe's unusual degree of interest in the processes by which the world of experience is ordered. While critics have continued to work along recognisably similar lines, it is fair to say that after 1985, with the entry into the academy of more radical versions of literary theory, consensus about the nature of fiction and its relation to the world began to evaporate. As we shall see in the next chapter, writing on Defoe began, accordingly, to explore some new, and occasionally hostile, angles.

CHAPTER SIX

Themes and Variations: Recent Criticism

DEFOE AND EMPIRICAL SCIENCE

Defoe has continued to be the subject of large-scale monographs which present his novels and other writings in relation to particular themes or areas of knowledge. In *Defoe and the New Sciences* (1996), Ilse Vickers seeks to place Defoe's 'realism' more squarely in the tradition of empirical science than Ian Watt did. Using a partial catalogue of Defoe's library to try to establish his reading practices, Vickers argues that Defoe was strongly in touch with the current of scientific thinking represented in the restoration and early eighteenth century by the Royal Society (founded 1662). So far as the fiction is concerned, Vickers concentrates largely on *Robinson Crusoe*, and especially on the island section, which demonstrates a 'belief in man's duty to study, alter and improve nature to his various uses'. Vickers associates this belief with the work of the empiricist philosopher and essayist Francis Bacon (1561–1626). Crusoe's 'objective and mathematically precise approach to reality' is demonstrated by his rationalistic, observant journal-keeping. The episode of the accidental crop of barley shows Crusoe learning from failure and responding by taking more accurate readings of the weather and seasons (which leads to success). He actually uses the word 'experiment' of this procedure and Vickers relates the process to the practical and often economically focused rationale for the experimental work of the Royal Society, which actively promoted the compilation and publication of Baconian 'Histories of Trades'. Crusoe's progress reinvents the learning processes of baking, ship-building, carpentry, poetry, basket-weaving, bakery, and farming. Crusoe forms a sort of one-man encyclopaedia of practical knowledge; he is '*homo faber*, the maker of things'. The book 'may stand as an allegory of the advancement of learning: a model of initiative and invention'.[1] His life on the island is supposed to begin in 1659 and his career thus parallels the early experiments and histories prepared by the fledgling Royal Society; Crusoe fulfils another obligation and ideal of the Royal Society, that of accurate environmental mapping (finding himself handily equipped with the necessary instruments). Crusoe enforces order and imposes his values upon his surroundings. Ultimately, the kingdom over which he presides is a huge, tidy 'magazine' of things and notions. Crusoe compiles, divides and ranks his collected data. Everything is inventoried, listed, enumerated – whether human, animal, or inanimate.

Vickers contends that the diary-keeping has been ascribed too narrowly to a Puritan tradition of self-examination, and wants instead to link Crusoe's scientific self-awareness with the theological strand available to contemporary science and known as 'natural theology', which advocates the study of nature as a means to understanding the wondrous mind of God. Restoration scientists saw no conflict between faith and reason in their work: experiments discovered divine ordering in the universe and found meaning in natural events and disasters (such as the great storm of 1703, Defoe's account of which includes both Baconian observation and theological reflection). This view of the study of nature was widespread in Anglican as well as dissenting circles and available in such well-known texts as John Ray's *The Wisdom of God Manifested in the Works of Creation* (1691), which offers a model for Crusoe's gradual increase in spiritual understanding alongside practical competence. Crusoe must therefore not only lord it over his island, using empirical knowledge as power, but must also learn to view the world in terms of God's ordering. Thus Vickers manages to resolve some of the tensions between the secular and the religious aspects of the novel identified by Watt and others.

The other element of Crusoe relevant to the argument is language. Defoe's indebtedness to utilitarian, non-figurative language that avoids (or claims to avoid) metaphor had been canvassed by various critics after Watt, but Vickers claims that Defoe had a direct link to the linguistic theories of the Royal Society through his teacher, Charles Morton. She also sees the occasional contradictions and imbalances in the style as giving a greater human authenticity to the moment of telling than an actual scientific account would: 'with one hand he gives accuracy, while with the other he disturbs the clarity to render a more life-like reality'; truthfulness demands repetition, modification, indecision, but 'it is exactly in these stylistic imperfections that we find the perfect rendering of the moment'.[2]

Vickers' account is in the line of traditional historicist scholarship, reconstructing an educational and social background to give a context for understanding the fiction. It is surprisingly innocent of any political interpretation, and even Crusoe's educational and spiritual dominance of Friday, which Vickers places as part of the project of mastery inherent in the Baconian advancement of learning, raises no postcolonial eyebrows. A monograph which comes closer to political questions is Karen Armstrong's *Defoe: Writer as Agent* (1996). This presents Defoe as a

consistent thinker, with *Robinson Crusoe* as a critique of the rush for over-
seas investment and *Moll Flanders* as a discussion of the rising crime rate
in early eighteenth-century London. But much of the work done on
Defoe since the 1980s has been influenced by literary theories which are
less concerned with the wholeness or unity of a work of art, or with its
intellectual coherence and background, and which tend by contrast to
celebrate the fractured or unstable elements of mind, body, and authority as incarnated and articulated in writing. Critics now tend to worry
less about the discoverable, unmixed intentions of the canonical author
Daniel Defoe and to concentrate instead on the rupture points in systems
of thinking that the novels may reveal. As we shall see shortly, the issue of
the colony is one such problematic area.

The sections that follow explore themes that have obvious continu-
ities with, and departures from, the earlier chapters. These loosely-
bounded areas are designed to suggest a sense of the variety and interest
of Defoe's writing, rather than compartmentalise his work reductively.
They show a developing debate, rather than a completed answer to any
issue, with radical lines of thought operating alongside more traditional
ones.

THE NOVEL CONTINUES TO RISE

As Novak remarks, 'the novel did not so much rise as it lurched in various directions'.[3] So has criticism of the 'rise' or 'origin' of the novel since
Watt's formulation of it, not least because of increased hostility towards
the teleology implied by 'rise' and the foundational truth suggested by
'origin'. John Richetti, for example, finds that Watt's model implies a false
hierarchy, a coming-to-maturity of 'the novel' as opposed to immature
popular forms of writing. The canon on which it is based is enormously
selective, and he is sceptical about the weight Watt gives to middle-class
influence.[4] Marthe Robert takes the term 'origin' as relatively unprob-
lematic because in her analysis there is such a foundational truth and
progress: the origin of the novel is the eternal psychodrama of the
unconscious. *Robinson Crusoe* features as a narcissistic foundling fantasy in
which the child repudiates its parents, dreams of nobler and more powerful ones to whom it really belongs, and elaborates a dream of omnipo-
tence in a paradisal world undisturbed by other people and (especially)
sexuality. For this reading the key theme is Crusoe's insatiable thirst for
power and mastery. He is reborn from the sea after a shipwreck, a painful
transition in which the fantasy turns out to be thwarted at every turn by
the obstacles of reality (not to mention the sentence of guilt from the
Oedipal court). He recapitulates growth afresh and achieves mastery
through work, while simultaneously regressing to a pre-sexual stage.

Friday becomes the son (born from the womb-like sea) who proves Crusoe's virile paternity once Crusoe's apprenticeship to reality is complete. The form of the novel appears to claim direct contact with reality, as if fantasy could be unproblematically accommodated within the world of experience, thus allowing the eternal family romance to continue functioning.[5]

Lennard J. Davis takes up Richetti's lead rather than Robert's in looking at a wider range of proto-novelistic material for the origins of the novel. He argues that the novel derives from history, journalism, and popular crime narratives, which offer 'factual fictions', as opposed to 'romance', which is aligned with epic and aristocratic idealisms. The novel distinguishes itself from romance by claiming documentary status, like journalism; and yet progressively and gradually distinguishes itself from the 'news/novels discourse' of everyday actuality by admitting that it is fiction and thus avoiding press censorship governing the dissemination of 'news'. Social and technological factors outweigh literary influences; printing gives new status to the immediacy of truth claims; political arguments about truth and authority catch emergent novelists in the crossfire. Davis's chapter on Defoe ('Lies as Truth') examines Defoe's fictions as works in progress within this process: 'his works remain odd to us because they seem not fully novels', and that is because they do not have a conscious, theorised generic status. Davis examines the prefatory materials accompanying all the fictions and finds that 'we can still sense the confusion of attitude toward fact and fiction'. Defoe's own personal career 'so filled with disguise, lies, indirection, forgery, deceit, and duplicity seems to place him constitutionally at the center of questions about the truthfulness of narratives, about the problem of framing and ambivalence, about the breakdown of signification and reliability'. Davis discerns a gradual rephrasing of prefatory statements about the factual basis of each novel in terms of an anxious and uneasy accommodation with the status of fiction: 'Defoe uses a series of dodges, feints, and poses to rationalize the use of fiction, and even in his last phase, he is very careful not to say outright that his work is not factual.'[6]

Michael McKeon analyses challenges to and reconstitutions of dominant ideologies in his study *The Origins of the English Novel* (1987), as does Stuart Sim in an article published in the same year.[7] McKeon finds Davis's explanations too mono-causal and tries to encompass a more fluid and unstable process within a complex Marxist analysis of 'dialectical engagements'. The novel as a form is an ideological answer to two crises: the problems of how narrative can be used to tell the truth; and of what happens when external social order and internal moral values do not appear any longer to equate. The novel mediates and negotiates these problems for a newly puzzled audience. As idealistic romances such as *Arcadia* (1581–93, by Sir Philip Sidney, 1554–86) came to be seen as too naïve to represent the world truly, a narrative mode of empirical fact-finding began to replace them in travel books and science writing. But this too was open to the accusation of naivety, in that all writing bears traces of artifice, conventionality and system; 'extreme scepticism' and parody were bound to undermine naïve empiricism. Like Watt, McKeon looks for social causes to these shifts, in a second strand of analysis. The aristocratic equation of rank with virtue began to look very questionable in the late seventeenth century and was countered by the claims of wit, money, intelligence, acquisition, industry. But this also generated a reactionary denial or scepticism. The novel does not exactly rise, and no one writer starts it off; it emerges from a dialectical interplay between these competing genres and truth claims. Eventually the novel achieves coherence and stability as a genre because of its ability to absorb, reflect and negotiate these contradictory impulses and highly diverse critiques.

McKeon's book has a theoretical first half and then a series of case studies, in a structure a little reminiscent of Watt. The chapter on Defoe takes *Robinson Crusoe* as a 'parable of the younger son' (perhaps picking up in part Robert's Oedipal theme). The problem of truth-telling in narrative is not solved by Defoe's claim to historicity since that already seemed like a naïve cover for subjective projection. McKeon sees the narrative voice split between the old Robinson and the young, or between Character and Narrator. Critical accounts have, in McKeon's view, also been split between the Wattian proponents of a materialist Crusoe and the Starr–Hunter line of an ideal Protestant narrative. McKeon takes these traditions to be conjoined, if contradictory, parts of the same intellectual complex. Defoe has gone a perilous step beyond Bunyanesque allegory in sanctioning a resistance to a spiritualised reading: that is, he makes it possible to read for the story rather than the meaning. The result is a literal narrative filled with the mutabilities of religion (providence) and romance (pirates, shipwreck), which do not so much undergo in themselves a transformation to a form of social mobility, in which the prodigal son can surmount his situation successfully, as engineer the conditions under which that mobility may transpire.

Defoe puts his hero on an island bereft of competition and exchange, which also excludes the potential sin of social advancement or excess. In this sense, all bets are off, and Crusoe has to refound his authority on claims that are often confused and specious. He cannot completely internalise either divine righteousness or socio-political versions of power:

■ *Robinson Crusoe* at times emits the aura of irony because, like all ideology, it is dedicated to the instrumental disclosure – in Defoe's case with unparalleled penetration and candor – of a complex of contradictions that it is simultaneously dedicated to mediating and rendering intelligible.[8] □

But when Crusoe returns to Brazil, McKeon senses 'an air of enchantment [. . .] as though the magic of providence had effected a merger with that of capitalism'. Nothing whatever is said about the labour which created the money: it is simply not seen, and the money is just magically there, as if the processes of laborious self-advancement outside society quietly merit labour-free self-advancement inside it. Defoe gives us 'the representation of the psychological state of being a principled possessive individualist, fully reconciled to the naturalness and morality of the pursuit of self-interest'.

■ The product of his experience first in the society of God and then, gradually, among other people, it represents the hard-won lesson that the metaphysical realm of the Spirit may be accommodated and rendered accessible as the psychological realm of Mind. It is Defoe's remarkable achievement not simply to have provided this psychological access to spiritual crisis but to have specified it [. . .] to the concrete dimension of material and social ambition.[9] □

Later histories of the novel in the eighteenth century have tended to emphasise the role of popular literature against the forces of social crisis. In his 1990 book *Before Novels*, J. Paul Hunter included an even wider range of non-imaginative writing as the matrix for the novel to emerge from.[10] Playing down romance and spiritual autobiography, Hunter looked, like Richetti, Davis and Bell before him, to the non-elite and non-classical forms of journalism: broadsheets, ephemera, travel writing, 'horrid news' pamphlets and ballads, criminal biography, conduct manuals, and didactic literature. The 'novelisation' of experience suggested contemporaneity and hereness; credibility and probability; familiarity; rejection of romance plot; individualism and subjectivity; character identification and empathy; and some degree of coherence and unity. Hunter argues that 'deep cultural desires' can be inferred from a study of these elements of popular reading, and that fiction as we know it came into existence to feed and satisfy these needs.

Feminist critiques suggest that Watt's distinction between novel and romance privileges male writers of 'serious' fiction over female writers of narratives of desire and seduction. Watt does not explain the widespread presence of the work of female novelists, nor of 'female' concerns with privacy and eroticism in the epoch covered by his study. Jane Spencer counters Watt by proposing *The Rise of the Woman Novelist* (1986) to take account of Aphra Behn, Jane Barker (1652–1732), Eliza Haywood (about 1693–1756) and others. In *Desire and Domestic Fiction: A Political History of the Novel* (1987), Nancy Armstrong sees the novel in relation to conduct literature and educational treatises and finds 'female' structures of feeling at its centre; it is a form which promotes and is promoted by women's sense of love, marriage and child-rearing. Watt sees the novel as mirroring a social shift, whereas Armstrong takes it as a space of struggle in which to appropriate key signs and practices. The novel is aligned with the history of sexuality, and domestic fiction disentangles sexuality from official power to construct a separate domestic zone of alternative politics.

Nonetheless, Defoe's role in the history of the novel continues to be taken as central. In *History and the Early English Novel* (1997), Robert Mayer puts 'history' on the agenda in a more self-conscious way by arguing that the early novel is actually in some ways about history. Defoe made 'the nexus of history and fiction a key element in the theory of the novel elaborated by writers and readers in the eighteenth century'. Mayer re-reads the tradition of seventeenth-century historiography in its various forms (biography, 'secret history', 'strange news') and discovers a tradition of Baconian history which did not wholly base itself on empirical evidence but absorbed hearsay, polemic, and fiction. Defoe's novels present themselves as 'histories' in this context. The novel emerges as a form not through particular literary performances themselves but in the theorisation that occurs around them. Crusoe represents the key epistemological rupture-point, a discursive realignment which makes readers think about and choose generic boundaries in ways which fictions such as those of Behn, whatever their claim to historicity, do not. In *The Cure of the Passions and the Origins of the English Novel* (2001), Geoffrey Sill aligns the emergent novel with a historically new kind of medical regulation of emotion. *Robinson Crusoe* and *Moll Flanders* are full of troubled and irrational passions and psychodramas, which call for a quasi-medical regimen and regulation. The novel comes into being to manage emotion: it has a kind of agenda, whereby the potential for pathological emotion is converted into the order of text.[11]

In January 2000 the journal *Eighteenth-Century Fiction* ran a special issue called 'Reconsidering the Rise of the Novel', with contributions from Richetti, Novak, McKeon, Hunter, Mayer, and Watt himself. Revisiting his own seminal work, Watt admitted that the slipperiness of the term 'realism' was obscuring and preventing actual debate, though his views were not in themselves hugely altered.[12] Watt's thesis is described as 'bloody but unbowed' in a recent account of the formation of the genre.[13]

ECONOMICS

It would perhaps have been a matter of pride to Defoe to know that *Robinson Crusoe* was taught in American business schools.[14] Defoe's origins were in trade and his businesses involved inventing, making, selling, importing and exporting a bizarre variety of commodities: wool, oysters, wine, tobacco, cheese, salt, linen, bricks, tiles, diving engines. He dreamed up projects on fishery, mining, and inland navigation. In addition, he wrote on a great many economic subjects and related social issues, such as taxation and what we would now call social security. Few novelists can have had such a thorough grounding in the economic business of the world, and few can have so foregrounded the importance of money to his protagonists. Watt's *Rise of the Novel* and Novak's *Economics and the Fiction of Daniel Defoe* brought more historical and critical acumen to bear on the issue, which has continued to interest critics. In 1970 Juliet McMaster published an article on Moll's obsessive totting-up of worldy goods, seeing the confusion between love and money in terms of an ironic indictment. In 1982 Lois Chaber produced a subtle Marxist reading of the presence of 'capital' in *Moll Flanders*.[15] Chaber takes issue with those who elevate Defoe's art at the expense of the moral status of his heroine, and argues instead that her 'indelicate, immoral, and illegal activities are emanations and illuminations of a burgeoning patriarchal capitalist community', of which the novel is taken to be a critique. Moll embodies a historical clash between bourgeois enterprise and the desire for gentility. She eludes the cycle of reproduction and enters the 'social cycle of production', becoming producer rather than product. This was a highly unusual path for the eighteenth-century literary heroine but one which seems to be based on female, matriarchal models of enterprise.

The role of economics in mapping the wider world is the theme of David Trotter's 1988 book on Defoe and Dickens.[16] Trotter finds that Defoe was fascinated by mechanisms of exchange and circulation which defined a formatted zone of pure 'economy'. The grid of navigation by which the world was known was formed by trade routes, a network less of exploration than of exploitation, locating points of exchange on coasts rather than in interiors. Defoe's novels test these boundaries and structures by pitting them against individual desire. Crusoe resists his father's inland format of settlement and struggles instead to make his way to networks of exchange in international trade. As a merchant, he rambles, and accumulates sometimes by accident; it is not an easy and regular progress. But there is a pattern, involving departure or escape from and subsequent return to set lines of correspondence, a pattern which forms his destiny and his significance: he continually reminds us of the world's grid by drifting off it catastrophically. He finds illegal routes, and faces dark interiors which have no co-ordinates. Like Defoe's other male protagonists, Crusoe experiences the hell of economic isolation in a way that reinforces the function of the rules.

This has consequences for the way selfhood is produced and perceived. The individuals prove there is life beyond the format of exchange, and yet all need to return to it. For Trotter, the conversion experience as discussed by Starr and Hunter cannot provide a complete significance for the novel. The journal which presents the core of the conversion narrative is symbolically limited and peters out. It mingles conversion with the slow degradation of Crusoe's structures, the falling apart of everything into elements: rope, nails, bits of sail. The conversion is not an adequate transformation of this brilliantly realised materiality and does not control or prefigure the shape or events of the rest of the novel. The alternative interpretation, stressing Crusoe's civilising programme, is also doubted because it lacks a sense of Crusoe's theatricality, his self-conscious performance of roles, which is more about identity formation than practical ethics. Even the disciplines of commercial exchange seem to be tested and exceeded by what Crusoe actually does: his histrionics are effective but not disciplined by economic principle. Trotter queries whether there is a regulatory power for the creation of the narrative of selfhood, since the novel seems to be about what defeats, obstructs, and stretches circulation: circuits of exchange lie forever around Crusoe's life without forming a solid basis for it.

Trotter's analysis of *Moll Flanders* finds 'an economy of trade' entering the lives of characters 'at every point'. Early on, Moll does not know how to trade properly with the elder brother, how to maximise potential, how to regulate the flow of desire and convert assets into a profitable contract. Sensible economic marriage to the brother is a transgression, both adulterous and incestuous: the 'discipline of the market supervenes on a transgression which has already formed her uneconomically'. The pattern for Moll is threefold: opportunity to exchange/circulate; reluctance; realisation of the consequences of failure. The formatted space of the marriage market is defined by the sober bank clerk and glamorous highwayman; like Crusoe, Moll scorns the given trade routes. She steals when not in economic need: adventure and transgression take over. Newgate awaits to fix those who disrupt exchange: it forms a psychological concentration of blockage and economic halt. The repentance associated with spiritual autobiography gains Moll advantage but does not define her selfhood or construe the rest of the narrative as a pattern. Transportation, the conversion of the criminal back into a legitimate economic individual, offers Moll a different opportunity to re-enter the formatted zone of exchange. As with Crusoe's return from his island, the voyage is part of her economic upsurge; she becomes rich. But she has not actually exchanged her way into a new selfhood. This route just takes her back to her criminal heritage (her mother) and emphasises the blockage in the marriage market (the brother).

Trotter is unconvinced by upbeat accounts of Moll's techniques of selfhood and survival. In this reading she does not achieve moral coherence and authority; circumstances mount up but do not deposit a self; opportunities for exchange arise but do not integrate her. Moll does not

have an intrinsic essence which survives the translations and constructions of economic exchange. We do not discover an essential self, just a
series of improvisations and displacements, with origins always already
insecure, removed, occulted. Moll, like Crusoe, ends indifferently, as
'unfinished business', incomplete, uncompletable, always moving on.
There is always something else, some supplement, some second thought,
some revision, something that cannot be satisfactorily incorporated and
fixed in a stable identity.

Moll Flanders has been to some degree more prominent than *Robinson
Crusoe* in recent discussions of these themes. Jacques Sohier sees the
heroine in relation to a notional 'rise' of the 'gentlewoman–
tradeswoman'.[17] Ann Kibbie studies the significance of the explicit link-
age of biological reproduction and capital increase in relation to persistent cultural anxieties about the tendency of money to beget money.
Such anxieties, often using female imagery as the model for unstable and
mysterious generation, were expressed in the economic theories that
Defoe drew on, and indeed by Defoe himself. Kibbie treats *Moll Flanders*
as the comic epic of this problem (where *Roxana* is the tragic version).
Calling attention to the eroticising of money, through flirtatious play
with purses, pockets, drawers and coins, and moving on to scenes of
gambling and theft, Kibbie suggests that monetary and biological reproduction are merged in a way which images both the power and the threat
of capitalism; Moll benefits from the association (a comic or optimistic
version), while Roxana crashes, showing the tragic side of the equation.[18]

More recent readings take us towards politics. Rebecca Connor links
Moll Flanders with the early political economist Sir William Petty
(1623–87). In the wake of Trotter's *Circulation*, Edward Copeland argues
that Defoe belongs partly to a tradition of cartography ('Moll' was the
surname of a famous mapmaker), and that the streets of London, as
mapped by Moll, are part of an effort to produce a grid of formatted
space at the centre of the globe. Amit Yahov-Brown contends that Defoe
conceived of a citizenship of rights in which earners provide support
through taxation for those who cannot earn, and that *Moll Flanders*
demonstrates the need for such a state. Moll is welcomed back into the
fold of citizenship by becoming economically productive as a transported
felon, rather than another executed thief.[19]

POLITICS

Robinson Crusoe has sometimes been seen as a narrative demonstrating
the generation of (Lockean) civil society. Ian Bell, for example, sees
Crusoe's stay on the island as a parable about the growth of government,
dismantling the patriarchal theories of Sir Robert Filmer (about

1588–1653) and aligning Crusoe with the free citizen of Locke's political theories. A savage, Hobbesian state of nature gives way to the
production of a god-fearing commonwealth through contractual
arrangements.[20]

Less often, *Robinson Crusoe* has been seen as a covert political statement in close relation to the shifting political climate of its decade, but
early assumptions that Defoe was a straightforward Lockean Whig have
become markedly less convincing as knowledge of what Defoe wrote has
increased. In a monograph published in 1984 Geoffrey Sill argued that
Defoe did attempt to maintain some kind of ideological consistency
amidst the stream of conflicting political pressures. Robert Harley,
Defoe's saviour and political master, is seen less as an instinctive 'moderate' than as a manager of complex political allegiances and forces; Defoe
wrote ideological fictions for him, promoting the ideal of above-party
consensus. Both were suspicious of heroic individualism as a simple solution for political problems. Ideology and fiction were, Sill argues, in some
ways not very distinct forms; ideology is not a principle but a fiction
'imposed on the world for particular ends'.[21] Sill's book concentrates on
Defoe's shift from propagandist to novelist in the decade preceding
Crusoe. Gradually Defoe learns, from the use of emblematic figures in
political writings, the novelistic habit of finding origins and psychology
for particular actions.

Defoe turns to fiction as a freer, more ideal zone in which to achieve
ideological aims, having exhausted the possibilities of more obviously
politically allegorical fiction and vividly-imagined biographical accounts
of the Duke of Marlborough (1650–1722), Harley, and other politicians.
Defoe's *Secret History of the White Staff* (1714), a defence of Harley, is full
of inaccuracies if treated as a political memoir but coherent as an ideological fiction, a mythic interpretation of 'faithful service and the tragedy
of good designs thwarted by fate and bad men'.[22] These memoirs are not
realistic in detail but do propose a psychology of characters in action,
with reflection over time making the significance of events clearer (as in
novels). Sill's analysis takes us away from charges that Defoe was just a
political liar by seeing him as generating fictional solutions to intractable
political problems: he was not a Machiavellian conspirator but a liberal
humanist. Sill reads Defoe's first novel as a hybrid between historical
biography and spiritual autobiography which forms the 'symbolic novel';
this form deliberately severs ties with the real historical world (to which
it alludes by date but nothing else) in order to plant an everyman Crusoe
in a pure environment to demonstrate how competing socio-political
claims might be reconciled.

Robinson Crusoe puts together all Defoe's ideas on kingship, nature,
providence, and self-restraint into a 'new model of personal and political
conduct with regard to one's sovereign and the public good'; it addresses

the difficulty of regulating a society of self-seeking individuals in a complex culture. Crusoe is not proposed as a model of monarchic hero-ism but prospers 'through the propagation of an ideology that stressed the virtues of moderation, reserve, self-restraint, and dependence on the counsel of knowledgeable advisors'. All the examples of Crusoe's mastery (of technology, of nature, of culture) are in essence signs of self-mastery, 'which he acquires through the discovery of his human limitations'. Crusoe's learning is not primarily economic; it is really about not exceeding necessary risk or accumulation. 'The point of Crusoe's discov-eries in economics, therefore, is not to support a particular theory of value, but to present in a new way the virtue of moderation and self-restraint.'[23] In the *Farther Adventures* Crusoe, having lost his 'pilot' Friday, and having experimented not very successfully with various forms of authority over his colony, finally cedes his wandering and conquering impulse to an exiled Russian politician in the wastes of Siberia, who teaches him that the greatest mastery is mastery of the self.

Sill was in part responding to an early formulation of an argument by Manuel Schonhorn which sees Crusoe more as the embodiment of a monarchic hero. In his subsequent monograph, Schonhorn took issue with the unexamined consensus that Defoe was a Lockean Whig, supporter of parliament and the sovereignty of the people, seeing him as a more maverick, complex figure. The Defoe who took arms in support of the Duke of Monmouth's abortive attempt to wrest the throne from James II in 1685, supported William III less as a king by consent than as a warrior monarch on biblical lines. Defoe defended William's powerful martial role; dissatisfied with the conflicting demands of parliament, Defoe was more attracted by the potent figure of a competent king. Since faction and violence are givens, the prince must be strong, must command prac-tically and with sufficient force. Schonhorn takes Defoe's immense poem *Jure Divino* (1706) as his fullest exploration of the origins of government and argues that Defoe is most attracted by God's model of kingship, from the First Book of Samuel in the Old Testament. 'Defoe's kingly ideal is the sword in the hands of a providential monarch; his crown, immediately derived from God, is a symbol of more than supreme earthly dignity; and his sceptre is the gift of a free and compliant people.'[24]

Robinson Crusoe stands as 'a political fable that emanated from an imagination that had been actively engaged in the most intense political debates in modern English history'. Schonhorn argues that Crusoe's vocabulary of rule is intended to represent 'his sustained consciousness of his political self', 'an imagination vibrantly afloat in regal waters'.[25] There is no irony in his lexicon of power (governor, king, reasons of state, commander, power, dominion, lord, estate, subjects). This hierarchy mirrors a political royalism; supreme power is already there, it is not granted by the people. Crusoe embodies the law of conquest. He is there, prior to his people, 'a naked Sword by my Side, two Pistols in my Belt, and a gun upon each Shoulder'. It is the complete control of a one-man army, enacting providential deliverance in the manner of a redemptive monarch. But Crusoe is not biologically a father-king, he is not a 'patriarch' in the biblical sense; like William III he is unable to perpetuate power, a true conqueror but still transitory.

More recent treatments have reverted to Hobbes as the key thinker in the struggle for political foundations. Sara Soncini sees *Robinson Crusoe* as based on a Hobbesian conception of the origin of societies and the relations between subjects and monarchs, with the *Farther Adventures* then exploring more complex, post-conquest issues in a Lockean way. Carol Kay suggests that Defoe's economics should be viewed in relation to Hobbes's politics, and downplays the influence of Locke. Kay manages to include Moll Flanders as a political player, an aspect other critics have largely neglected. She sees the novels as engaging with, or conspicuously evading, public arguments; they are not in some free private zone but in the same culture as Defoe's pamphleteering and his arguments about social management.[26]

In an essay called 'Crusoe's Secret' (2005), Tom Paulin returns us to specific political questions.[27] Paulin sees *Robinson Crusoe* as an extended allegory of the anxiety experienced by the oppressed dissenters under the Stuarts. Others have noted the correspondence of dates between Crusoe's exile and the return of Charles II, and speculated about the kind of exile that represents for Defoe's kind, but Paulin finds a number of further parallels, particularly in accounts of the Duke of Monmouth's Protestant rebellion against the Catholic James II, in which Defoe participated. The strong vein of prison and execution imagery in the book reminds Paulin that Defoe was lucky to escape the bloody judicial reprisals after the rising failed. Paulin sees the presence of Newgate and Tyburn in Defoe's fiction as part of his 'survivor's guilt', an ongoing anxiety about punishment reinforced by subsequent arrests and the spell in the pillory. Defoe's political writings support the reading: the fact that Crusoe, the definitive imperial Englishman, is in fact descended from a family from Bremen, can be linked to Defoe's *The True-Born Englishman* (1701), his anti-xenophobic satire in support of the Dutch William III. Paradisal scenes remind Paulin of the work of Puritan forebears such as John Milton (1608–74) and Andrew Marvell (1621–78), a radical MP, from 1659 until his death, for Hull – a place which is also a key part of Crusoe's background.

SEXUAL POLITICS AND GENDER TROUBLE

Charles Dickens commented to his biographer that 'De Foe's women too – Robinson Crusoe's wife for instance – are terrible dull commonplace fellows without breeches; and I have no doubt he was a precious dry disagreeable article himself – I mean De Foe: not Robinson.'[28] We know from his other writings that Defoe had a profound interest in family mechanics and sexual behaviour and it has always been a matter of surprise that Crusoe appears quite without sexual desire or trouble through his 28 years on the island – in strong contrast to possible sources such as *The Isle of Pines* (1668), where the narrator, shipwrecked with four women, enjoys a highly patriarchal sexual utopia. Crusoe's longing for company appears assuaged by the appearance of his male servant Friday. On his return to civilisation Crusoe marries and is widowed in the space of half a sentence. On the other hand, he marries when well over fifty, and embarks for further adventures after his wife's death, in a sign of virile continuance. He also grieves more pointedly for his wife in the *Farther Adventures*, and sends wives for the men in his colony, as if noticing a deficiency in the first adventure.

Moll, by contrast, uses sex as a weapon of control and as an economic product. E. M. Forster, preparing for his *Aspects of the Novel* lectures, noted that *Moll Flanders* was 'A puzzling book – gynomorphic [woman-shaped], not one stitch of the man-made' and asked himself '(By the way, why is D. only keen on the sexual life of women? His approach to men's [. . .] is perfunctory. Only when there is a woman in the case does he warm up.)'[29] Virginia Woolf celebrated the femininity of Defoe's heroine more loudly, linking the book to his other writings on the position of women. This aspect was picked up in articles about *Moll Flanders*, particularly in relation to the theme of marriage, by Tommy Watson, David Blewett and John Richetti.[30] Attempts to see Defoe as a kind of early pornographer, or as the proponent of an 'androgynous vision', have been isolated.[31] Feminist criticism in the 1970s largely took Woolf's point about Defoe's progressive views on the social position of women seriously, though often with some ambivalence about male assumptions of what constituted 'woman'. Kathleen McCoy scrutinised patriarchal readings of the novel which took as signs of eternal femininity aspects of experience and identity which could be seen to be historically and culturally determined. Miriam Lerenbaum defended Defoe's presentation of motherhood and femininity on experiential and historical grounds. Katherine Rogers argued that Defoe's 'recognition of [women's] full humanity and his wish to free them from sexual as well as economic dependence on men' constituted 'feminism beyond the bounds of respectable thought'.[32]

In 1978 Shirlene Mason published the first full monograph on these issues, looking at the social history of female roles in tandem with Defoe's social writings (especially those on economics and family).[33] Defoe himself had many daughters to provide for and was intensely aware of the lack of institutional or social support and education for the offspring of poor families. He knew that women lacked power in relation to marriage and property laws; his bankruptcy had erased his own wife's dowry. Defoe's *Essay upon Projects* picked up ideas from the early feminist Mary Astell (1666–1731) and proposed much-extended female education on the grounds that there would be economic advantage to men if women were properly trained; this had nothing to do with 'Female Government'. Moll's education is clearly low-level, accidental and unsupported – essentially an imitation of education for the rich, which itself contained nothing useful. In other works Defoe was highly critical of socially mobile servants but Mason thinks he was clearly attracted by Moll's go-getting aspirations. Most of Moll's marriages are a disaster by the standards set out in Defoe's social pamphlets, from the first 'matrimonial whoredom' (the subtitle of Defoe's *Conjugal Lewdness*) enacted when Moll marries the younger brother while in love with the elder. The second marriage is to a fool, the third is bigamous and incestuous, the fourth is bigamous and based on false premises, and the fifth is mercenary but sexually successful. But these are in effect social problems rather than individual ones, in Mason's reading; instead of turning Moll into a bitter and quarrelsome woman like those of *Conjugal Lewdness*, Defoe (eventually) rewards her survival instinct with a happy marriage. Indeed Moll conducts a series of do-it-yourself divorces, going freelance on the marriage market: this represents Defoe's awareness of the potential for huge unfairness and unhappiness in marital arrangements.

Moll Flanders was therefore a kind of case study in the failure of marriage laws and social security, and the poverty of educational and business opportunities for women. In conclusion, Mason underscores a basic paradox about Defoe's writings on women. He is comparatively free of the satirical misogyny of the time, he advocated education and support for women, he was open to the view that women might well have intellectual superiority over men in at least some areas of life, he deplored abuses of women in marriage and in certain legal situations. But he was not advocating any wholesale reform of the status quo, and was not looking for female suffrage or real economic or professional independence. Marriage remained the main destination for women in his thinking. Moll (and Roxana) are provocative in this connection because 'his real interest seems to lie with the woman who is clever and independent, living on her wit and plucking the good things from life'.[34] But his successful women remain exceptions, social outcasts: the possibilities opened by fiction, for women's independent survival and self-making, are not thought through into any programme of social action.

Feminist arguments about the status of Moll have continued to emerge. Mona Scheuermann celebrates Defoe's heroine for her human normality, independence, resistance to victimhood and determination to achieve financial, as opposed to spiritual, security. Srividhya Swaminathan finds that Moll outstrips the narrow moral that Defoe intends her to illustrate and forges links of solidarity with other women, providing a gendered social network that supports rather than oppresses. Melissa Ganz has recently returned to the historical moment of the novel, and its force as a kind of social tract about the plight of women abandoned in marriages which they had no means of formally ending.[35] But gender-based criticism is not so straightforwardly politicised as it once was, and examinations of sexual politics have often taken a different turn.

In 1979 Robert Erickson produced a study of the figure of 'Mother Midnight' in *Moll Flanders*, later using this material as the foundation for a book on 'birth, sex and fate' in the fictions of Defoe and later novelists. Erickson examines the role of Moll's midwife, later re-imagined as her 'Governess', a mutable bawd/fence/midwife intermediary who facilitates Moll's initiation into and progress through various kinds of illegality. Using midwifery manuals and medical discourses about childbirth, Erickson shows that by insistently drawing attention to the processes of childbirth, swaddling, the weaving of cloth and so on, the 'Mother Midnight' figure comes to oversee the making of the individuated, responsible body. The body is not taken for granted as the central legal unit of identity but forever produced, abused, imperilled, dressed, and sent forth. Novelists from Defoe onwards were fascinated by the reproductive body as the site of a conflicted and troubled selfhood. Individuation is thus linked to an explicitly gendered social body image, appropriated and constructed by the male 'fathers' of the novel.[36] Carol Houlihan Flynn sees *Moll Flanders* as a text preoccupied with appetite and sexuality. The body's presence is continually signalled by the recurrent child problem, which prevents or inhibits escape from the economic situation: Moll is forced to recognise the body in ways confirmed elsewhere by the criminal law which has ultimate power over it. The body becomes the site of attention for the ordering of desire and consumption; bodily sensations present a threatening arena of chaos and disorder, a reality not automatically structured into meaning.[37]

One of the challenging things the body does in *Moll Flanders* is commit incest, a theme recently brought to the fore by Defoe critics. Thomas Grant Olsen regards *Moll Flanders* as an investigation into the rules governing kinship and language, with incest acting as a kind of irrepressible unconscious remnant of the control over the unruly female figure exerted by the male pen. While the preface imposes order, sexual activity subverts the bourgeois family. An extremely sophisticated reading of the situation is given by Ellen Pollak, who regards the incest as a crucial discursive event, not simply a handy plot device. Referring to early debates on incest, case histories, and literary representations, Pollak suggests that incest could be seen as liberating and transgressive, engaging with and obscuring shifts between patriarchal, kin-based systems and

Lockean, class-based ones. Moll's incest is emblematic, a symptom of her desire to elude the normal bourgeois systems of exchange whereby women are circulated among men as objects of consumption; it blocks both patriarchal and capitalist modes of exchange, though Pollak also finds the subsequent treatment of the moment to be conservative and containing.[38]

Family matters are also of interest to Crusoe, though not quite to the same degree. Chris Flint points out that Defoe uses conjugal models as normative in his social writings, yet all his fictional characters flee traditional family arrangements, marginalising the family romance and refusing to 'domesticate the text'. *Robinson Crusoe* makes up strange replica families, while the *Farther Adventures* appears to compensate, in a displaced way, for the deficiencies of the earlier volume; but this island living, annulling the original family, still constitutes a powerful exclusion of the female. Richard Braverman sees Friday less as Crusoe's 'colonial prize' than as his deeply-needed son, projecting forward the father–son line submerged in the text and giving Crusoe's accumulated knowledge an heir (then exponentially increased by the arrival of Friday's actual father and the other colonists). Ian Bell revisits the marginal and spectral female figures, against Crusoe's remarkable lack of sexual interests: society appears male. But there are wives and daughters in the shadows, and they appear rather as steadfast and trustworthy, surprisingly strong figures in fact, compared with the squabbling self-seeking of the men they are condemned to serve: 'Crusoe's women represent the stable and enduring features of a world constantly put out of balance by the aggressive forces of male impulsiveness.'[39] George Haggerty reminds us that masculinity is a cultural process, not a biological given, and sees the novel as a series of trials through which Crusoe tries, not always successfully, to attain what is at best a contingent male power, deeply riven by castration anxiety. Haggerty builds in part on work by Hans Turley, who comments on the homoerotic aspects of Crusoe's subjugation of Friday and the thorough 'sublimation' of sexual desire in Crusoe's colonial trilogy. Turley has also written on the trilogy as an attempt to envisage a piratical and homosocial self, as opposed to the domestic and feminised type of bourgeois subjectivity. Readings of the novel as a case history of homosexual repression have recently started to appear.[40]

CRIME

It has long been a tenet of Defoe criticism that his experiences in Newgate and in the pillory conditioned the settings of his fiction, especially in *Moll Flanders* and *Colonel Jack*. In 1954 Brian Fitzgerald claimed that Defoe 'was entertained by thieves, highwaymen, and pirates, by coiners and [. . .]

pretty whores. He admired their energy and their intelligence; the skill and courage with which they had faced up to circumstances and conquered them. They were, after all, expert tradesmen and tradeswomen – in their own line.' According to this argument, Defoe saw criminals as enjoying an enviable freedom of self-invention, in contrast to his own trammelled business failures.[41] It used to be thought that Defoe wrote for John Applebee, a publisher specialising in criminal biography, and while this is no longer universally accepted, Defoe clearly had a strong social interest in crime and punishment, which were matters for comment in the *Review* and other writings. His novels emerged into a culture of semi-official crime literature, including transcripts of trials, the 'sessions papers' from the central criminal court at the Old Bailey, criminal biographies issued by the Ordinary (chaplain) of Newgate, and collections such as Captain Alexander Smith's *The History of the Lives of the Most Noted Highway-Men, Foot-pads, House-Breakers, Shoplifts, and Cheats of both Sexes [. . .] for above fifty Years last past*, which reached a second edition in 1714. A letter from a pickpocket, 'Moll of Rag-Fair', dated 16 July 1720, appeared in Applebee's *Weekly Journal*, and in Mist's *Weekly Journal* for 22 September 1722 there was a story about Moll King, 'a most notorious Offender, famous for stealing gold Watches from the Ladies' Sides in Churches, for which she has been several times convicted, being lately return'd from Transportation, has been taken, and is committed to Newgate'. Defoe might, or might not, have had something to do with these texts, but at any rate they form part of the context for his novel. In 1968 Gerald Howson suggested that Moll King, who crossed the Atlantic more often even than Moll Flanders and also managed to escape execution, could have supplied Defoe with stories while she was in jail, including anecdotes of another criminal, Callico Sarah, named, like Moll, after contraband cloth.[42]

Much work has been done on this criminal context. In 1976 Robert Singleton looked at the novel in relation to the spiritual presence and literary endeavours of the Ordinary of Newgate.[43] Paula Backscheider's introductory study announced itself as *Moll Flanders: The Making of a Criminal Mind* (1990) and gave some historical and sociological background about transportation, trials, fences, gangs, and highwaymen, in presenting the novel as a kind of policy document with a developing criminal psychology. Gregory Durston, a barrister rather than an academic, sees the book (or at any rate, the story of Moll's criminal career) as largely accurate in its depiction of the crime scene of Defoe's day (rather than Moll's).[44] Durston cites a range of contemporary and historical material in support of Defoe's depiction of crime and policing. He works methodically through an entire catalogue of criminal kinds: the thefts Moll will and will not commit, Newgate and other prisons, criminal legislation, informers and accomplice evidence, constables, receiving of stolen goods, magistrates, mobs and street punishment, civil actions, attorneys, counterfeiting (as in the case of Barbara Spencer, burned for coining in 1721), grand juries, trial procedures at the Old Bailey, the role of the Ordinary, commutation of sentence and transportation, and female criminality. Moll is not a 'typical' London thief: she starts too late, is too preternaturally skilfull, and makes too much money. But

> ■ her experiences of crime and the penal process in London are illustrative of a policing and criminal justice system that was already under severe structural stress and which was not fully able to cope with the rapid changes under way in the wider society.[45] □

Some procedural aspects have prompted more extensive investigation, as with Brett McInelly's examination of transporation.[46] Beth Swan takes the historical point that prisoners did not normally have counsel, representing their own case, and argues that the whole novel is a kind of plea in mitigation, to its readers; Moll represents herself in the court of our judgement, just as (under the legal procedures in the period) she represents herself in the actual court. Her splitting of hairs in court is like her moral wriggles in the story as a whole.[47]

Some work lies in another slightly different line, deriving from the older criminal tradition of 'the counterfeit lady', otherwise known as Mary Carleton, an imposter, bigamist and thief eventually hanged, after returning early from transportation, in 1673. Her case provoked an astounding series of popular narratives seeking the truth behind the various illusions and disguises she promoted herself in. Her story has obvious similarities to Moll's, and as long ago as 1914 it was proposed as a 'missing chapter' in the history of the novel.[48] Some of the narratives are very close to the picaresque tradition of the witty rogue who prospers through intelligent manipulation of circumstance, and Moll has also been aligned with, and differentiated from, that model.[49] Mary Carleton is used by John Rietz as the prototype of a female criminal, in contextualising Defoe's difficulties in producing a convincing unification of the categories of 'woman' and 'criminal'; for Rietz, figures like Carleton were 'unfamiliar social hybrids'. John Zomchick, however, sees Moll's liberatingly deviant career as finally cornered into a 'normative female subject with a sexuality dedicated to the production of domestic tranquillity'. Mary Jo Kietzman also contests Rietz's reading of the material, arguing that it gives too much weight to fixed categories of 'the feminine', and suggesting that female felons were constructed as hybrid subjects even by the law. Kietzman sees Carleton as the exponent of 'serial subjectivity', compulsively reinventing the self as a form of resistance to social limitation and oppression. What Defoe does is to impose a limited human subjectivity on Moll's pragmatic, relational and contingent version of potential serial identities.[50]

Robinson Crusoe features alongside *Moll Flanders* in John Bender's innovative *Imagining the Penitentiary* (1987). Bender sees fiction as a prime site for the re-imagining of social discipline along reformist lines.[51] He contrasts the old style of prisons like Newgate – chaotic, promiscuous, randomised, placed liminally between the order of judgement and the execution of punishment – with the style of confinement that displaced it in the later eighteenth century: the 'penitentiary', which was founded on rules, schedules, timetables, surveillance, and the notion that prison life was about reformation. In the old prison, life was lived by reference to a 'structurally inarticulate' authority, powerful but sporadic; a prisoner's story might be published at the execution which was its natural culmination. In the new penitentiary, life would be lived according to an ordered model of reclamation and internalisation of discipline, in which power was pervasive; the story, with all its progress and regression, was to be lived *inside* the prison. Bender contends that fiction actually imagined these changes before they happened in penal practice. Defoe (once a prisoner, latterly an agent of surveillance) took the crucial step of providing 'detailed narrative articulation' of private experience, and thus showing the novel's potential for control; he also showed that during confinement, 'the internal forces of psychological motivation fuse dynamically with the physical details of perceptual experience'. He does not propose penitentiaries, but he does give expression to the kind of subjective order later institutionalised by the penitentiary, and he does make visible the power that lies latent in 'the minutely sequential representations of realist narrative'.[52]

Moll's prison experience is in one sense old-fashioned: Newgate is a dangerous, otherworldly hell, carnivalesque and unpredictable. But Moll's private consciousness takes her in a different direction: 'at the very same instant Defoe's plots represent the old prison in all of its externally arbitrary, emblematic circumstance, he is reimagining punishment causally and sequentially as the reformation of inner thought'. Moll's reaction implies a conception of a new type of imprisonment, structured like a story, imitating the architectural lines of the autobiographical, realistic, consciousness-centred novel. The conversion experience is really a kind of reversal of the Puritan allegorisation of the world, for Defoe contrives 'fictional lives that could be construed as material validations of spiritual order. With Defoe, salvation becomes a matter of self-confirmation through psychological insight.'[53] His idea of what constitutes personality is materialistic in the way that Locke's theory of mind is; and these ideas, with their educational and governmental programmes attached, are not only instrumental in the rise of the novel, but a prefiguring of the mechanical operations of pleasure and pain on which penitentiary discipline is founded.

■ The penitentiary, which uses the material instruments of architecture and daily regime to recreate the convict, who has been sentenced for a crime that signifies failure to extract moral order from experience, parallels the novel in which a facsimile of the material world is shaped by a central consciousness discovering ordering principles among contradictions.[54] □

This works for *Robinson Crusoe* as well, since it is full of the imagery of prisons and executions, despite its remote setting, and it 'presents a materially realistic delineation of consciousness shaped through the narration of confinement'. Crusoe subjects his entire life to reflective criticism in a place of confinement, as a prisoner in the penitentiary is supposed to do. His random wanderings (crimes) begin to make sense as part of a larger pattern, and when this is realised the inmate can take over the prison.

■ We see the mythology of reform taking shape here. Prison, now equated with solitary reflection, is first viewed as negative, random, punitive, vengeful; but it slides into another thing entirely – something salubrious, beneficent, reformative, and productive of wealth and social integration. Crusoe's illness can be read [. . .] as a prospective allegory of the move from the old, fever-ridden jails to the clean, healthy, contemplative solitude of the penitentiaries.[55] □

Crusoe's narrative also incorporates several of the elements of civic life, including racial and religious diversity, in a structure of dominance which contains, without (in Bender's reading) quite eliminating this range of conflicting elements and voices. Crusoe rises to a position of governmental authority, which includes the right to commute the death sentence on the mutineers into an enforced colonisation: 'Upon Crusoe's departure, the island and its furniture exchange their metaphorical standing as prison for that of an actual penal colony with his fortress at its civic center and his story as its master narrative.'[56]

In *Crime and Defoe* (1993) Lincoln Faller examines the relationship between Defoe's narratives and standard-issue criminal biography, arguing that Defoe's novels are much more complex and require more flexible reading strategies. His texts both invoke and transcend generic markers, finding in their 'literariness' ways to deal with some of the moral and intellectual problems raised by crime in his period. The fictions liberate readers expecting certain kinds of ideologically pre-packaged accounts of criminal transgression, that is, the readers of criminal biography as it developed in the late seventeenth century, with stories of actual criminals as opposed to the tricks and 'pranks' of generic rogues. Criminal biography normally provided a socially acceptable gloss on the executed criminal's life-history, showing the progress of deviation and the infallibility of punishment, and providing a kind of answer to the question of criminal motivation in the absence of any existing theory of abnormal psychology. Faller argues that Defoe found normal criminal biography (whether extracting a rigorously pious moral, or hectically totting up grotesque adventures) lacking in explanatory force and authenticity (as witness the drunken uselessness of the Ordinary in *Moll Flanders*). The novels extend the field, produce new (novel) heroes who are not merely criminals and who are untouched by previously established discourses of trial and execution.

■ Defoe's novels are more teasing, provoking, and capacious than actual criminal biography, and more taking and inviting. Encouraging strategies of reading far more complicated than anything required by their putative genre, they can put readers into highly complicated, highly self-conscious, highly abstracted 'reading positions'.[57] □

Defoe's criminal heroes differ from 'real' criminals in the manner of the telling, in 'voices peculiar to themselves', in subjectivities much deeper than that allowed in standard popular literature. Against the pattern and coherence of criminal biography, which often celebrates religious conversion and an attendant sense of meaning after crime, Defoe's heroes allow themselves a 'polyvalent' view of their pasts and incorporate other points of view (as bystanders, husbands, witnesses). They do not always say what they ought to be saying. Defoe's criminals have to be taken seriously, but cannot be viewed through the normative lens of standard biography. The narratives resist conformity to pattern, while not quite granting the narrators the autonomy of later novels. Moll gets away with saying a great deal that the Ordinary of Newgate would not have allowed her to say: only the reader is in a position to question her: 'Challenged by voices from the alleyways and margins, readers are prompted (and long before there actually was any such thing in England) to become their *own* policemen.' Readers must look through and around the details of the story to find 'the reality behind it and its larger meaning': the partiality and blindness of the narrators is not so much morally ironic as strategically designed to provoke readers into imaginative response.[58]

Moll does not see the patterns and coincidences that govern her; 'Moll is the luckiest and the blindest of all Defoe's criminal protagonists', which means that we have to answer the question of why God has been 'so good to her'.[59] The secularisation which modern readers sense could also be seen in the period as a loss of a traditional interpretative model. Faller argues that where criminal biography makes providence cut-and-dried, Defoe reminds us that the Grace of God is a lot more unpredictable and mysterious: you cannot simply buy it. There is always hope: God may be merciful even where mercy is not deserved. But on the other hand, it is not clear that God has been so good to her anyway: the recovery of one child reminds us that her 'spectacular fecundity' has been thrown away for a final barren liaison, while her energy has dwindled to restlessness. The book can be read all ways: 'A punished Moll is a warning, a saved Moll an encouragement, and an exhausted Moll an admonition not to leave off repenting too long.'[60] Providence is not so easy to read (no wonder, Faller remarks, that the Panopticon or all-seeing penitentiary was invented to do God's job better). Faller offers a complex discussion of how readers, granted a kind of space for play as well as an enhanced moral responsibility and power, might be expected to organise the threads, themes and perspectives of the story in 'an order teasingly beyond comprehension'.[61] In a further chapter, he offers a close analysis of Moll's false arrest by the mercer and his journeyman as a case study in the multiple points of view and lines of sympathy operative for Defoe's commercially-minded readers. Faller finds the 'criminal psychology' delineating Moll and Defoe's other transgressive heroes to be actually rather static and undeveloped, and he does not agree that they represent go-getting individualism; if anything, they become 'increasingly alienated and fragmented'.[62] Defoe is suspicious of the 'characterological core' of being that criminal biography offered; rather, the fictions challenge such stable versions of selfhood by stimulating readers to think beyond received or 'official' patterns of meaning, and come up with their own, always provisional, answers.

EXOTIC AND COLONY

Most of Defoe's novels are in large measure constituted by a geographical adventure: Captain Singleton walks across Africa; Colonel Jack reorganises the slave economy in America; Moll dies as a rich Virginia planter, and in her repeated crossings of the Atlantic travels almost as much as Crusoe. But above all, *Robinson Crusoe* locates a civilised western man in an environment utterly without connection to his home, and it ends, after a process of gradual acclimatisation and adaptation, by claiming a new colony for Britain. In the process Crusoe disposes of a slave but acquires an entirely submissive indigenous servant, the haunting and increasingly interesting figure of Friday. Clearly, for most early readers the exotic setting was part of the pleasure of the fantasy, with little sense of disturbance from the political issues of slavery or colonialism; Samuel Johnson admired the book as much as he denounced slavery (and defended the rights of Britain to administer its American colonies). The poet and essayist Walter Savage Landor (1775–1864), writing in the 1840s, linked the boyhood love of Crusoe with the expanding empire in poems of sentimental patriotism, suggesting that Defoe's text might have been a crucial stimulus to the naval victories of Lord Rodney (1719–92) and Lord Nelson (1758–1805):

> ■ What boy is there who never laid
> Under his pillow, half afraid,
> That precious volume, lest the morrow
> For unlearnt lesson might bring sorrow?
> But nobler lessons he has taught
> Wide-awake scholars who fear'd naught:
> A Rodney and a Nelson may
> Without him not have won the day. □

Indeed, Sir Alexander Ball (1756–1809), a naval commander with Nelson at the Battle of the Nile (1798), told Coleridge that he had entered the navy precisely because 'of the deep impression and vivid images which were left on his mind by the perusal of *Robinson Crusoe*'.[63] Aside from military conquest, Crusoe became a metaphor and a prompt for exploration: René Caillié (1799–1838), a French explorer of then unmapped regions of Africa, said: 'The History of Robinson Crusoe, in particular, inflamed my young imagination: I was impatient to encounter adventures like him; nay, I already felt an ambition to signalize myself by some important discovery springing up in my heart.' The poet William Cox describes a scene in which the Swiss anthropologist and explorer J. L. Burckhardt (1784–1817) reads *Crusoe* 'to his Arabs in the Desert', in a completely unabashed colonial gesture: as Burckhardt, clothed in 'the sheepskin and the turban', reads the book to the 'wild swarthy forms, that wore / The Bedouin's garb', the light of western adventure transforms their hint of threat into docile admiration: 'the blaze, streaming up, showed joy in each dark look'.[64] The master/servant relationship of Crusoe and Friday is bizarrely replicated in a quite different geographical locale but with strangely similar effects. It is known that *Robinson Crusoe* was sometimes quite directly used in a colonial administrative context. In 1852 it was translated into Maori, for example, as part of an attempt to educate the native peoples of New Zealand in European models of thrift and industry. On the other hand, it was also read by the colonised in radical ways: Jay Fliegelman shows how the American revolutionaries read Crusoe as being against the patriarchal authority of the British king.[65]

The 'personal' island has been one of the dominant fantasies of the island race. The poet Walter de la Mare (1873–1956), in *Desert Islands and Robinson Crusoe* (1930), with illustrations by Rex Whistler (1905–44), produced a subtle and appreciative account of the presence of castaways in literature. Imaginary voyaging remains part of the pleasure of Defoe's book. Novak and others have explored Crusoe's island fantasy, exotic setting, cannibal fantasies and symbolic relation to animals, in a number of articles not specifically related to the issue of colonialism.[66] Daniel Peck studied Crusoe's educational processes and his gradual engagement with his surroundings; in digging a home, he is digging into himself; he acquires a sense of limit and place, and thereby a new sense of himself. In *Farther Adventures*, the colony fails because of his neglect, and Friday is killed, severing the living link. Losing the purity of the island, he gathers the world's guilt, as a wanderer, in contrast to the exiled Russian prince in Siberia, who has lost his territorial claim but gained a sense of personal selfhood and home. Pat Rogers sees Crusoe as 'homo domesticus' (rather than 'economicus'), 'a Caribbean nabob who makes a little England in remote surroundings [. . .]; his narrative, the epic of home-making, and housekeeping'. In this reading Crusoe is linked to the early eighteenth-century culture of landscape gardening; he is less an aggressive, land-grabbing grandee than a contemplative gentleman.[67]

Another way of looking at the island novel is as a story of exile. In several essays Michael Seidel stresses the strangeness and surprise of the adventures, as Defoe had done on the title page. But always exile is para-doxical: Crusoe is from home and at home at the same time; he is always discovering himself when he encounters others. Exile promotes a kind of pattern, a determination or temptation to push at the boundaries of experience. Hence Crusoe's gradual exploration around concentric circles of safety, a model of analysis and imagination. There is a political element to this, since Defoe's narratives all work on the principle of 'self-propulsion' and 'self-extension'. Defoe's Crusoe is like a government in exile, in reversal of Charles II's landing from the sea on the island of England. Crusoe is 'restored', restocked, by the wreck. Seidel makes a comparison with Shakespeare's island play *The Tempest* (1611): Crusoe is a sort of Prospero, with Friday in the Ariel role, a magical monarch who returns from exile on certain conditions. The print in the sand is the ulti-mate limit of exile: its singleness suggests an unseen other, elsewhere: it requires completion in society. Solitude is not in the end sustainable, and Crusoe must learn sovereignty in order to go home as a man of substance, knowing the limits of the symbolic island which constitutes himself. Seidel's 1991 introductory study also stresses the symbolic importance of the island story and island living, making the book 'a primer for the new science of man, a field study for the anthropologist, the psychologist, the economist, the political scientist, the sociologist, the geographer, the engineer, the agronomist, the theologian [. . .] the mili-tary strategist'.[68] As a story which localises the epic wanderer to a partic-ular zone of control and order, it is the foundational text in the history of the novel, but also a story of principled exile, holding land in trust pending return at the right moment.

Diana Loxley's *Problematic Shores:The Literature of Islands* (1990) declares that island narratives are essentially the literary projection of British colonialism. For Swift and for Joyce, writing from the perspective of a colonised Ireland, colonies meant exploitation, and there is a long tradition which examines Crusoe's activities on the island in a more interrogative light; issues of exploration and colonial dominance are now one of the major features of Defoe criticism. For Defoe himself, writing during the expansion of the British Empire, there was very little embarrassment about proposing colonial development. Novak's chapter on 'Fiction as Colonial Propaganda' looks at Defoe's promotion of colonisation as a means to British commercial prosperity. His fictions explore and familiarise areas of the world that he thought could profitably be colonised, especially in South America. Crusoe's island is situated near the mouth of the Orinoco, where Ralegh had prospected, always a favourite subject for Defoe's colonial fantasies. Crusoe fails as a colonist where he might, Defoe implies, have succeeded, and this represents a kind of reflection on Britain's failure to look after its colonists. Moll does rather better, eventually prospering as a colonist in Virginia, and Defoe is clearly inspired by the 'Transportation Act' of 1718, which opened Virginia and Maryland to the transportation of convicted felons once more as a means to convert economic transgression into economic profit. J. A. Downie argues that Defoe capitalised on the vogue for travel literature to push for imperial expansion in his fictions.[69]

More directly politicised is Peter Hulme's *Colonial Encounters* (1986), which summarises the differences between 'spiritual' and 'colonial' readings and then 'returns Robinson Crusoe to the Caribbean' by giving a central place to Caribbean history and Friday's origins, in contrast to Crusoe's cannibal fantasies.[70] Some political readings of the issue turn inwards, to psychoanalysis. In 1976 Elihu Pearlman used the theories of the French psychoanalyst Jacques Lacan (1901–81) to propose a reading of Crusoe's infantilism, paternal ambivalence and weak ego boundaries, linked to colonial and imperial fantasy: Crusoe is 'a radical individualist and the prototype of new economic man, but he is also an authoritarian of a dangerous kind and an unredeemed, uncivilised colonialist'. This was followed up by other psychodramatic readings, with varying degrees of hostility. Martin Gliserman calls attention to the psychic patterns and enclosures that govern Crusoe's experience and imagining on the island. Gary Hentzi sees *Robinson Crusoe* as an Enlightenment text that measures and counts everything from the point of view of Crusoe as the centre of attention. But in the footprint episode, in which Crusoe quite literally attempts to impose his physique on the signature imprint of a local inhabitant, which resists and exceeds him, the triggering of a 'sublime' terror and an aggressive and imperial response suggests to Hentzi a link to the Lacanian reading of the infantile mirror-phase and its fragile and troubled sense of self-possession. Crusoe is caught between narcissistic gratification and a threatened collapse. His violent despair, converted to imperial power and desire for dominance, gives us also the island as fantasy of the body as a kind of ideal unity.[71]

Similarly fusing political and psychological readings, Carol Houlihan Flynn writes on Defoe and alienation, with the footprint as the sign of the loneliness of the modern condition. This brings the encounter with a savagely cannibal 'other' into highly problematic focus, and Flynn examines the crucial encounter between Crusoe and Friday, in which Crusoe is seen to threaten Friday with death as the means of civilising him. Additionally, he shoots a goat kid and a talking parrot in order to demonstrate a level of power to his servant (Friday's initiation into this form of violence against nature is later re-enacted and confirmed by the encounter with the bear). Crusoe is terrified of savagery, of the castration and random dismemberment enacted by cannibalism. At the same time, he is clearly the most efficiently violent man there, becoming the 'most professionally savage' inhabitant as he struggles to supply his complicated needs. Crusoe saves himself from the condition of the beast by rescuing an order of civilisation from the ship; yet he clothes himself in the skin of the beasts from which he is trying to distinguish himself, placing himself at the top of the food chain in a protective endeavour and disguising his inner savagery. For Flynn, this is analytic (if not ironic). The novel shows that the colony depends 'on slavery, upon violence, upon death'. Crusoe must eat or be eaten. Defoe's characters are not exceptionally ruthless; but if necessary they will eat anyone and anything to preserve themselves. This is how civilisation works: 'Defoe would not stop looking hard at what was being mastered [. . .] Crusoe compulsively ranges about the world to order an economy bigger than himself, one that incorporates fear into its triumphs and demands that freedom depend upon slavery.'[72]

Such niceties are scorned by Patrick J. Keane in his 1994 study of Coleridge's marginalia to *Robinson Crusoe*. Keane starts from the surprising silence of Coleridge, a lifelong abolitionist, on the matter of slavery in the book, which he read early and annotated late in life. Keane's own views are clear enough:

■ the deepest emotions of Robinson Crusoe, an unloving and sexually apathetic mercantilist, are stirred by money, and his friends tend to be those with whom he has some economic arrangement – the widow in England, the Portuguese Captain, his partner in Brazil.[73] □

There is no substantial difference between Defoe the colonist and Crusoe the coloniser, with his cold failures to appreciate the natural and human world around him except in terms of its propensity for exploitation, nor any real irony in Crusoe's assumptions of power. Crusoe repents of many things, but not of being involved in the slaving voyage which ends in shipwreck, or of having a financial stake in slavery; Friday simply provides him with an ideally unresisting, naturalised slave.

Several other critics have taken up the issue of Crusoe's relationship with Friday, cannibalism and slavery. Comparing *Robinson Crusoe* with one of its possible sources, Aphra Behn's *Oroonoko* (1688), which features a 'Europeanised' black prince/slave for a hero, Gary Gautier finds that Defoe's novel shows inherited ideologies under stress from the individualistic culture of commerce, and resorting to race rather than class as a justification (or 'naturalisation') of slavery; a kind of racial essentialism, extended and developed through time and history rather than simply imposed at a given moment. Others have seen Friday as crucially inhabiting a boundary between legitimate Caribs and demonised cannibals, or demonstrating the fissure-points in early racial ideologies.[74] Ellis Markman describes how fear of cannibals was used in empire-building mythology; Lincoln Faller suggests that Crusoe's colony fails through fears of miscegenation and the threatening confusions of mixed-race marriages.[75] Robert Marzec uses *Robinson Crusoe* as the foundational text for literary treatments of the control and enclosure of land, while Brett McInelly sees Crusoe as the primary type of the emerging colonist, with Defoe producing (as Joyce suggested) a kind of premonition of empire. As the first proper novelist, Defoe imagines the kind of expansive, individualist selfhood required for colonial exploration and dominance. But the model is also made benevolent and tolerant, in political contradistinction to the demonised atrocities of the Spanish (with whom Britain was competing).[76] Everett Zimmerman, finding Crusoe cast up on an island 'somewhere between Hobbes and Locke', examines how numeration and measurement offer partial, if weak, structures for the ordering of violence which lies outside the normal grids of control.[77]

With political ground cleared, attention has slightly turned towards matters of trade and contemporary international law. Anna Neill argues that the absolute authority of *Robinson Crusoe* shifts to a more doubtful position in the *Farther Adventures*, reflecting the position that 'absolute colonial rule is in conflict with national duty, as well as with the international law which regulates colonial trade'. Aparna Dharwadker looks at the ways in which trade pushes definitions of self and race beyond ordinary geography, unsettling fixed identities; the colonialist is exposed to the orientalist in *Farther Adventures*. Lydia H. Liu finds in the earthenware pot (Woolf's prime example of Defoe's intensity) a metonymy of European relations with China, embodying a 'poetics of colonial disavowal' whereby the coloniser learns through trade and then claims the new commodities as the result of prior ingenuity. Robert Markley also reminds us of the greater geography, including Russia and China, which is envisaged by Defoe's mapping project in the trilogy as a whole, and the consequences this ought to have for our reading of the first 'adventures'.[78]

It is a timely reminder: as the world shrinks, Defoe's novels offer us a way of remembering what it might have been like to pursue discovery (both external and internal) beyond known limits. The remainder of this Guide offers a Conclusion, in which the main areas of Defoe criticism to date are summarised, with some thoughts about possible future directions; and an Appendix which maps some of the many ways in which Defoe's creations have been extended, rewritten, and taken to places Defoe himself did not imagine.

Conclusion

Defoe's novels have enjoyed a critical history not unlike that of their protagonists: born in rebellion against the proffered forms of literary authority (like Crusoe rebelling against his father) or at extreme social disadvantage (Moll's birth in Newgate to a criminal mother), the novels took time to establish themselves as legitimate objects of study. They could only be identified as agents of 'the Rise of the Novel', once it had become clear that there was any such thing as 'the Novel' and that it could be argued to have 'risen' out of something. The early status of Defoe's novels was unclear in all sorts of ways, from their anonymity to their generic classification. Essentially they made their way, in pre-academic days, by popular readership; *Robinson Crusoe* appearing to offer to men (especially) of widely differing social classes and political leanings a sustained dream of solitude, power, and male completeness, sufficient to enchant generations of readers through to Victorian times. In the early days of critical attention, it was Defoe's realism and verisimilitude that dominated discussion. *Robinson Crusoe* induced a state of naïve identification with the hero in which island fantasies were imaginatively worked out. There was no real question of art: the novel put its readers completely in the picture and no one worried about 'Defoe'. If justification for this kind of reading were needed, there were plenty of commentators, from Rousseau to Wordsworth, capable of justifying its moral or theological tendencies.

Moll Flanders, always suspect because of its criminal milieu, sexual pragmatism and incest motif, only gradually attained a similar canonical status, and then in part through its pairing with *Robinson Crusoe*. Charles Lamb's advocacy of *Moll Flanders* did not gain much of a hearing until Virginia Woolf and E. M. Forster took the novel up in the early twentieth century. Since then it has gained steadily on its male-centred forebear, partly as a result of an increasingly sophisticated sexual politics of reading, and partly because of a growing unease about the colonial content and context of *Robinson Crusoe*. Many would now see *Moll Flanders* as the more complete, contained, artistically-modelled novel, a study of the individual in society which surmounts some of Defoe's problems with his earlier fiction.

But there has always been a counter-tradition in criticism of Defoe, partly derived from his uniquely embattled political manoeuvrings. Some critics have thought of his novels as essentially rather accidental or contingent texts in which various kinds of force and idea meet and conflict; Defoe could, famously, write on either side of a question. For some, 'realism' was simply not enough: as the nineteenth-century Defoe industry produced ever more editions and collected works, voices began to be raised from the perspective of the later development of the novel, with its more knowing and confident use of art. Defoe's naturalistic materialism came to look like a lack of high art, or intense feeling, or profound thought.

Twentieth-century academic criticism has in the main attempted to deal with this problem in several ways. One kind of study finds high art in the fiction, notably in the use of careful perspective and ironic distancing between reader and protagonist, especially in *Moll Flanders*, which has never enjoyed the degree of imaginative identification that *Robinson Crusoe* inspired. Secondly, research has often concentrated on setting Defoe's fictions in the context of his other writings, to show how they interact with his programmes for social reform or with his thinking on matters of marriage, sex, trade, or politics. A third way has been to accept the fictions as brilliantly improvised experiments, inter-acting with other forms of writing, exploring the interfaces of self and world and settling for an always-provisional sense of engagement rather than aiming for a fixed target. The decline in reverential criti-cism, attendant on the increased use of overtly theoretical positions since the 1980s, has in addition enhanced a readiness to confront polit-ical issues in the fictions: capitalism, colonialism, slavery. In one sense we almost find ourselves back where we were in the very early read-ings, with a kind of (often political) hostility to Defoe's projects more or less built into criticism. Ian Watt, indeed, was scarcely a respecter of persons when it came to looking for unresolved tensions or unfinished business in Defoe's narratives. There is, it should be stressed, no final wall between these ways of thinking, which often feed from each other.

Representatives of all these positions can still be found in recent criticism of Defoe. Most of the old questions have not gone away. Studies continue to look in the novels for evidence of Defoe's general thinking on religion and society: Nicholas Hudson, for example, finds that Defoe is as baffled as Crusoe by Friday's questions about God's failure to scotch the Devil. 'Crusoe's hesitant shifting between reason and impulse, between a desire to reduce the universe to some logical order and grudging acceptance of a universe beyond comprehension, reflects dilemmas that persist throughout Defoe's later writings on reli-gion.'[1] James Foster thinks that the apparent conflict between secu-lar–economic and religious–allegorical readings of *Robinson Crusoe* is superficial, and that the real problem is located in a widespread early eighteenth-century ambivalence about the imagination. The deep tension is between

■ the imaginative presentation of a fictionalized self which interacts with, and attempts to escape, the limitations imposed by ethical, religious and national environments, and [. . .] a superimposed spiritualizing framework of meaning which attempts – and finally fails – to circumscribe Crusoe's behaviour and to control his destiny.[2] □

Jeffrey Hopes thinks we can take Defoe's prefaces to the *Crusoe* novels seriously as a quasi-religious guide to interpretation, aligned with the Calvinist doctrine of election: if we get our interpretations wrong, we were never going to get them right. Janis Svilpis revisits the question of Crusoe as a bourgeois isolationist, while Richard Barney argues that his selfhood is always conceived as improvised between private and public states, with a 'lucidly public and political identity' emerging.[3] Freudian interpretations of Crusoe's mental life have continued to emerge, with his landscape allegorised by Geoffrey M. Sill as the generation of a super-ego capable of commanding meaning.[4] *Moll Flanders* attracts a similar range of attention. Michael Suarez tries to close the case on the long-standing argument about the authenticity of Moll's repentance by using theological and legal background to show that she does not fulfil the conditions for conversion required by someone of Defoe's time and training; but it seems likely that the argument about her status will shift rather than reach a formal consensus. The novel stimulates critical reflec-tions on everything from Moll's 'onomaphobia' – her fear of names – as an aspect of personal identity to the significance of the equivocations in the editorial preface.[5]

It has perhaps become more normal to think of the novels as texts, writings or narratives rather than novels or 'literature'. Carl Lovitt finds that Defoe laces *Moll Flanders* with 'flagrantly artificial' devices (such as Moll's calling Jemy telepathically) to foreground the authorial basis of the fiction in a rather postmodern way; Sandra Sherman thinks that the *Robinson Crusoe* trilogy sets up a series of mutually deferring sources of prior authority which always deflect questions of authenticity, in the manner that Defoe's 'secret' political writings did.[6] Cameron McFarlane argues that Crusoe's sense of himself as interpreter of providential design relocates meaning in subjectivity, in a kind of prescient discovery of the constructed nature of reality. Steven Michael sees *Moll Flanders* as a self-deconstructing rhetorical text in which language is used like money, for benefit, rather than truth; its persistent denial of any final or central tran-scendent truth constitutes its meaning. The statement, insofar as there is one, is always a kind of deferral; the absence of centre is the presence or 'lesson' of the book.[7] One flamboyant celebration of Defoe's lack of termination is Kevin Cope's 'All Aboard the Ark of Possibility: or, Robinson Crusoe returns from Mars as a small-footprint, multi-channel indeterminacy machine' (1998). Where everything is so open, Defoe can be co-opted to more or less anything, including modern continental ethical philosophy.[8]

But such positions can be taken only because Defoe is still firmly a canonical figure of the academy, especially in America. The Modern Language Association of America in 2005 published a book of essays from scholars round the world, on the issues involved in teaching *Robinson Crusoe* to students.[9] A new Defoe Society, with its own website, is being launched; a roundtable discussion of the 'Future of Defoe Studies' took place in March 2007, with contributions from several of the scholars represented in this Guide, including John Richetti, Maximillian E. Novak, Robert Mayer, and Geoffrey Sill.[10]

The production of editions prepared by scholars but priced for student and general readership shows no signs of debility. More monumentally, the Stoke Newington Edition, published by AMS Press, has issued some large-scale scholarly editions of Defoe's writings. It is true that the Defoe canon has undergone a radical reassessment in recent times, in large measure due to the arguments of P. N. Furbank and W. R. Owens. In a series of studies, Furbank and Owens have challenged the list of Defoe's works published by J. R. Moore, on which generations of more or less sceptical scholars have based their studies. Moore's 550 items are reduced to about 250, excluding journalism (the fictions are not affected). While this sounds like diminution, or another assault on canonicity, and while some of the 'de-attributions' remain controversial, a good deal of what has been assigned to other authors, or no author at all, was fairly peripheral in the first place. What remains has the added weight of careful deliberation: in some ways, it can be seen as a confirmation of Defoe as canonical author. Furbank and Owens are now general editors of a series of modern editions of Defoe's works. In some ways, he is easier to read now than he has been since his own day; though the canon has been cut, what Defoe can be reasonably safely considered actually to have written is now more available than it has been for centuries. This is likely to produce further shifts in the way the novels are viewed, quite possibly including a resurgence of the sense that he wrote cumulatively, to a thought-out and consistent plan; certainly it will encourage the reading of the fiction alongside the non-fiction.[11]

Defoe himself appears to be able to withstand any amount of biographical treatment. Very substantial scholarly biographies of him by Backscheider and Novak have been joined most recently by John Richetti's 2005 volume.[12] Other biographies take a more thematic line. The psychoanalytic interpretation of Defoe's life and works by Leo Abse, and John Martin's shock-horror detection of Defoe's bizarre sex life as (supposedly) allegorised by the novels, seem unlikely to disturb the monolith unduly.[13] They do, however, suggest that interest in Defoe in non-scholarly circles remains high; and this represents another important sense in which Defoe's novels continue to live beyond their original determinate limits. Moll Flanders and Robinson Crusoe have always been labile, shapeshifting figures and their cultural presence has appropriately enough been mediated by critical rewriting in other forms: they are not only the colonists of early empire, but subjects of colonisation, infiltration and transformation in other genres. Robinson Crusoe in his goatskin cap rapidly became an emblem of the desert island fantasy, and the image has been presented in art, on stage, in poems, in popular song, in television adaptations and on film, in various degrees of closeness to Defoe's original text. Crusoe is a figure both instantly recognisable and infinitely malleable: something like a brand. He turns up in cartoons in the *New Yorker*; he was subjected to the *Mad Magazine* treatment in 1956; he has featured in Bugs Bunny animations; several computer games with Crusoesque situations are available. While naïve boyish excitement about the story is unlikely to be maintained in the modern world, actual tourism has taken over: in 1966 the Chilean government renamed Más a Tierra, the main island of the Juan Fernández archipelago, Isla Robinson Crusoe, with a smaller one named after Selkirk, the sailor who was actually marooned there. A small permanent population is supported partly by tourism. In October 2005 *National Geographic* reported that the ruins of Selkirk's hut had been found, shifting the focus from the suspect Crusoe to the more acceptable 'original' castaway. One Robinson Crusoe website straightforwardly advertises fish products; another tells tourists of the delights of Robinson Crusoe island – in Fiji.[14]

Moll Flanders has been less readily transformed by popular culture, partly because it lacks the fantasy setting of the earlier novel and partly because of moral problems attending the activities of its heroine. The literary influence has been much more covert and hard to define, and as a brand, Moll products seem a good deal more desperate: there is an internet shopping service for those with historical interests ('Mall Flanders') – surely an ironic gesture, given Moll's propensity for shoplifting; there is a Moll Flanders cocktail recipe; and, despite the book's notable lack of interest in anything culinary, we can purchase Sandra Sherman's *Flesh from the Past: Recipes and Revelations from Moll Flanders' Kitchen* (2004). Moll is apparently something of a figure of personal therapy on the web.[15] Rumours that a long-delayed project by director Ken Russell (born 1927) to turn Moll Flanders into a film might actually materialise, after much litigation and dispute, began to circulate in 2006; if true, the story behind the film would be, appropriately enough, one of survival and return.[16]

Popular culture was, after all, the literary matrix from which Defoe emerged – or at least, it was one of the elements without which his fictions could not have been achieved. The Appendix to this Guide offers a brief summary of some of these efforts at remapping Defoe's fictional territory; some ludicrous, some hostile, some cheap, and some sufficiently 'literary' to generate their own scholarship. Parasitic in one sense, they testify to the enduring and apparently endlessly mutating stimulus that Defoe's stories have given to the human imagination since 1719.

Appendix: Adaptations and Appropriations

This appendix lists some of the more important, as well as some of the more bizarre, manifestations of Defoe's characters and settings. In a notable example of the hybridity of much modern scholarship, such adaptations have been attracting considerable attention from cultural historians and others students of Defoe's work.[1]

CHAPBOOKS AND ABRIDGEMENTS

Robinson Crusoe was quickly pirated and abridged, appearing in cheap chapbook versions into the nineteenth century, sometimes in as little as eight pages. Pat Rogers's study of these abridgements suggests that certain key elements (storm, shipwreck, island living, Friday) were soon recognised and packaged as the 'Crusoe myth'. Chapbook versions of *Moll Flanders* were also quick to appear, often with illustrations, chapter divisions and extra details: of Moll's 'real' name, family background, death, will and funeral, as if attempting to put the lid on something that Defoe deliberately left open. *Moll Flanders* was to some extent kept going in such abridged versions, having not been maintained in full authorised texts to the same extent as *Robinson Crusoe*. Rogers finds that the chapbooks quickly lost touch with Defoe's novel, treating 'their subject as a legend, an object of common property'.[2]

THE 'ROBINSONADE' TRADITION

Robinson Crusoe has been very widely translated, not only into the major European languages, but also into Arabic, Turkish, Hebrew, Pharsi, Coptic and Sudanese – not to mention into 'words of one syllable', by 'Mary Godolphin', pseudonym of Lucy Aikin (1781–1864). The novel also defined a castaway trope which was rapidly identified as an imitable source and reference point for a seemingly unending stream of imitations and versions. The basic elements (shipwreck, pirates, cannibals, climatic catastrophes, rescue) can be found across almost three centuries of subsequent fiction, rarely without some consciousness of Defoe's novel. Early imitations and rewritings tend to treat the story as an opportunity for adventure; most of the later examples treat it as a text for rewriting in the light of postcolonial or feminist theory.[3]

Peter Longueville (dates unknown), *The Hermit* (1727)
Robert Paltock (1697–1767), *The Life and Adventures of Peter Wilkins, a Cornish Man* (1751)
Anonymous, *The Female American* (1767)
Johann David Wyss (1743–1818) and Johann Rudolf Wyss (1781–1830), *Der Schweizerische Robinson* (1812–13), translated as *The Swiss Family Robinson*
Agnes Strickland (1796–1874), *The Rival Crusoes* (1826)
Anonymous, *The Arctic Crusoe* (1854)
R. M. Ballantyne (1825–94), *Coral Island* (1858)
R. M. Ballantyne, *The Dog Crusoe* (1860)
Anonymous, *The Catholic Crusoe* (1860)
Robert Louis Stevenson (1850–94), *Treasure Island* (1883)
Alfred Séguin (dates unknown), *Robinson Noir* (1877)
Jules Verne (1828–1905), *L'Ecole des Robinsons* (1882)
Jean-Richard Bloch (1884–1947), *Le Robinson Juif* (1925)
Jean Giraudoux (1822–1944), *Suzanne et le Pacifique* (1921)
William Golding (1911–93), *Lord of the Flies* (1954)
William Golding, *Pincher Martin* (1956)
Muriel Spark (1918–2006), *Robinson* (1958)
Michel Tournier (born 1924), *Vendredi ou les limbes du Pacifique* (1967)[4]
Angela Carter (1940–92), 'Master' (from *Fireworks*, 1981)
Jane Gardam (born 1928), *Crusoe's Daughter* (1985)
Gaston Compère (born 1924), *Robinson '86* (1986)
J. M. Coetzee (born 1940), *Foe* (1986)[5]

POETIC LICENCE

Despite his own ambitions as a poet and the occasional Victorian lyrical outburst, some of which we have quoted in context, most readers have considered Defoe's fictions to be as prosaic as prose can be. *Moll Flanders* in particular has not tended to prompt thoughts of poetry, though Roger McGough (born 1937) produced a tart little ditty on the 'Nice timing' of her penitence.[6] *Robinson Crusoe*, however, has produced a small range of poetic transformations, which, like the fictional appropriations, increasingly dismantle Crusoe's fenced-in masculinism and imperial power:

Thomas Bailey Aldrich (1836–1907), 'Like Crusoe Walking by the Lonely Strand', from *The Poems* (1907)
Robert Graves (1895–1985), 'Robinson Crusoe cut his coats', from *The Penny Fiddle* (1960)
Thomas Merton (1915–69), 'Crusoe', from *Collected Poems of Thomas Merton* (1977)

Adrian Mitchell (born 1932), 'Crusoe Dying in England', from *Heart on the Left: Poems, 1953–1984* (1997)

Elizabeth Bishop (1911–79), 'Crusoe in England', from *Geography III* (1977)[7]

Derek Walcott (born 1930), 'Crusoe's Journal', from *The Castaway and Other Poems* (1965)[8]

Charles Martin (born 1942), *Passages from Friday* (1983)

A. D. Hope (1907–2000), 'Man Friday', from *The Age of Reason* (1985)

STAGE

Moll Flanders has not had much stage presence, though a version was performed in 2005–6 by the Kaos theatre company, who describe their play as 'Daniel Defoe's classic tale of adventure & debauchery, an eye-popping account of one woman's journey through poverty, prostitution, pick pocketing & penitence.'[9] *Robinson Crusoe*, meanwhile, has characteristically found its way into a bizarre variety of stage versions, beginning with *Robinson Crusoe: or Harlequin Friday*, performed as a comic afterpiece to *The Winter's Tale* at Drury Lane Theatre, London, on 29 January 1781, a version perhaps part-authored by Richard Brinsley Sheridan (1751–1816). The song 'Where Did Robinson Crusoe Go with Friday on Saturday Night?' by Al Jolson (1886–1950) was interpolated into a Broadway musical, *Robinson Crusoe, Jr.*, with a book by Edgar Smith and music by Sigmund Romberg (1887–1951), indicating once again the story's labile popular currency. Other stage versions include:

Charles Guilbert de Pixérécourt (1773–1844), *Robinson Crusoé* (1805)[10]

Isaac Pocock (active 1810–67), *Robinson Crusoe: or, The Bold Bucaniers, A Romantic Melo-Drama* (1817)

Thomas William Robertson (1829–71), *Robinson Crusoe: A Burlesque in One Act* (1856)

Jacques Offenbach (1819–80), *Robinson Crusoé* (1867) (opera)

Adrian Mitchell, *Man Friday* (1973) (for the film version of this see next section)

Derek Walcott, *Pantomime* (1978)[11]

FILM

Robinson Crusoe's visual appeal has been strong since its first publication, with a frontispiece coming before the title page. Even William Blake (1757–1827), arch-Romantic and anti-materialist, drew Crusoe, and illustrations of the novel have emphasised different aspects of the character and setting as literary fashions have changed.[12] Film-makers have taken advantage of the story's scenic potential.[13] Silent film versions of the story, now lost, were made in 1913, 1916 and 1922; the earliest surviving print is of an unpretentious film from 1926, called straightforwardly *Robinson Crusoe*, to which sound was added in 1936 in the form of a voice-over. Subsequent adaptations include:

> *Mr. Robinson Crusoe*, directed by Edward Sutherland (1932)
>
> *Robinson Crusoeland*, directed by Leo Joannon, starring Laurel and Hardy (1952)
>
> *The Adventures of Robinson Crusoe*, directed by Luis Buñuel (1952)
>
> *Robinson Crusoe on Mars*, directed by Byron Haskin (1964)
>
> *The Erotic Adventures of Robinson Crusoe*, directed by Ken Dixon (1975)
>
> *Man Friday*, directed by Jack Gold (1975), based on Adrian Mitchell's play (1973)
>
> *Crusoe*, directed by Caleb Dechanel (1988)[14]
>
> *Robinson Crusoe*, directed by Rod Hardy and George Miller (1997)
>
> *The Adventures of Robinson Crusoe* was shown on television in 13 episodes from 12 October to 30 December 1965, in a version thought to be suitable for children.

Moll Flanders was slower to reach a screen version, probably because of the moral codes operative in the cinema, but as obscenity laws were relaxed, film and television versions began to appear:

> *The Amorous Adventures of Moll Flanders*, directed by Terence Young (1965)
>
> *Moll Flanders*, directed by Pen Densham (1995)
>
> *Moll Flanders*, adapted for television in two episodes by Hugh Whitemore, directed by Donald McWhinnie (1975)
>
> *The Fortunes and Misfortunes of Moll Flanders*, adapted for television in four parts by Andrew Davies, directed by David Attwood (1996)[15]

Notes

1 Introduction

1 Information on the publication of *Robinson Crusoe* is very usefully gathered together in Pat Rogers, *Robinson Crusoe* (London: George, Allen & Unwin, 1979), pp. 7–11.

2 See, however, Robert Markley, 'Teaching the Crusoe Trilogy', in *Approaches to Teaching Defoe's Robinson Crusoe*, ed. Maximillian E. Novak and Carl Fisher (New York: Modern Language Association of America, 2005), pp. 96–104.

2 Early Responses

1 It was anonymous; an annotated edition, by Paul Dottin, was published under the title *Robinson Crusoe Examin'd and Criticis'd: Or, A New Edition of Charles Gildon's Famous Pamphlet Now Published with an Introduction and Explanatory Notes Together with an Essay on Gildon's Life* (1719) (London and Paris: J. M. Dent, 1923). For an excellent collection of early material on Defoe generally, including much that bears on the novels, see *Defoe: The Critical Heritage*, ed. Pat Rogers (London: Routledge and Kegan Paul, 1972); the same author's *Robinson Crusoe* (London: George Allen and Unwin, 1979) provides a useful overview of the critical reception of that novel, in chapter 7.

2 Gildon (1923), pp. iii, x.

3 Gildon (1923), p. 25.

4 *The Highland Rogue* (1723), sig A2^v; the book is sometimes, though less and less plausibly, ascribed to Defoe himself.

5 James Arbuckle, *A Collection of Letters and Essays [. . .] Lately Published in the Dublin Journal* (1729), i. 71; originally published in 1725. Sally Salisbury, a high-class prostitute, died in Newgate in 1724 after stabbing a client; Jack Sheppard was a burglar who achieved much notoriety by breaking out of Newgate prison before being caught and executed in 1724. Defoe may have written about them.

6 Alexander Pope, *The Dunciad*, ii. 139, and see ii. 383, and note; edited by James Sutherland, 2nd edn (London: Methuen, 1953), pp. 117, 148. Defoe did not lose his ears in the pillory, though such a punishment for seditious libel had occasionally been inflicted on Puritan writers in the seventeenth century.

7 Jonathan Swift's jeering reference to the pillory came in *A Letter Concerning the Sacramental Test* (1709). Rogers, *Robinson Crusoe*, p. 107; Michael Seidel, *Robinson Crusoe: Island Myths and the Novel* (Boston, MA: G. K. Hall, 1991), p. 18.

8 Joseph Spence, *Observations, Anecdotes, and Characters of Books and Men Collected from Conversation*, ed. James M. Osborn, 2 vols (Oxford: Clarendon Press, 1966), i. 213.

9 Theophilus Cibber, et al., *Lives of the Poets*, 5 vols (1753), iv. 325.

10 Quoted in Walter Wilson, *Memoirs of the Life and Times of Daniel De Foe*, 3 vols (1830), iii. 441.

11 *Boswell's Life of Johnson*, 2 vols (London: Oxford University Press, 1927), ii. 202 (10 April 1778); Hesther Lynch Piozzi, *Anecdotes of the late Samuel Johnson, LL.D. During the last twenty Years of his Life*, 4th edn (1786), p. 281.

12 Hugh Blair, *Lectures on Rhetoric and Belles Lettres* (1783), ii. 309.

13 James Beattie, *Dissertations Moral and Critical* (1783), pp. 566–7; *A Memoir of Thomas Bewick, Written by Himself*, ed. Iain Bain (Oxford: Oxford University Press, 1979), p. 11.

14 Clara Reeve, *Progress of Romance*, 2 vols (1785), i. 124–7. For another early female reading, see Anna Laetitia Barbauld's essay on Defoe in volume 16 of her series *The British Novelists* (London, 1810), pp. i–vii.

15 Quoted from *Defoe: The Critical Heritage*, pp. 52–3.

16 Elsewhere, Scott suggested that Swift's detailed verisimilitude in *Gulliver's Travels* was learned from Defoe's manner: see *Swift: The Critical Heritage*, ed. Kathleen Williams (London: Routledge & Kegan Paul, 1970), p. 307.

17 *The Miscellaneous Works of Sir Walter Scott, Bart.* (Edinburgh, 1834), iv. 248–81.

18 Quoted in James Gillman, *The Life of Samuel Taylor Coleridge*, 2 vols (1838), i. 20.

19 *Coleridge's Miscellaneous Criticism*, ed. T. M. Raysor (London: Constable, 1936), pp. 194, 292–300. Coleridge's ironic reading of the 'money' moment depends on a famous punctuation crux; see Irving N. Rothman, 'Coleridge on the Semi-Colon in *Robinson Crusoe*: Problems in Editing Defoe', *Studies in the Novel*, 27 (1995), 320–40.

20 *Prose Works of William Wordsworth*, ed A. B. Grosart (1876), iii. 468; the remark dates from around 1840.

21 William Drennan, 'Written in a copy of Robinson Crusoe', from *Glandalloch, and other Poems*, 1859); Napoleon died in 1821, and the poem appears to have been written before then.

22 Edgar Allan Poe, reviewing a new edition of *Robinson Crusoe*, *Southern Literary Messenger*, January 1836, in *Complete Works of Edgar Allan Poe*, ed. James A. Harrison, 15 vols (New York: Crowell, 1902), viii. 169–73.

23 Charles Lamb to Walter Wilson, 16 December 1822; *Works of Charles and Mary Lamb*, ed. E. V. Lucas, 7 vols (London, 1903–5), vii. 586–7 and i. 326–7. Lamb also wrote a mock-pindaric 'Ode to the Treadmill' (1825), comparing modern forms of punishment with the pillory as suffered by the 'Historiographer of deathless Crusoe'; he imagines Defoe accompanied by his heroes – 'Here Flandrian Moll her brazen incest brags', and so on; *Works*, ed. Lucas, v. 67–70.

24 Wilson (1830), iii. 442–3.

25 Wilson (1830), iii. 492.

26 *Collected Works of William Hazlitt*, ed. A. R. Waller and A. Glover, 13 vols (London, 1902–6), x. 379–80 and xiii. 367.

27 *British Critic*, viii (1830), 100; Hazlitt's 'Memoir', prefixed to *Works of Daniel De Foe*, 3 vols (1840), i. cviii–cix.

28 Bernard Barton's poem was, for example, attached to the 1896 edition of *Robinson Crusoe*. As a Quaker, Barton was more alive to the issue of slavery than most, and alluded to Crusoe's intent to purchase 'Poor Blacks' in stanza 8.

29 John Ruskin, *Præterita*, 3 vols (1886) i. 1–2; Mill, *Autobiography* (1873), p. 9; G. O. Trevelyan, *The Life and Letters of Lord Macaulay*, 2 vols (New York, 1877), ii. 383; John Clive, *Thomas Babington Macaulay: The Shaping of the Historian* (London: Secker and Warburg, 1973), p. 403.

30 George Borrow, *Lavengro: The Scholar, The Gypsy, The Priest* (1851; London: J. M. Dent, 1911), pp. 22–5.

31 Borrow (1911), pp. 190, 228, 241–3. For commentary on Borrow's stories see Maximillian E. Novak, *Realism, Myth and History in Defoe's Fiction* (Lincoln, NE: University of Nebraska Press, 1983), pp. 71–5, and Pat Rogers, 'Moll in the Chapbooks', in *Literature and Popular Culture in Eighteenth-Century England* (Brighton: Harvester, 1985), pp. 183–97.

32 Wilkie Collins, *The Moonstone*, ed. J. I. M. Stewart (Harmondsworth: Penguin, 1966), p. 41.

33 Robert Louis Stevenson, 'A Gossip on Romance', originally in *Longman's Magazine*, November 1882, reprinted in *Memories and Portraits; Memoirs of Himself; Selections from his Notebooks*, volume 29 of the Tusitala edition (London: Heinemann, 1924).

34 John Forster, *Daniel De Foe and Charles Churchill* (1855), p. 140.

35 Anonymous essay, 'Novels and Novelists – Daniel De Foe', *Dublin University Magazine*, xlviii (July 1856), 57–71.

36 *The National Review*, iii (October 1856), pp. 380–410; Rogers (*Defoe: The Critical Heritage*, p. 21) considers that this unsigned review may be by Walter Bagehot.

37 *British Quarterly Review*, xxvii (1858), 85–105.

38 Karl Marx, *Das Kapital* (1867), tr. Samuel Moore and Edward Aveling, 2 vols (1915), i. 88–91.

39 John Forster, *The Life of Charles Dickens*, 3rd edn, 3 vols (London, 1872), iii. 112–13.

40 *Cornhill Magazine*, xxiii (March 1871), 310–20; Rogers (*Critical Heritage*, p. 199) suggests it is by John Dennis.

41 William Minto, *Daniel Defoe* (1879), chapter 9, pp. 133–57.

42 Stephen's remarks appeared in the *Cornhill Magazine* in 1868 and were reprinted as 'Defoe's Novels' in *Hours in a Library* (1874), and in a revised edn, 3 vols (1892), i. 17–46. In *The Great Tradition* (1948; repr. Harmondsworth: Penguin, 1977), p. 10 n. 3, F. R. Leavis used Stephen's comments as a conveniently drastic way of ruling Defoe out of serious consideration as a novelist.

43 Quoted in Novak (1983), p. 46.

44 Franz Kafka, cited in Leopold Damrosch, Jr, *God's Plot and Man's Stories* (Chicago: University of Chicago Press, 1985), p. 81; André Malraux, cited in Ian Watt, *The Rise of the Novel: Studies in Defoe, Richardson and Fielding* (London: Chatto and Windus, 1957; repr. Harmondsworth: Pelican Books, 1976), p. 150.

45 Frank Budgen, *James Joyce and the Making of Ulysses* (Bloomington, IN: Indiana University Press, 1960), p. 181.

46 James Joyce, *Daniel Defoe*, ed. and tr. Joseph Prescott (Buffalo: State University of New York, 1964).

47 Virginia Woolf, 'Defoe', in *The Common Reader* (1925; repr. London: Hogarth Press, 1951), pp. 121–31; 'Robinson Crusoe', in *The Second Common Reader* (1932; repr. London: Pelican Books, 1944), pp. 39–44. For a reading which compares Woolf's techniques for the production of selfhood with Defoe's in *Moll Flanders*, see Peter Hühn, 'The Precarious Autopoiesis of Modern Selves: Daniel Defoe's *Moll Flanders* and Virginia Woolf's *The Waves*', *European Journal of English Studies*, 5 (2001), 335–48.

48 *Chicago Tribune*, 16 July 1927.

49 E. M. Forster, *Aspects of the Novel* (1927), ed. Oliver Stallybrass (Harmondsworth: Penguin, 1978), pp. 64–8, 157, 163–4.

3 The Rise of Novel Criticism

1 Gustaf Lannert, *An Investigation into the Language of Robinson Crusoe as Compared with that of other 18th Century Works* (Uppsala: Almqvist & Widsells Boktryckeri-A.B., 1910).

2 Pat Rogers gives a reliable summary of Selkirk's experience and other narrative sources in *Robinson Crusoe*, pp. 17–21, 27–33.

3 J. R. Moore, *A Checklist of the Writings of Daniel Defoe* (Bloomington, IN: Indiana University Press, 1960).

4 P. N. Furbank and W. R. Owens, *A Critical Bibliography of Daniel Defoe* (London: Pickering and Chatto, 1998), lists about half as many items as Moore.

5 J. R. Moore, *Daniel Defoe, Citizen of the Modern World* (Chicago: University of Chicago Press, 1958). Moore's earlier collection, *Defoe in the Pillory and other Studies* (Bloomington, IN: Indiana University Publications, 1939), contains scattered observations on the two novels.

6 James Sutherland, *Defoe* (1937; 2nd edn, London: Methuen, 1950).

7 Sutherland (1950), pp. 231–3.

8 Sutherland (1950), pp. 239, 245.

9 James Sutherland, *Defoe* (London: Longmans, 1954), pp. 22, 26.

10 James Sutherland, *Daniel Defoe: A Critical Study* (Cambridge, MA: Harvard University Press, 1971), pp. 129–33.

11 Sutherland (1971), pp. 175, 179.

12 Sutherland (1971), pp. 182–4, 187, 194.

13 Mark Schorer, 'A Study in Defoe: Moral Vision and Structural Form', *Thought*, 25 (1950), 275–87, and 'Introduction' to *Moll Flanders* (New York: The Modern Library, 1950).

14 Dorothy van Ghent, *The English Novel: Form and Function* (New York: Holt, Rinehart & Winston, 1953), pp. 33–43.

15 Brian Fitzgerald, *Daniel Defoe: A Study in Conflict* (London: Secker & Warburg, 1954), pp. 188–91.

16 Benjamin Boyce, 'The Question of Emotion in Defoe', *Studies in Philology*, 1 (1953), 45–53.

17 Edwin Benjamin, 'Symbolic Elements in *Robinson Crusoe*', *Philological Quarterly*, 30 (1951), 205–11; Eric Berne, 'The Psychological Structure of Space with Some Remarks on *Robinson Crusoe*', *The Psychoanalytic Quarterly*, 25 (1956), 549–67.

18 E. M. W. Tillyard, *The Epic Strain in the English Novel* (London: Chatto & Windus, 1958), pp. 31–50.

19 A. D. McKillop, *The Early Masters of English Fiction* (Lawrence: University of Kansas Press, 1956), pp. 20–33.

20 Ian Watt, '*Robinson Crusoe* as Myth', *Essays in Criticism*, 1 (1951), 95–119. Watt was not of course alone in seeing Robinson Crusoe in economic terms; see also Irving Howe, '*Robinson Crusoe*: Epic of the Middle Class', *Tomorrow*, 8 (1949), 51–4.

21 Ian Watt, *The Rise of the Novel: Studies in Defoe, Richardson and Fielding* (London: Chatto & Windus, 1957; repr. Harmondsworth: Pelican Books, 1976), p. 54.

22 Watt (1976), p. 80.

23 Watt (1976), p. 72.

24 Watt (1976), p. 102.

25 Watt (1976), pp. 148, 124.

26 Watt (1976), pp. 110, 118.

27 Watt (1976), p. 126.

28 Watt (1976), pp. 122, 126, 128.

29 E. M. Forster, *Aspects of the Novel* (1927), ed. Oliver Stallybrass (Harmondsworth: Penguin, 1978), pp. 157, 67.

30 Watt (1976), pp. 129, 144.

31 Watt (1976), pp. 131, 134.

32 Watt (1976), p. 140.

33 Watt (1976), p. 143.

34 Watt (1976), p. 146.

35 Watt (1976), p. 147.

36 For a more strictly Marxist reading of the ideological formatting and silences of *Robinson Crusoe*, see Pierre Macherey, *A Theory of Literary Production* (1966), tr. Geoffrey Wall (London: Routledge & Kegan Paul, 1978), pp. 240–9.

37 Diana Spearman, *The Novel and Society* (London: Routledge & Kegan Paul, 1966), pp. 154–72.

38 Ian Watt, 'Serious Reflections on *The Rise of the Novel*', *Novel: A Forum on Fiction*, 1 (1968), 205–18.

4 The Art of Fiction (1960–75)

1 Terence Martin, 'The Unity of *Moll Flanders*', *Modern Language Quarterly*, 22 (1961), 115–24.

2 Dennis Donoghue, 'The Values of Moll Flanders', *Sewanee Review*, 71 (1963), 287–303.

3 Howard Koonce, 'Moll's Muddle: Defoe's Use of Irony in *Moll Flanders*', *ELH: A Journal of English Literary History*, 30 (1963), 377–94. Wayne Booth's classic *Rhetoric of Fiction* (Chicago: University of Chicago Press, 1961) sets out the technical grounds on which irony can be deployed and detected in early fiction, including *Moll Flanders*, and tends to agree with Watt that very often a definitive answer cannot be given.

4 Robert Columbus, 'Conscious Artistry in *Moll Flanders*', *Studies in English Literature, 1500–1900*, 3 (1963), 415–32.

5 Arnold Kettle, 'In Defence of *Moll Flanders*', in *Of Books and Humankind*, ed. John Butt (London: Routledge & Kegan Paul, 1964), pp. 55–67.

6 R. A. Donovan, *The Shaping Vision: Imagination in the English Novel from Defoe to Dickens* (New York: Cornell University Press, 1966), pp. 34–45.

7 M. A. Goldberg, '*Moll Flanders*: Christian Allegory in a Hobbesian Mode', *University Review*, 33 (1967), 267–78.

8 Ian Watt, 'The Recent Critical Fortunes of *Moll Flanders*', *Eighteenth-Century Studies*, 1 (1967), 109–26.

9 Maximillian E. Novak, 'Conscious Irony in *Moll Flanders*: Facts and Problems', *College English*, 26 (1964), 198–204. For Novak's later perspective on the irony question see his contribution to *The Uses of Irony: Papers on Defoe and Swift read at a Clark Library Seminar* (Los Angeles: University of California, 1966); and a further article on the novel, 'Defoe's Indifferent Monitor: the Complexity of *Moll Flanders*', *Eighteenth-Century Studies*, 3 (1973), 351–65.

10 Maximillian E. Novak, 'Defoe's Theory of Fiction', *Studies in Philology*, 61 (1964), 650–68.

11 Maximillian E. Novak, *Economics and the Fiction of Daniel Defoe* (Berkeley and Los Angeles: University of California Press, 1962), p. ix. See also his 'Robinson Crusoe and Economic Utopia', *Kenyon Review*, 25 (1963), 474–90. James Sutherland supported Novak against Watt in his 1971 study (pp. 136–7), seeing Crusoe's transgressive and buccaneering ventures as driven by something deeper and perhaps more pathological than capitalist accumulation. See also Stephen Hymer, '*Robinson Crusoe* and Primitive Accumulation', *Monthly Review*, 23 (1971), 11–36.

12 Novak (1962), p. 37.

13 Novak (1962), pp. 47–8.

14 Novak (1962), p. 144.

15 Maximillian E. Novak, 'Robinson Crusoe's Fear and the Search for Natural Man', *Modern Philology*, 58 (1961), 238–44.

16 Maximillian E. Novak, *Defoe and the Nature of Man* (Oxford: Oxford University Press, 1963), pp. 2, 5.

17 Novak (1963), p. 37.

18 Novak (1963), pp. 70, 71, 88.

19 William H. Halewood, 'Religion and Invention in *Robinson Crusoe*', *Essays in Criticism*, 14 (1964), 339–51.

20 George A. Starr, *Defoe and Spiritual Autobiography* (Princeton, NJ: Princeton University Press, 1965), pp. 27, 44, 72.

21 Starr (1965), pp. 79, 100.

22 Starr (1965), p. 103.

23 Starr (1965), p. 123.

24 Starr (1965), p. 161.

25 Starr (1965), pp. 157, 160.

26 J. Paul Hunter, *The Reluctant Pilgrim: Defoe's Emblematic Method and Quest for Form in Robinson Crusoe* (Baltimore, MD: Johns Hopkins Press, 1966).

27 Hunter (1966), p. 19.

28 Hunter (1966), pp. 36, 47.

29 Hunter (1966), pp. 102, 119.

30 Hunter (1966), p. 126.

31 Hunter (1966), p. 151.

32 Hunter (1966), p. 175.

33 Hunter (1966), p. 188.

34 Hunter (1966), p. 198.

35 George A. Starr, *Defoe and Casuistry* (Princeton, NJ: Princeton University Press, 1971), p. x.

36 Starr (1971), pp. ix–x.

37 Starr (1971), p. 155.

38 Robert W. Ayers, 'Robinson Crusoe: "Allusive Allegorick History"', *PMLA*, 82 (1967), 399–407; see also Martin J. Greif, 'The Conversion of Robinson Crusoe', *Studies in English Literature, 1500–1900*, 6 (1966), 551–74; Robert Bell, 'Moll's Grace Abounding', *Genre*, 8 (1975), 267–82.

39 Douglas Brooks, *Number and Pattern in the Eighteenth-Century Novel* (London: Routledge & Kegan Paul, 1973), pp. 18–64; 'Moll Flanders: an Interpretation', *Essays in Criticism*, 19 (1969), 46–59, with a rejoinder by Arthur Sherbo in the same journal, *Essays in Criticism*, 19 (1969), 351–4.

40 Michael Shinagel, *Daniel Defoe and Middle-Class Gentility* (Cambridge, MA: Harvard University Press, 1968).

41 Shinagel (1968), p. 141.

42 Shinagel (1968), pp. 149, 154–5.

43 Michael Shinagel, 'The Maternal Theme in *Moll Flanders*: Craft and Character', *Cornell Library Journal*, 7 (1969), 3–23.

44 William Bowman Piper, 'Moll Flanders as a Structure of Topics', *Studies in English Literature, 1500–1900*, 9 (1969), 489–502; Lee Edwards, 'Between the Real and the Moral: Problems in the Structure of *Moll Flanders*', in R. C. Elliott (ed.), *Twentieth-Century Interpretations of Moll Flanders* (Englewood Cliffs, NJ: Prentice Hall, 1970), pp. 95–107.

45 William J. Krier, 'A Courtesy which Grants Integrity: a Literal Reading of *Moll Flanders*', *English Literary History*, 38 (1971), 397–410; Frederick R. Karl, 'Moll's Many-Colored Coat: Veil and Disguise in the Fiction of Defoe', *Studies in the Novel*, 5 (1973), 87–97; J. A. Michie, 'The Unity of *Moll Flanders*', in *Knaves and Swindlers: Essays on the Picaresque Novel in Europe*, ed. C. J. Whitbourn (London: Oxford University Press, 1974), pp. 75–93.

46 Ralph Rader, 'Defoe, Richardson, Joyce, and the Concept of Form in the Novel', in *Autobiography, Biography and the Novel*, by William Matthews and Ralph Rader (Los Angeles: William Andrews Clark Memorial Library, 1973), pp. 45–7; Pat Rogers, 'Moll's Memory', *English*, 24 (1975), 65–72.

47 John Preston, *The Created Self: The Reader's Role in Eighteenth-Century Fiction* (London: Heinemann, 1970), pp. 8, 14, 19–20.

48 Preston (1970), pp. 22, 26, 28.

49 Preston (1970), pp. 34–5, 37.

50 Homer O. Brown, 'The Displaced Self in the Novels of Daniel Defoe', *ELH: A Journal of English Literary History*, 38 (1971), 562–90.

51 George A. Starr, 'Defoe's Prose Style: I – The Language of Interpretation', *Modern Philology*, 71 (1974), 277–94.

52 E. Anthony James, *Defoe's Many Voices: A Rhetorical Study of Prose Style and Literary Method* (Amsterdam: Rodopi, 1972).

53 Leo Braudy, 'Daniel Defoe and the Anxieties of Autobiography', *Genre*, 6 (1973), 76–90.

5 Traditions and Innovations

1 Everett Zimmerman, *Defoe and the Novel* (Berkeley and Los Angeles: University of California Press, 1975); John J. Richetti, *Defoe's Narratives: Situations and Structures* (Oxford: Oxford University Press, 1975). See also John J. Richetti's introductory survey *Daniel Defoe* (Boston, MA: Twayne, 1987).

2 Zimmerman (1975), p. 5.

3 Zimmerman (1975), p. 26.

4 Zimmerman (1975), p. 32.

5 Zimmerman (1975), p. 37.

6 Zimmerman (1975), p. 44.

7 Zimmerman (1975), pp. 85, 88.

8 Zimmerman (1975), pp. 90, 95.

9 Zimmerman (1975), p. 100.

10 Zimmerman (1975), pp. 106.
11 Richetti (1975), pp. 11–13.
12 Richetti (1975), p. 17.
13 Richetti (1975), p. 23.
14 Richetti (1975), pp. 30–1.
15 Richetti (1975), pp. 51–6.
16 Richetti (1975), pp. 96, 101, 105.
17 Richetti (1975), pp. 108, 109, 111.
18 Richetti (1975), pp. 116, 118.
19 Richetti (1975), pp. 122, 126, 128.
20 Richetti (1975), p. 134.
21 Richetti (1975), p. 144.
22 Paul Alkon, *Defoe and Fictional Time* (Athens, GA: University of Georgia Press, 1979), p. 9.
23 Earlier work on this problem includes David Higdon, 'The Chronology of *Moll Flanders*', *English Studies*, 56 (1975), 316–19.
24 Alkon (1979), p. 64.
25 Alkon (1979), p. 89.
26 Alkon (1979), p. 132.
27 Alkon (1979), p. 247.
28 David Blewett, *Defoe's Art of Fiction* (Toronto: University of Toronto Press, 1979). Robert J. Merrett, *Daniel Defoe's Moral and Rhetorical Ideas* (Victoria, BC: University of Victoria, 1980), sees the fiction more directly as a vehicle for Defoe's social thought.
29 Blewett (1979), p. 27.
30 Blewett (1979), p. 28.
31 Blewett (1979), p. 42.
32 Blewett (1979), p. 64.
33 Blewett (1979), p. 80.
34 Pat Rogers, *Robinson Crusoe* (London: George Allen & Unwin, 1979).
35 Mary Butler, 'The Effect of the Narrator's Rhetorical Uncertainty on the Fiction of *Robinson Crusoe*', *Studies in the Novel*, 15 (1983), 77–90.
36 James H. Maddox, 'Interpreter Crusoe', *ELH: A Journal of English Literary History*, 51 (1984), 33–52.
37 Leopold Damrosch, Jr, *God's Plot and Man's Stories* (Chicago: University of Chicago Press, 1985), pp. 187–213.
38 Laura Curtis, *The Elusive Daniel Defoe* (London: Vision Press, 1984), p. 14.
39 Curtis (1984), pp. 32, 39.
40 Curtis (1984), pp. 72, 81, 85.
41 Curtis (1984), p. 139.
42 Paula Backscheider, *A Being More Intense: A Study of the Prose Works of Bunyan, Swift, and Defoe* (New York: AMS Press, 1984); *Daniel Defoe: Ambition and Innovation* (Lexington, KY: University of Kentucky Press, 1986).
43 Ian A. Bell, *Defoe's Fiction* (London and Sydney: Croom Helm, 1985).
44 Bell (1985), pp. 39, 42.
45 John J. Richetti, *Popular Fiction before Richardson* (Oxford: Clarendon Press, 1969).
46 Bell (1985), pp. 69–70.
47 Bell (1985), p. 118.
48 Bell (1985), p. 127.
49 Bell (1985), pp. 141, 144.
50 Bell (1985), p. 190.
51 Virginia Ogden Birdsall, *Defoe's Perpetual Seekers: A Study of the Major Fiction* (Lewisburgh, PA: Bucknell University Press, 1985), p. 13.
52 Birdsall (1985), pp. 14, 23.
53 Birdsall (1985), p. 73.

6 Themes and Variations: Recent Criticism

1 Ilse Vickers, *Defoe and the New Sciences* (Cambridge: Cambridge University Press, 1996), pp. 99, 105.

2 Vickers (1996), pp. 128, 130.

3 Maximillian E. Novak, *Realism, Myth, and History in Defoe's Fiction* (Lincoln, NE, and London: University of Nebraska Press, 1983), p. 7.

4 John J. Richetti, *Popular Fiction Before Richardson* (Oxford: Clarendon Press, 1969), chapter 1, 'The Rise of the Novel Reconsidered'.

5 Marthe Robert, *Roman des Origines et Origines du Roman* (1972), tr. Sacha Rabinovitch (Bloomington: Indiana University Press, 1980), pp. 81–113.

6 Lennard J. Davis, *Factual Fictions: The Origins of the English Novel* (New York: Columbia University Press, 1983), pp. 155–6.

7 Michael McKeon, *The Origins of the English Novel, 1600–1740* (Baltimore, MD: Johns Hopkins University Press, 1987), chapter 9, pp. 315–37; Stuart Sim, 'Interrogating an Ideology: Defoe's *Robinson Crusoe*', *British Journal for Eighteenth-Century Studies*, 10 (1987), 163–73.

8 McKeon (1987), p. 332.

9 McKeon (1987), p. 336.

10 J. Paul Hunter, *Before Novels: The Cultural Contexts of Eighteenth-Century Fiction* (New York: W. W. Norton, 1990). On early definitions of the novel, see also Alan Downie, 'The Making of the English Novel', *Eighteenth-Century Fiction*, 9 (1996–7), 249–66.

11 Robert Mayer, *History and the Early English Novel: Matters of Fact from Bacon to Defoe* (Cambridge: Cambridge University Press, 1997); Geoffrey M. Sill, *The Cure of the Passions and the Origins of the English Novel* (Cambridge: Cambridge University Press, 2001).

12 Ian Watt, 'Flat-Footed and Fly-Blown: the Realities of Realism', *Eighteenth-Century Fiction*, 12:2 (January 2000), pp. 147–66; Watt further re-states his views in the section on Crusoe in his *Myths of Modern Individualism* (Cambridge: Cambridge University Press, 1996), which sees Crusoe as the first hero to rebel against religious and secular structures without suffering a form of damnation.

13 Brean Hammond and Shaun Regan, *Making the Novel: Fiction and Society in Britain, 1660–1789* (Basingstoke: Palgrave Macmillan, 2006), p. 4 For their views on how *Robinson Crusoe* and *Moll Flanders* fit (or lie athwart) the patterns of the early novel, see pp. 52–74.

14 Cheryl Nixon, 'Accounting for the Self: Teaching *Robinson Crusoe* at a Business School', in *Approaches to Teaching Robinson Crusoe*, ed. Maximillian E. Novak and Carl Fisher (New York: Modern Language Association of America, 2005), pp. 207–15.

15 Juliet McMaster, 'The Equation of Love and Money in *Moll Flanders*', *Studies in the Novel*, 2 (1970), 131–44; Lois Chaber, 'Matriarchal Mirror: Women and Capital in *Moll Flanders*', *PMLA*, 97 (1982), 212–26.

16 David Trotter, *Circulation: Defoe, Dickens, and the Economies of the Novel* (Basingstoke: Macmillan, 1988).

17 Jacques Sohier, '*Moll Flanders* and the Rise of the Complete Gentlewoman–Tradeswoman', *Eighteenth-Century Novel*, 2 (2002), 1–21.

18 Ann Louise Kibbie, 'Monstrous Generation: the Birth of Capital in Defoe's *Moll Flanders* and *Roxana*', *PMLA*, 110 (1995), 1023–34. For a recent general assessment of Defoe's mercantile economics, see Sandra Sherman, *Finance and Fictionality in the Early Eighteenth Century: Accounting for Defoe* (Cambridge: Cambridge University Press, 1996).

19 Rebecca E. Connor, '"Can you Apply Arithmetick to Every Thing?": Moll Flanders, William Petty, and Social Accounting', *Studies in Eighteenth-Century Culture*, 27 (1998), 169–94; Edward Copeland, 'Defoe and the London Wall: Mapped Perspectives', *Eighteenth-Century Fiction*, 10 (1998), 407–28; Amit Yahov-Brown, 'At Home in England, or Projecting Liberal Citizenship in *Moll Flanders*', *Novel*, 35 (2001), 24–45.

20 Ian A. Bell, 'King Crusoe: Locke's Political Theory in *Robinson Crusoe*', *English Studies*, 69 (1988), 27–36; see also Maximillian E. Novak, 'Crusoe the King and the Political Evolution of his Island', *Studies in English Literature, 1500–1900*, 2 (1962), 337–50.

21 Geoffrey M. Sill, *Defoe and the Idea of Fiction, 1713–1719* (Newark: University of Delaware Press, 1983), p. 78.

22 Sill (1983), p. 88.

23 Sill (1983), pp. 158–62.

24 Manuel Schonhorn, *Defoe's Politics: Parliament, Power, Kingship, and Robinson Crusoe* (Cambridge: Cambridge University Press, 1991), p. 130.

25 Schonhorn (1991), pp. 141–2.

26 Sara Soncini, 'The Island as Social Experiment: a Reappraisal of Daniel Defoe's Political Discourse(s) in *Robinson Crusoe* and *The Farther Adventures*', in *Wrestling with Defoe: Approaches from a Workshop on Defoe's Prose*, ed. Marialuisa Bignami (Bologna: Instituto Editoriale Universitario, 1997); Carol Kay, *Political Constructions: Defoe, Richardson and Sterne in Relation to Hobbes, Hume and Burke* (Ithaca and London: Cornell University Press, 1998).

27 Tom Paulin, *Crusoe's Secret: The Aesthetics of Dissent* (London: Faber, 2005), pp. 80–104.

28 John Forster, *The Life of Charles Dickens*, 3rd edn, 3 vols (London, 1872), iii. 112–13.

29 E. M. Forster, *Aspects of the Novel* (1927), ed. Oliver Stallybrass (Harmondsworth: Penguin, 1978), pp. 157, 164: the comments do not make it into the published lectures.

30 Tommy Watson, 'Defoe's Attitude toward Marriage and the Position of Women as Revealed in *Moll Flanders*', *Southern Quarterly*, 3 (1964), 1–8; David Blewett, 'Changing Attitudes towards Marriage in the Time of Defoe: the Case of *Moll Flanders*', *Huntington Library Quarterly*, 44 (1981), 77–88; John J. Richetti, 'The Family, Sex and Marriage in Defoe's *Moll Flanders* and *Roxana*', *Studies in the Literary Imagination*, 15 (1982), 19–35.

31 LeRoy Smith, 'Daniel Defoe: Incipient Pornographer', *Literature and Psychology*, 22 (1972), 165–78; Marsha Brodner, 'Defoe's Androgynous Vision in *Moll Flanders* and *Roxana*', *Gypsy Scholar*, 2 (1974), 76–93.

32 Paula Backscheider, 'Defoe's Women: Snares and Prey', *Studies in Eighteenth-Century Culture*, 5 (1976), 103–19; Kathleen McCoy, 'The Femininity of Moll Flanders', *Studies in Eighteenth-Century Culture*, 7 (1978), 413–22; Miriam Lerenbaum, 'Moll Flanders: a Woman on Her Own Account', in *The Authority of Experience: Essays in Feminist Criticism*, ed. Arlyn Diamond and Lee R. Edwards (Amherst: University of Massachusetts Press, 1977), pp. 106–11; Katherine M. Rogers, 'The Feminism of Daniel Defoe', in *Women in the 18th Century and Other Essays*, ed. Paul Fritz and Richard Morton (Toronto: Samuel Stevens Hakkert, 1976), pp. 3–24.

33 Shirlene Mason, *Daniel Defoe and the Status of Women* (St. Alban's, VT: Eden Press Women's Publications, 1978).

34 Mason (1978), p. 104.

35 Mona Scheuermann, *Her Bread to Earn: Women, Money and Society from Defoe to Austen* (Lexington, KY: University Press of Kentucky, 1993); and 'An Income of One's Own: Woman and Money in *Moll Flanders* and *Roxana*', *Durham University Journal*, 80 (1988), 225–39; Srividhya Swaminathan, 'Defoe's Alternative Conduct Manual: Survival Strategies and Female Networks in *Moll Flanders*', *Eighteenth-Century Fiction*, 15 (2003), 185–206; Melissa J. Ganz, '*Moll Flanders* and English Marriage Law', *Eighteenth-Century Fiction*, 17 (2005), 157–82.

36 Robert A. Erickson, 'Moll's Fate: "Mother Midnight" and *Moll Flanders*', *Studies in Philology*, 76 (1979), 75–100; *Mother Midnight: Birth, Sex, and Fate in Eighteenth-Century Fiction (Defoe, Richardson, and Sterne)* (New York: AMS Press, 1986).

37 Carol Houlihan Flynn, *The Body in Swift and Defoe* (Cambridge: Cambridge University Press, 1990), pp. 61–76.

38 Thomas Grant Olsen, 'Reading and Righting *Moll Flanders*', *Studies in English Literature, 1500–1900*, 41 (2001), 467–81; Ellen Pollak, '*Moll Flanders*, Incest, and the Structure of Exchange', *The Eighteenth Century: Theory and Interpretation*, 30 (1989), 3–21; and see her *Incest and the English Novel, 1684–1814* (Baltimore: Johns Hopkins University Press, 2003).

39 Chris Flint, 'Orphaning the Family: the Role of Kinship in *Robinson Crusoe*', *ELH: A Journal of English Literary History*, 55 (1988), 381–419; Richard Braverman, *Plots and Counterplots: Sexual Politics and the Body Politic in English Literature, 1660–1730* (Cambridge: Cambridge University Press, 1993), pp. 248–71; Ian A. Bell, 'Crusoe's Women: Or, the Curious Incident of the Dog in the Night-Time', in *Robinson Crusoe: Myths and Metamorphoses*, ed. Lieve Spaas and Brian Stimpson (Basingstoke: Macmillan, 1996), pp. 28–44.

40 George Haggerty, 'Thank God It's Friday: the Construction of Masculinity in *Robinson Crusoe*', in Novak and Fisher, eds, *Approaches to Teaching Defoe's Robinson Crusoe* (2005), pp. 78–87; Hans Turley, 'The Sublimation of Desire to Apocalyptic Passion in Defoe's *Crusoe* Trilogy', in *Imperial Desire: Dissenting Sexualities and Colonial Literature*, ed. Philip Holden and Richard J. Ruppel (Minneapolis: University of Minnesota Press, 2003), pp. 3–20; Hans Turley, 'Protestant Evangelism, British Imperialism, and Crusoian Identity', in *The New Imperial History: Culture, Identity and Modernity in Britain and the Empire, 1660–1836*, ed. Kathleen Wilson (Cambridge: Cambridge University Press, 2004); DeeAnn DeLuna, 'Robinson Crusoe, Virginal Hero of the Commercial North', *Eighteenth-Century Life*, 28 (2004), 69–91.

41 Brian Fitzgerald, *Daniel Defoe: A Study in Conflict* (London: Secker & Warburg, 1954), p. 190.

42 Gerald Howson, 'Who was Moll Flanders?', *Times Literary Supplement*, 18 January 1968.

43 Robert R. Singleton, 'Defoe, *Moll Flanders*, and the Ordinary of Newgate', *Harvard Library Bulletin*, 24 (1976), 407–13.

44 Gregory Durston, *Moll Flanders: An Analysis of an Eighteenth-Century Criminal Biography* (Chichester: Barry Rose, 1997).

45 Durston (1997), p. 229.

46 Brett McInelly, 'Exile or Opportunity? The Plight of the Transported Felon in Daniel Defoe's *Moll Flanders* and *Colonel Jack*', *Genre*, 22 (2001), 210–17.

47 Beth Swan, '*Moll Flanders*: the Felon as Lawyer', *Eighteenth-Century Fiction*, 11 (1998), 33–48.

48 See Ernest Bernbaum, *The Mary Carleton Narratives, 1663–1673: A Missing Chapter in the History of the English Novel* (Cambridge, MA: Harvard University Press, 1914).

49 Richard Bjornson, 'The Ambiguous Success of the Picaresque Hero in Defoe's *Moll Flanders*', in *The Picaresque Hero in European Fiction* (Madison, WI: University of Wisconsin Press, 1977); Lou Caton, 'Doing the Right Thing with Moll Flanders: a "Reasonable" Difference between the Picara and the Penitent', *College Language Association Journal*, 40 (1997), 508–16; Tina Kuhlisch, 'The Ambivalent Rogue: Moll Flanders as Modern Picara', in *Rogues and Early Modern English Culture*, ed. Craig Dionne and Steve Mentz (Ann Arbor: University of Michigan Press, 2004), pp. 337–60.

50 John Rietz, 'Criminal Ms-Representation: *Moll Flanders* and Female Criminal Biography', *Studies in the Novel*, 23 (1991), 183–95; John P. Zomchick, '"A Penetration which Nothing Can Deceive": Gender and Judicial Discourse in Some Eighteenth-Century Narratives', *Studies in English Literature, 1500–1900*, 29 (1989), 535–53; M. J. Kietzman, 'Defoe Masters the Serial Subject', *ELH: A Journal of English Literary History*, 66 (1999), 677–705.

51 John Bender, *Imagining the Penitentiary: Fiction and the Architecture of Mind* (Chicago: University of Chicago Press, 1987). An earlier suggestive account of Crusoe's imprisonment, not specifically linked to crime, can be found in W. B. Carnochan's *Confinement and Flight: An Essay on English Literature of the Eighteenth Century* (Berkeley: University of California Press, 1977).

52 Bender (1987), pp. 43, 45.

53 Bender (1987), pp. 47, 48.

54 Bender (1987), p. 50.

55 Bender (1987), pp. 52, 55.

56 Bender (1987), p. 56.

57 Lincoln B. Faller, *Crime and Defoe: A New Kind of Writing* (Cambridge: Cambridge University Press, 1993), p. 31.

58 Faller (1993), p. 73.

59 Faller (1993), p. 119.

60 Faller (1993), p. 127.

61 Faller (1993), p. 135.

62 Faller (1993), p. 254.

63 Landor's poems were written c.1840 and published in 1897; *Complete Works of Walter Savage Landor*, ed. Stephen Wheeler, 16 vols (Oxford: Clarendon Press, 1927–36), 3.216; and see Patrick J. Keane, *Coleridge's Submerged Politics: The Ancient Mariner and Robinson Crusoe* (Columbia and London: University of Missouri Press, 1994), p. 139.

64 John Robert Moore, *Daniel Defoe* (1958), p. 282; William Cox, 'Burckhardt reading Robinson Crusoe to his Arabs in the Desert', from *My Sonnets* (1843); sonnet dated 16 November 1842.

65 Shef Rogers, 'Crusoe among the Maori: Translation and Colonial Acculturation in Victorian New Zealand', *Book History*, 1 (1998), 182–95; Jay Fliegelman, *Prodigals and Pilgrims: The American Revolution against Patriarchal Authority* (Cambridge: Cambridge University Press, 1983), pp. 67–90; Benjamin Franklin acknowledges both Defoe novels as sources of his own literary style, in his *Autobiography*.

66 Maximillian E. Novak, 'Imaginary Islands and Real Beasts: the Imaginative Genesis of *Robinson Crusoe*', *Tennessee Studies in Literature*, 19 (1974), 57–78; William Bysshe Stein, 'Robinson Crusoe: the Trickster Tricked', *Centennial Review*, 90 (1965), 271–88.

67 H. Daniel Peck, '*Robinson Crusoe*: the Moral Geography of Limitation', *Journal of Narrative Theory*, 3 (1973), 20–31; Pat Rogers, 'Crusoe's Home', *Essays in Criticism*, 24 (1974), 375–90. See also Hugh Jenkins, 'Crusoe's Country House(s)', *Eighteenth Century: Theory and Interpretation*, 38 (1997), 118–33.

68 Michael Seidel, *Robinson Crusoe: Island Myths and the Novel* (Boston, MA: G. K. Hall, 1991), p. 9; and see his 'Crusoe in Exile', *PMLA*, 96 (1981), 363–74, and *Exile and the Narrative Imagination* (New Haven, CT: Yale University Press, 1986).

69 Maximillian E. Novak, *Economics and the Fiction of Daniel Defoe* (Berkeley and Los Angeles: University of California Press, 1962), pp. 140–55; see also Pat Rogers, *Robinson Crusoe*, pp. 40–6; J. A. Downie, 'Defoe, Imperialism, and the Travel Books Reconsidered', *Yearbook of English Studies*, 13 (1983), 66–83.

70 Peter Hulme, *Colonial Encounters: Europe and the Native Carribean, 1492–1797* (New York and London: Methuen, 1987), pp. 175–222. In *Culture and Imperialism* (London: Chatto & Windus, 1993), Edward Said sees Crusoe as the archetypal or originating novel of colonialism since it stakes a symbolic cultural claim on non-European territory (p. 84). See also Srinivas Aravamudan, *Tropicopolitans: Colonialism and Agency, 1688–1804* (Durham, NC: Duke University Press, 1999).

71 Elihu Pearlman, 'Robinson Crusoe and the Cannibals', *Mosaic: A Journal for the Interdisciplinary Study of Literature*, 10 (1976), 42–54; Martin Gliserman, 'Robinson Crusoe: the Vicissitudes of Greed – Cannibalism and Capitalism', *American Imago: A Psychoanalytic Journal for Culture, Science, and the Arts*, 47 (1990), 197–231; Gary Hentzi, 'Sublime Moments and Social Authority in *Robinson Crusoe* and *A Journal of the Plague Year*', *Eighteenth-Century Studies*, 26:3 (1993), 419–34.

72 Flynn, *The Body in Swift and Defoe* (1990), pp. 149–59. On these complex interactions, see further Minaz Jooma, 'Robinson Crusoe Inc(corporates): Domestic Economy, Incest, and the Trope of Cannibalism', *Lit: Literature, Interpretation, Theory*, 8 (1997), 61–81.

73 Keane, *Coleridge's Submerged Politics* (1994), pp. 47, 52.

74 Gary Gautier, 'Slavery and the Fashioning of Race in *Oroonoko*, *Robinson Crusoe*, and Equiano's *Life*', *Eighteenth Century: Theory and Interpretation*, 42 (2001), 161–79. See also Roxann Wheeler, '"My Savage" My Man: Racial Multiplicity in *Robinson Crusoe*', *ELH: A Journal of English Literary History*, 62 (1995), 821–61, and Maximillian E. Novak, 'Friday: or, the Power of Naming', in *Augustan Subjects*, ed. Albert J. Riveiro (Newark, DE: Delaware University Press, 1997), pp. 110–22.

75 Ellis Markman, 'Crusoe, Cannibalism and Empire', in Spaas and Stimpson (eds), *Robinson Crusoe: Myths and Metamorphoses* (1996), pp. 95–61; Lincoln B. Faller, 'Captain Misson's Failed Utopia, Crusoe's Failed Colony: Race and Identity in New, Not Quite Imaginable Worlds', *Eighteenth Century: Theory and Interpretation*, 43 (2002), 1–17.

76 Robert Marzec, 'Enclosures, Colonization, and the *Robinson Crusoe* Syndrome', *boundary 2*, 29.2 (2002), 129–56; Brett McInelly, 'Expanding Empires, Expanding Selves: Colonialism, the Novel, and *Robinson Crusoe*', *Studies in the Novel*, 35 (2003), 1–21.

77 Everett Zimmerman, 'Robinson Crusoe and No Man's Land', *Journal of English and Germanic Philology*, 102 (2003), 506–29, and see his 'Contexts for Crusoe: Colonial Adventure and Social Disintegration', in Novak and Fisher (eds), *Approaches to Teaching Defoe's Robinson Crusoe*, pp. 152–60.

78 Anna Neill, 'Crusoe's Farther Adventures: Discovery, Trade, and the Law of Nations', *Eighteenth Century: Theory and Interpretation*, 38 (1997), 213–30; Aparna Dharwadker, 'Nation, Race, and the Ideology of Commerce in Defoe', *Eighteenth Century: Theory and Interpretation*, 39 (1998), 63–84; Lydia H. Liu, 'Robinson Crusoe's Earthenware Pot', *Critical Inquiry*, 25 (1999), 728–57; Robert Markley, '"I Have Now Done with My Island, and All Manner of Discourse about It": Crusoe's Farther Adventures and the Unwritten History of the Novel', in *The Blackwell Companion to the Eighteenth-Century Novel*, ed. Paula Backscheider and Catherine Ingrassia (Oxford: Blackwell, 2005), pp. 506–28.

Conclusion

1 Nicholas Hudson, '"Why God no kill the Devil?": the Diabolical Disruption of Order in *Robinson Crusoe*', *Review of English Studies*, 39 (1988), 494–501. On this theme see also Timothy C. Blackburn, 'Friday's Religion', *Eighteenth-Century Studies*, 18 (1984–5), 360–82.

2 James Foster, '*Robinson Crusoe* and the Uses of the Imagination', *Journal of English and Germanic Philology*, 90 (1992), 179–202. For another view of the secular–economic debate see Robert Maniquis, 'Teaching *The Pilgrim's Progress* and *Robinson Crusoe*; or, from filthy mire to the glory of things', in *Approaches to Teaching Defoe's Robinson Crusoe*, ed. Maximillian E. Novak and Carl Fisher (New York: Modern Language Association of America, 2005), pp. 25–36.

3 Jeffrey Hopes, 'Real and Imaginary Stories: *Robinson Crusoe* and the *Serious Reflections*', *Eighteenth-Century Fiction*, 8 (1996), 313–28; Janis Svilpis, 'Bourgeois Solitude in Robinson Crusoe', *English Studies in Canada*, 22 (1996), 35–43; Richard A. Barney, *Plots of Enlightenment: Education and the Novel in Eighteenth-Century England* (Stanford, CA: Stanford University Press, 1999), pp. 203–52.

4 Geoffrey M. Sill, 'Crusoe and the Cave: Defoe and the Semiotics of Desire', *Eighteenth-Century Fiction*, 6 (1994), 215–32.

5 Mary Butler, '"Onomaphobia" and Personal Identity in *Moll Flanders*', *Studies in the Novel*, 22 (1990), 377–91; Larry Langford, 'Retelling Moll's Story: the Editor's Preface to *Moll Flanders*', *Journal of Narrative Technique*, 22 (1992), 167–75; Michael Suarez, 'The Shortest Way to Heaven? Moll Flanders's Repentance Reconsidered', *1650–1850: Ideas, Aesthetics, and Inquiries on the Early Modern Era*, 3 (1997), 3–28.

6 Carl Lovitt, 'Defoe's "Almost Invisible Hand": Narrative Logic as a Structuring Principle in *Moll Flanders*', *Eighteenth-Century Fiction*, 6 (1993), 1–28; Sandra Sherman, 'The Secret History of *The Secret History*: Grub Street Decorum in *Robinson Crusoe*', *Prose Studies*, 17 (1994), 1–22.

7 Cameron McFarlane, 'Reading Crusoe Reading Providence', *English Studies in Canada*, 21 (1995), 257–67; Steven Michael, 'Thinking Parables: What Moll Flanders Does Not Say', *ELH: A Journal of English Literary History*, 63 (1996), 367–95.

8 Kevin Cope, 'All Aboard the Ark of Possibility: or, Robinson Crusoe returns from Mars as a small foot-print, multi-channel indeterminacy machine', *Studies in the Novel*, 30 (1998), 150–63; John Llewelyn, 'What is Orientalism in Thinking: Facing the Fact in *Robinson Crusoe*', in *Proximity: Emmanuel Levinas and the Eighteenth Century*, ed. Melvyn New with Robert Bernasconi and Richard A. Cohen (Lubbock, TX: Texas Tech, 2001), pp. 69–90. In this

connection, the yet-to-be-published *Robinson Crusoe's Economic Man: A Construction and Deconstruction*, ed. Ulla Grapard and Gillian Hewitson and announced for October 2007, should provide interesting material.

9 Maximillian E. Novak and Carl Fisher (eds), *Approaches to Teaching Defoe's Robinson Crusoe* (New York: Modern Language Association of America, 2005).

10 The 38th annual meeting of the American Society for Eighteenth-Century Studies took place at Atlanta, Georgia, in March 2007; the Defoe Society (http://www.defoesociety.org) has a discussion list at defoe@lists.whitman.edu

11 P. N. Furbank and W. R. Owens, *The Canonisation of Daniel Defoe* (New Haven, CT: Yale University Press, 1988); *Defoe De-Attributions: A Critique of J. R. Moore's Checklist* (London: Hambledon Press, 1994); *Critical Bibliography of Daniel Defoe* (London: Pickering & Chatto, 1998). The series of Defoe editions is published by Pickering & Chatto.

12 Details of these biographies are given in the appropriate section of the Bibliography.

13 Leo Abse, *The Bi-Sexuality of Daniel Defoe: A Psychoanalytic Survey of the Man and his Works* (London: Karnac Books, 2006); John Martin, *Beyond Belief: The Real Life of Daniel Defoe* (London: Accent Press, 2006).

14 See www.rcrusoe.org/; www.robinsoncrusoe.com; www.robinsoncrusoeislandfiji.com/; and Diana Souhani, *Selkirk's Island* (London: Weidenfeld & Nicolson, 2001); Tim Severin, *Seeking Robinson Crusoe* (Basingstoke: Palgrave Macmillan, 2002).

15 See Catherine N. Parke, 'Adaptations of Defoe's *Moll Flanders*', in *Eighteenth-Century Fiction on Screen*, ed. Robert Mayer (Cambridge: Cambridge University Press, 2002), pp. 52–69, notes 19–21.

16 Ken Russell began negotiations with Bob Guccione to film the novel in about 1982; the failure of the project to materialise ended in an abortive court case, itself later the subject of a television documentary. See *Sundries: An Eighteenth-century Newsletter*, 35 (17 June 2006), www.chezjim.com/sundries/s35.html; the production is also reported on IMDb: www.imdb.com/title/tt0847747. The documentary ('Your Honour, I Object!') was screened on Channel 4, on 27 November 1987. Russell discusses the project in his autobiography *A British Picture* (1989).

Appendix: Adaptations and Appropriations

1 See the essays collected in Lieve Spaas and Brian Stimpson (eds), *Robinson Crusoe: Myths and Metamorphoses* (Basingstoke: Macmillan, 1996); and Maximillian E. Novak and Carl Fisher (eds), *Approaches to Teaching Defoe's Robinson Crusoe* (New York: Modern Language Association of America, 2005), pp. 25–36.

2 Pat Rogers, 'Classics and Chapbooks' and 'Moll in the Chapbooks', in *Literature and Popular Culture in Eighteenth-Century England* (Brighton: Harvester, 1985), pp. 162–82, 183–97. Some of the 'Moll' illustrations and chapbook verses are printed in Maximillian E. Novak, *Realism, Myth and History*. See also Michael J. Preston, 'Rethinking Folklore, Rethinking Literature: Looking at *Robinson Crusoe* and *Gulliver's Travels* as Folktales, a Chapbook-Inspired Inquiry', in *The Other Print Tradition: Essays on Chapbooks, Broadsides, and Related Ephemera* (New York: Garland, 1995), pp. 19–73.

3 See Pat Rogers, *Robinson Crusoe* (London: George Allen & Unwin, 1979), pp. 12–13, citing H. Ullrich, *Robinson and Robinsonaden* (Weimar, 1898); see also Carl Fisher, 'The Robinsonade: an Intercultural History of an Idea', in Novak and Fisher (eds), *Approaches to Teaching Defoe's Robinson Crusoe*, pp. 129–39. Kevin Carpenter, *Desert Isles and Pirate Islands* (Frankfurt am Main, 1984), lists some 500 English stories of desert islands from the period 1788–1910. See also Martin Green, *The Robinson Crusoe Story* (Philadelphia: Pennsylvania State University Press, 1990); and Patrick J. Keane, *Coleridge's Submerged Politics: The Ancient Mariner and Robinson Crusoe* (Columbia and London: University of Missouri Press, 1994), pp. 106–23.

4 Michel Tournier, *Vendredi*, tr. Norman Denny as *Friday or the Other Island* (Harmondsworth: Penguin Books, 1969); *Vendredi ou la vie sauvage* (1971; tr. R. Manheim as *Friday and Robinson:*

Life on Esperanza Island (London: Aldus, 1972). For criticism see Lorna Milne, 'Myth as Microscope: Michel Tournier's *Vendredi ou les limbes du Pacifique*'; Anthony Purdy, '"Skilful in the usury of time"': Michel Tournier and the Critique of Economism'; Emma Wilson, 'Vendredi ou les limbes du Pacifique: Tournier, Seduction and Paternity', in Spaas and Stimpson (eds), *Robinson Crusoe: Myths and Metamorphoses* (1996), pp. 167–81, 182–98, 199–209.

5 Paula Burnett, 'The Ulyssean Crusoe and the Quest for Redemption in J. M. Coetzee's *Foe* and Derek Walcott's *Omeros*'; Patrick Corcoran, '*Foe*: Metafiction and the Discourse of Power', in Spaas and Stimpson (eds), *Robinson Crusoe: Myths and Metamorphoses* (1996), pp. 239–55 and 256–66.

6 Roger McGough, 'Moll Flanders', in McGough's *The State of Poetry* (London: Penguin, 2005), p. 7.

7 See Anne Ferry, 'The Naming of Crusoe', *Eighteenth-Century Life*, 16 (1992), pp. 195–207.

8 See Stewart Brown, '"Between me and thee is a great gulf fixed": the Crusoe Presence in Walcott's Early Poetry', in Spaas and Stimpson (eds), *Robinson Crusoe: Myths and Metamorphoses*, pp. 210–24; and Charles W. Pollard, 'Teaching Contemporary Responses to *Robinson Crusoe*: Coetzee, Walcott and Others in a World Literature Survey', in Novak and Fisher (eds), *Approaches to Teaching Robinson Crusoe*, pp. 161–8.

9 www.kaostheatre.com/moll.php

10 See C. N. Smith, 'Charles Guilbert de Pixérécourt's, *Robinson Crusoé* (1805)', in Spaas and Stimpson (eds), *Robinson Crusoe: Myths and Metamorphoses*, pp. 127–40.

11 Bridget Jones, '"With Crusoe the slave and Friday the boss": Derek Walcott's *Pantomime*', in Spaas and Stimpson (eds), *Robinson Crusoe: Myths and Metamorphoses*, pp. 225–38.

12 David Blewett, *The Illustrations of Robinson Crusoe* (New York: Oxford University Press, 1996). A web resource giving access to many of these images, and based in part on information in Blewett's book, can be found at www.camden.rutgers.edu/Camden/Crusoe/Pages/crusoe.html. See also Maximillian E. Novak, '"Picturing the Thing Itself, or Not: Defoe, Painting, Prose Fiction, and the Arts of Describing', *Eighteenth-Century Fiction*, 9 (1996), 1–20, for an account of Defoe's possible interest in landscape painting.

13 Robert Mayer, 'Three Cinematic Robinsonades', in *Eighteenth-Century Fiction on Screen*, ed. Robert Mayer (Cambridge: Cambridge University Press, 2002), pp. 35–51. Mayer also treats Robert Zemeckis's *Cast Away* (2000) as a modern take on the symbolic alienation of economic man, in the Crusoe tradition. See also his 'Robinson Crusoe in Hollywood', in Novak and Fisher (eds), *Approaches to Teaching Robinson Crusoe*, pp. 169–74.

14 Sharon Meagher, 'Resisting *Robinson Crusoe* in Dechanel's Film', in Spaas and Stimpson (eds), *Robinson Crusoe: Myths and Metamorphoses*, pp. 148–56.

15 Catherine N. Parke, 'Adaptations of Defoe's *Moll Flanders*', in *Eighteenth-Century Fiction on Screen*, ed. Robert Mayer, pp. 52–69. For a behind-the-scenes account of the 1996 television version, with stills and interviews, see Anthony Hayward, *The Making of 'Moll Flanders'* (London: Headline Publishing, 1996).

Bibliography

EDITIONS

Robinson Crusoe, ed. Michael Shinagel, 2nd edition (New York: W. W. Norton, 1994).
Robinson Crusoe, ed. John Richetti (London: Penguin, 2003).
Robinson Crusoe, ed. Thomas Keymer and James Kelly (Oxford: Oxford University Press, 2007).
Moll Flanders, ed. Albert J. Rivero (New York: W. W. Norton, 2003).
Moll Flanders, ed. David Blewett (London: Penguin Books, 1989).
Moll Flanders, ed. G. A. Starr (Oxford: Oxford University Press, 1998).
Moll Flanders, ed. Paul A. Scanlon (Peterborough, Ont.: Broadview, 2005).

BIBLIOGRAPHIES AND STUDY GUIDES

Furbank, P. N. and W. R. Owens, *Critical Bibliography of Daniel Defoe* (London: Pickering & Chatto, 1998).
Hutchins, Henry Clinton, *Robinson Crusoe and its Printing, 1719–1731* (New York: Columbia University Press, 1925).
Maslen, K. D., 'The Printers of *Robinson Crusoe*', *The Library*, 7 (1952), 124–31.
Moore, John Robert, *A Checklist of the Writings of Daniel Defoe* (Bloomington, IN: Indiana University Press, 1960).
Peterson, Spiro, *Daniel Defoe: A Reference Guide, 1731–1924* (Boston: G. K. Hall, 1987).
Rogers, Pat, *Robinson Crusoe* (London: George Allen & Unwin, 1979).
Spackman, I. J., W. R. Owens and P. N. Furbank, eds, *A KWIC Concordance to Daniel Defoe's Robinson Crusoe* (New York: Garland, 1987).
Stoler, John A., *Daniel Defoe: An Annotated Bibliography of Modern Criticism, 1900–1980* (New York: Garland, 1984).

BIOGRAPHIES

Backscheider, Paula, *Daniel Defoe: His Life* (Baltimore, MD: Johns Hopkins University Press, 1989).
Furbank, P. N., and W. R. Owens, *A Political Biography of Daniel Defoe* (London: Pickering & Chatto, 2006).
Moore, John Robert, *Daniel Defoe, Citizen of the Modern World* (Chicago: University of Chicago Press, 1958).
Novak, Maximillian E., *Daniel Defoe: Master of Fictions* (Oxford: Oxford University Press, 2001).
Owens, W. R., and P. N. Furbank, *A Political Biography of Daniel Defoe* (London: Pickering & Chatto, 2006).
Richetti, John, *The Life of Daniel Defoe* (Oxford: Blackwell, 2005).
Sutherland, James, *Defoe* (1937; 2nd edn, London: Methuen, 1950).

CRITICISM: COLLECTIONS OF ESSAYS AND CRITICAL MATERIAL

Bloom, Harold (ed.), *Daniel Defoe: Modern Critical Views* (New York: Chelsea House, 1987).
Bloom, Harold (ed.), Daniel Defoe's *Moll Flanders: Modern Critical Interpretations* (New York: Chelsea House, 1987).

Bloom, Harold (ed.), *Daniel Defoe's Robinson Crusoe: Modern Critical Interpretations* (New York: Chelsea House, 1988).

Byrd, Max (ed.), *Daniel Defoe: A Collection of Critical Essays* (Englewood Cliffs, NJ: Prentice Hall, 1976).

Elliott, R. C. (ed.), *Twentieth-Century Interpretations of Moll Flanders* (Englewood Cliffs, NJ: Prentice Hall, 1970).

Ellis, F. H. (ed.), *Twentieth-Century Interpretations of Robinson Crusoe* (Englewood Cliffs, NJ: Prentice Hall, 1969).

Lamoine, Georges (ed.), *Lectures d'un Oeuvre: Moll Flanders de Daniel Defoe* (Paris: Editions du Temps, 1997).

Lund, Roger D. (ed.), *Critical Essays on Daniel Defoe* (New York: G. K. Hall, 1997).

Mayer, Robert (ed.), *Eighteenth-Century Fiction on Screen* (Cambridge: Cambridge University Press, 2002).

Novak, Maximillian E., and Carl Fisher (eds), *Approaches to Teaching Defoe's Robinson Crusoe* (New York: Modern Language Association of America, 2005).

Rogers, Pat (ed.), *Defoe: The Critical Heritage* (London: Routledge & Kegan Paul, 1972).

Spaas, Lieve, and Brian Stimpson (eds), *Robinson Crusoe: Myths and Metamorphoses* (Basingstoke: Macmillan, 1996).

CRITICISM: MONOGRAPHS AND ARTICLES

CHAPTER 2 EARLY RESPONSES

Dottin, Paul (ed.), *Robinson Crusoe Examin'd and Criticis'd: Or, A New Edition of Charles Gildon's Famous Pamphlet Now Published with an Introduction and Explanatory Notes Together with an Essay on Gildon's Life* (London and Paris: J. M. Dent, 1923).

Hühn, Peter, 'The Precarious Autopoiesis of Modern Selves: Daniel Defoe's *Moll Flanders* and Virginia Woolf's *The Waves*', *European Journal of English Studies*, 5 (2001), 335–48.

Rothman, Irving R., 'Coleridge on the Semi-Colon in *Robinson Crusoe*: Problems in Editing Defoe', *Studies in the Novel*, 27 (1995), 320–40.

CHAPTER 3 THE RISE OF NOVEL CRITICISM

Benjamin, Edwin, 'Symbolic Elements in *Robinson Crusoe*', *Philological Quarterly*, 30 (1951), 205–11.

Berne, Eric, 'The Psychological Structure of Space with Some Remarks on *Robinson Crusoe*', *Psychoanalytic Quarterly*, 25 (1956), 549–67.

Boyce, Benjamin, 'The Question of Emotion in Defoe', *Studies in Philology*, 1 (1953), 45–53.

Fitzgerald, Brian, *Daniel Defoe: A Study in Conflict* (London: Secker & Warburg, 1954).

Ghent, Dorothy van, *The English Novel: Form and Function* (New York: Holt, Rinehart & Winston, 1953).

Howe, Irving, '*Robinson Crusoe*: Epic of the Middle Class', *Tomorrow*, 8 (1949), 51–4.

Lannert, Gustaf, *An Investigation into the Language of Robinson Crusoe as Compared with that of Other 18th Century Works* (Uppsala: Almqvist & Widsells Boktryckeri-A.B., 1910).

McKillop, A. D., *The Early Masters of English Fiction* (Lawrence, KS: University of Kansas Press, 1956).

Schorer, Mark, 'A Study in Defoe: Moral Vision and Structural Form', *Thought*, 25 (1950), 275–87.

Secord, A. W., *Studies in the Narrative Method of Defoe* (University of Illinois, Studies in Language and Literature, 1924; reissued, New York: Russell & Russell, 1963).

Sutherland, James, *Defoe* (London: Longmans, 1954).

Sutherland, James, *Daniel Defoe: A Critical Study* (Cambridge, MA: Harvard University Press, 1971).

Tillyard, E. M. W., *The Epic Strain in the English Novel* (London: Chatto & Windus, 1958).

Watt, Ian, 'Robinson Crusoe as Myth', Essays in Criticism, 1 (1951), 95–119.
Watt, Ian, The Rise of the Novel: Studies in Defoe, Richardson and Fielding (London: Chatto & Windus, 1957; repr. Harmondsworth: Pelican Books, 1976).
Watt, Ian, 'The Recent Critical Fortunes of Moll Flanders', Eighteenth-Century Studies, 1 (1967), 109–26.
Watt, Ian, 'Serious Reflections on The Rise of the Novel', Novel: A Forum on Fiction, 1 (1968), 205–18.

CHAPTER 4 THE ART OF FICTION

Ayers, Robert W., 'Robinson Crusoe: "Allusive Allegorick History"', PMLA, 82 (1967), 399–407.
Bell, Robert, 'Moll's Grace Abounding', Genre, 8 (1975), 267–82.
Braudy, Leo, 'Daniel Defoe and the Anxieties of Autobiography', Genre, 6 (1973), 76–90.
Brooks, Douglas, 'Moll Flanders: an Interpretation', Essays in Criticism, 19 (1969), 46–59.
Brooks, Douglas, Number and Pattern in the Eighteenth-Century Novel: Defoe, Fielding, Smollett, and Sterne (London: Routledge & Kegan Paul, 1973).
Brown, Homer O., 'The Displaced Self in the Novels of Daniel Defoe', ELH: A Journal of English Literary History, 38 (1971), 562–90.
Columbus, Robert R., 'Conscious Artistry in Moll Flanders', Studies in English Literature, 1500–1900, 3 (1963), 415–32.
Donoghue, Dennis, 'The Values of Moll Flanders', Sewanee Review, 71 (1963), 287–303.
Donovan, R. A., The Shaping Vision: Imagination in the English Novel from Defoe to Dickens (New York: Cornell University Press, 1966).
Edwards, Lee, 'Between the Real and the Moral: Problems in the Structure of Moll Flanders', in R. C. Elliott (ed.), Twentieth-Century Interpretations of Moll Flanders (Englewood Cliffs, NJ: Prentice Hall, 1970), pp. 95–107.
Goldberg, M. A., 'Moll Flanders: Christian Allegory in a Hobbesian Mode', The University Review, 33 (1967), 267–78.
Greif, Martin J., 'The Conversion of Robinson Crusoe', Studies in English Literature, 1500–1900, 6 (1966), 551–74.
Halewood, William H., 'Religion and Invention in Robinson Crusoe', Essays in Criticism, 14 (1964), 339–51.
Hunter, J. Paul, The Reluctant Pilgrim: Defoe's Emblematic Method and Quest for Form in Robinson Crusoe (Baltimore, MD: Johns Hopkins Press, 1966).
Hymer, Stephen, 'Robinson Crusoe and Primitive Accumulation', Monthly Review, 23 (1971), 11–36.
James, E. Anthony, Defoe's Many Voices: A Rhetorical Study of Prose Style and Literary Method (Amsterdam: Rodopi, 1972).
Karl, Frederick R., 'Moll's Many-Colored Coat: Veil and Disguise in the Fiction of Defoe', Studies in the Novel, 5 (1973), 87–97.
Kettle, Arnold, 'In Defence of Moll Flanders', in Of Books and Humankind: Essays and Poems Presented to Bonamy Dobrée, ed. John Butt (London: Routledge & Kegan Paul, 1964), pp. 55–67.
Koonce, Howard, 'Moll's Muddle: Defoe's Use of Irony in Moll Flanders', ELH: A Journal of English Literary History, 30 (1963), 377–94.
Krier, William J., 'A Courtesy which Grants Integrity: a Literal Reading of Moll Flanders', ELH: A Journal of English Literary History, 38 (1971), 397–410.
Martin, Terence R., 'The Unity of Moll Flanders', Modern Language Quarterly, 22 (1961), 115–24.
Michie, J. A., 'The Unity of Moll Flanders', in Knaves and Swindlers: Essays on the Picaresque Novel in Europe, ed. C. J. Whitbourn (London: Oxford University Press, 1974), pp. 75–93.

Novak, Maximillian E., 'Robinson Crusoe's Fear and the Search for Natural Man', *Modern Philology*, 58 (1961), 238–44.

Novak, Maximillian E., 'Crusoe the King and the Political Evolution of His Island', *Studies in English Literature, 1500–1900*, 2 (1962), 337–50.

Novak, Maximillian E., *Economics and the Fiction of Daniel Defoe* (Berkeley and Los Angeles: University of California Press, 1962).

Novak, Maximillian E., 'Robinson Crusoe and Economic Utopia', *Kenyon Review*, 25 (1963), 474–90.

Novak, Maximillian E., *Defoe and the Nature of Man* (Oxford: Oxford University Press, 1963).

Novak, Maximillian E., 'Conscious Irony in *Moll Flanders*: Facts and Problems', *College English*, 26 (1964), 198–204.

Novak, Maximillian E., 'Defoe's theory of fiction', *Studies in Philology*, 61 (1964), 650–68.

Novak, Maximillian E., 'Defoe's Indifferent Monitor: the Complexity of *Moll Flanders*', *Eighteenth-Century Studies*, 3 (1973), 351–65.

Novak, Maximillian E., *Realism, Myth and History in Defoe's Fiction* (Lincoln, NE, and London: University of Nebraska Press, 1983).

Piper, William Bowman, '*Moll Flanders* as a Structure of Topics', *Studies in English Literature, 1500–1900*, 9 (1969), 489–502.

Preston, John, *The Created Self: The Reader's Role in Eighteenth-Century Fiction* (London: Heinemann, 1970).

Rader, Ralph, 'Defoe, Richardson, Joyce and the Concept of Form in the Novel', in *Autobiography, Biography and the Novel*, by Ralph Rader and William Matthews (Los Angeles: William Andrews Clark Memorial Library, 1973).

Richetti, John, *Defoe's Narratives: Situations and Structures* (Oxford: Oxford University Press, 1975).

Richetti, John, *Daniel Defoe* (Boston, MA: Twayne, 1987).

Rogers, Pat, 'Moll's Memory', *English*, 24 (1975), 67–72.

Shinagel, Michael, *Daniel Defoe and Middle-Class Gentility* (Cambridge, MA: Harvard University Press, 1968).

Shinagel, Michael, 'The Maternal Theme in *Moll Flanders*: Craft and Character', *Cornell Library Journal*, 7 (1969), 3–23.

Starr, G. A., *Defoe and Spiritual Autobiography* (Princeton, NJ: Princeton University Press, 1965).

Starr, G. A., *Defoe and Casuistry* (Princeton, NJ: Princeton University Press, 1971).

Starr, G. A., 'Defoe's Prose Style: 1. The Language of Interpretation', *Modern Philology*, 71 (1974), 277–94.

Zimmerman, Everett, *Defoe and the Novel* (Berkeley and Los Angeles: University of California Press, 1975).

CHAPTER 5 TRADITIONS AND INNOVATIONS

Alkon, Paul, *Defoe and Fictional Time* (Athens, GA: University of Georgia Press, 1979).

Backscheider, Paula, *A Being More Intense: A Study of the Prose Works of Bunyan, Swift, and Defoe* (New York, AMS Press, 1984).

Backscheider, Paula, *Daniel Defoe: Ambition and Innovation* (Lexington, KY: University of Kentucky Press, 1986).

Bell, Ian A., 'Narrators and Narrative in Defoe', *Novel: A Forum on Fiction*, 18 (1985), 154–72.

Bell, Ian A., *Defoe's Fiction* (London and Sydney: Croom Helm, 1985).

Birdsall, Virginia Ogden, *Defoe's Perpetual Seekers: A Study of the Major Fiction* (Lewisburgh, PA: Bucknell University Press, 1985).

Blewett, David, *Defoe's Art of Fiction* (Toronto: University of Toronto Press, 1979).

Boardman, Michael, *Defoe and the Uses of Narrative* (New Brunswick: Rutgers University Press, 1983).

Curtis, Laura, *The Elusive Daniel Defoe* (London: Vision Press, 1984).

Damrosch, Leopold, *God's Plot and Man's Stories* (Chicago: University of Chicago Press, 1985).

Hammond, Brean S., 'Repentance: Solution to the Clash of Moralities in *Moll Flanders*', *English Studies*, 61 (1980), 329–37.

Merrett, Robert J., *Daniel Defoe's Moral and Rhetorical Ideas* (Victoria, BC: University of Victoria, 1980).

Rogers, Henry N., 'The Two Faces of Moll', *Journal of Narrative Technique*, 9 (1979), 117–25.

Rogers, Pat, 'Crusoe's Home', *Essays in Criticism*, 24 (1975), 375–90.

CHAPTER 6 THEMES AND VARIATIONS

Alter, Robert, 'A Bourgeois Picaroon', in *Rogue's Progress: Studies in the Picaresque Novel* (Cambridge, MA: Harvard University Press, 1964).

Armstrong, Nancy, *Desire and Domestic Fiction: A Political History of the Novel* (New York: Oxford University Press, 1987).

Backscheider, Paula, 'Defoe's Women: Snares and Prey', *Studies in Eighteenth-Century Culture*, 5 (1976), 103–19.

Backscheider, Paula, *Moll Flanders: The Making of a Criminal Mind* (Boston, MA: Twayne, 1990).

Bell, Ian A., 'King Crusoe: Locke's Political Theory in *Robinson Crusoe*', *English Studies*, 69 (1988), 27–36.

Bender, John, *Imagining the Penitentiary: Fiction and the Architecture of Mind* (Chicago: University of Chicago Press, 1987).

Bjornson, Richard, 'The Ambiguous Success of the Picaresque Hero in Defoe's *Moll Flanders*', *The Picaresque Hero in European Fiction* (Madison: University of Wisconsin Press, 1977).

Blewett, David, 'Changing Attitudes towards Marriage in the Time of Defoe: the Case of Moll Flanders', *Huntington Library Quarterly*, 44 (1981), 77–88.

Braverman, Richard, 'Crusoe's Legacy', *Studies in the Novel*, 18 (1986), 1–26.

Braverman, Richard, *Plots and Counterplots: Sexual Politics and the Body Politic in English Literature, 1660–1730* (Cambridge: Cambridge University Press, 1993).

Brodner, Marsha, 'Defoe's Androgynous Vision in *Moll Flanders* and *Roxana*', *Gypsy Scholar*, 2 (1974), 76–93.

Butler, Mary, 'The Effect of the Narrator's Rhetorical Uncertainty on the Fiction of *Robinson Crusoe*', *Studies in the Novel*, 15 (1983), 77–90.

Butler, Mary, '"Onomaphobia" and Personal Identity in *Moll Flanders*', *Studies in the Novel*, 22 (1990), 377–91.

Caton, Lou, 'Doing the Right Thing with Moll Flanders: a "Reasonable" Difference between the Picara and the Penitent', *College Language Association Journal*, 40 (1997), 508–16.

Chaber, Lois A., 'Matriarchal Mirror: Women and Capital in *Moll Flanders*', *PMLA*, 97 (1982), 212–26.

Connor, Rebecca E., '"Can You Apply Arithmetick to Every Thing?": Moll Flanders, William Petty, and Social Accounting', *Studies in Eighteenth-Century Culture*, 27 (1998), 169–94.

Copeland, Edward, 'Defoe and the London Wall: Mapped Perspectives', *Eighteenth-Century Fiction*, 10 (1998), 407–28.

Davis, Lennard. J., *Factual Fictions: The Origins of the English Novel* (New York: Columbia University Press, 1983).

DeLuna, DeeAnn, 'Robinson Crusoe, Virginal Hero of the Commercial North', *Eighteenth-Century Life*, 28 (2004), 69–91.

Détis, Elisabeth, *Daniel Defoe: Moll Flanders* (Paris: Didier Érudition–CNED, 1997).

Dharwadker, Aparna, 'Nation, Race, and the Ideology of Commerce in Defoe', *Eighteenth Century: Theory and Interpretation*, 39 (1998), 63–84.

Downie, J. A., 'Defoe, Imperialism and the Travel Books Reconsidered', *Yearbook of English Studies*, 13 (1983), 66–83.

Downie, J. A., 'The Making of the English Novel', *Eighteenth-Century Fiction*, 9 (1996–7), 249–66.

Durston, Gregory, *Moll Flanders: An Analysis of an Eighteenth-Century Criminal Biography* (Chichester: Barry Rose, 1997).

Erickson, Robert A., *Mother Midnight: Birth, Sex, and Fate in Eighteenth-Century Fiction (Defoe, Richardson, and Sterne)* (New York: AMS Press, 1986).

Faller, Lincoln B., *Crime and Defoe: A New Kind of Writing* (Cambridge: Cambridge University Press, 1993).

Faller, 'Captain Misson's Failed Utopia, Crusoe's Failed Colony: Race and Identity in New, Not Quite Imaginable Worlds', *Eighteenth Century: Theory and Interpretation*, 43 (2002), 1–17.

Flint, Chris, 'Orphaning the Family: the Role of Kinship in *Robinson Crusoe*', *ELH: A Journal of English Literary History*, 55 (1988), 381–419.

Flynn, Carol Houlihan, *The Body in Swift and Defoe* (Cambridge: Cambridge University Press, 1990).

Ganz, Melissa J., '*Moll Flanders* and English Marriage Law', *Eighteenth-Century Fiction*, 17 (2005), 157–82.

Gautier, Gary, 'Slavery and the Fashioning of Race in *Oroonoko*, *Robinson Crusoe*, and Equiano's *Life*', *Eighteenth Century: Theory and Interpretation*, 42 (2001), 161–79.

Gliserman, Martin, 'Robinson Crusoe: the Vicissitudes of Greed – Cannibalism and Capitalism', *American Imago: A Psychoanalytic Journal for Culture, Science, and the Arts*, 47 (1990), 197–231.

Green, Martin, *The Robinson Crusoe Story* (Philadelphia: Pennsylvania State University Press, 1990).

Hammond, Brean, and Shaun Regan, *Making the Novel: Fiction and Society in Britain, 1660–1789* (Basingstoke: Palgrave Macmillan, 2006).

Hentzi, Gary, 'Sublime Moments and Social Authority in *Robinson Crusoe* and *A Journal of the Plague Year*', *Eighteenth-Century Studies*, 26 (1993), 419–34.

Hopes, Jeffrey, 'Real and Imaginary Stories: *Robinson Crusoe* and the *Serious Reflections*', *Eighteenth-Century Fiction*, 8 (1996), 313–28.

Howson, Gerald, 'Who was Moll Flanders?' *Times Literary Supplement*, 18 January 1968.

Hulme, Peter, *Colonial Encounters: Europe and the Native Caribbean, 1492–1767* (New York and London: Methuen, 1986).

Hunter, J. Paul, *Before Novels: The Cultural Contexts of Eighteenth-Century Fiction* (New York: W. W. Norton, 1990).

Jenkins, Hugh, 'Crusoe's Country House(s)', *Eighteenth Century: Theory and Interpretation*, 38 (1997), 118–33.

Jooma, Minaz, 'Robinson Crusoe Inc(orporates): Domestic Economy, Incest, and the Trope of Cannibalism', *LIT: Literature, Interpretation, Theory*, 8 (1997), 61–81.

Kay, Carol, *Political Constructions: Defoe, Richardson and Sterne in Relation to Hobbes, Hume and Burke* (Ithaca and London: Cornell University Press, 1998).

Keane, Patrick J., *Coleridge's Submerged Politics: The Ancient Mariner and Robinson Crusoe* (Columbia and London: University of Missouri Press, 1994).

Kibbie, Ann Louise, 'Monstrous Generation: the Birth of Capital in Defoe's *Moll Flanders* and *Roxana*', *PMLA*, 110 (1995), 1023–34.

Kietzman, M. J., 'Defoe Masters the Serial Subject (Criminal Biography, *Moll Flanders*)', *ELH: A Journal of English Literary History*, 66 (1999), 677–705.

Kuhlisch, Tina, 'The Ambivalent Rogue: Moll Flanders as Modern Picara', in *Rogues and Early Modern English Culture*, ed. Craig Dionne and Steve Mentz (Ann Arbor: University of Michigan Press, 2004), pp. 337–60.

Langford, Larry L., 'Retelling Moll's Story: the Editor's Preface to *Moll Flanders*', *Journal of Narrative Technique*, 22 (1992), 164–79.

Lerenbaum, Miriam, 'Moll Flanders: a Woman on Her Own Account', *The Authority of Experience: Essays in Feminist Criticism*, ed. Arlyn Diamond and Lee R. Edwards (Amherst: University of Massachusetts Press, 1977), pp. 101–17.

Liu, Lydia H., 'Robinson Crusoe's Earthenware Pot', *Critical Inquiry*, 25 (1999), 728–57.

Lovitt, Carl R., 'Defoe's "Almost Invisible Hand": Narrative Logic as a Structuring Principle in *Moll Flanders*', *Eighteenth-Century Fiction*, 6 (1993), 1–28.

Loxley, Diana, *Problematic Shores: The Literature of Islands* (New York: St Martin's Press, 1990).

McCoy, Kathleen, 'The Femininity of Moll Flanders', *Studies in Eighteenth-Century Culture*, 7 (1978), 413–22.

McFarlane, Cameron, 'Reading Crusoe Reading Providence', *English Studies in Canada*, 21 (1995), 257–67.

McInelly, Brett C., 'Exile or Opportunity? The Plight of the Transported Felon in Daniel Defoe's *Moll Flanders* and *Colonel Jack*', *Genre*, 22 (2001), 210–17.

McInelly, Brett C., 'Expanding Empires, Expanding Selves: Colonialism, the Novel, and *Robinson Crusoe*', *Studies in the Novel*, 35 (2003), 1–21.

McKeon, Michael, *The Origins of the English Novel, 1600–1740* (Baltimore, MD: Johns Hopkins University Press, 1987).

McMaster, Juliet, 'The Equation of Love and Money in *Moll Flanders*', *Studies in the Novel*, 2 (1970), 131–44.

Markley, Robert, '"I Have Now Done with My Island, and All Manner of Discourse about It": Crusoe's Farther Adventures and the Unwritten History of the Novel', in *Blackwell Companion to the Eighteenth-Century Novel*, ed. Paula Backscheider and Catherine Ingrassia (Oxford: Blackwell, 2005), pp. 506–28.

Marzec, Robert, 'Enclosures, Colonization, and the Robinson Crusoe Syndrome', *boundary 2*, 29 (2002), 129–56.

Mason, Shirlene, *Daniel Defoe and the Status of Women* (St Alban's, VT: Eden Press Women's Publications, 1978).

Michael, Steven, 'Thinking Parables: What Moll Flanders Does Not Say', *ELH: A Journal of English Literary History*, 63 (1996), 367–95.

Neill, Anna, 'Crusoe's Farther Adventures: Discovery, Trade, and the Law of Nations', *Eighteenth Century: Theory and Interpretation*, 38 (1997), 213–30.

Novak, Maximillian E., 'Imaginary Islands and Real Beasts: the Imaginative Genesis of *Robinson Crusoe*', *Tennessee Studies in Literature*, 19 (1974), 57–78.

Novak, Maximillian E., 'Friday: or, the Power of Naming', in *Augustan Subjects*, ed. Albert J. Riveiro (Newark: Delaware University Press, 1997), pp. 110–22.

Olsen, Thomas Grant, 'Reading and Righting *Moll Flanders*', *Studies in English Literature, 1500–1900*, 41 (2001), 467–81.

Paulin, Tom, *Crusoe's Secret: The Aesthetics of Dissent* (London: Faber, 2005).

Pearlman, Elihu, 'Robinson Crusoe and the Cannibals', *Mosaic: A Journal for the Inter-disciplinary Study of Literature*, 10 (1976), 42–54.

Peck, H. Daniel, '*Robinson Crusoe*: the Moral Geography of Limitation', *Journal of Narrative Technique*, 3 (1973), 20–31.

Pollak, Ellen, '*Moll Flanders*, Incest, and the Structure of Exchange', *Eighteenth Century: Theory and Interpretation*, 30 (1989), 3–21.

Pollak, Ellen, *Incest and the English Novel, 1684–1814* (Baltimore, MD: Johns Hopkins University Press, 2003).

Richetti, John, *Popular Fiction before Richardson* (Oxford: Clarendon Press, 1969).

Richetti, John, 'The Family, Sex and Marriage in Defoe's *Moll Flanders* and *Roxana*', *Studies in the Literary Imagination*, 15 (1982), 19–35.

Rietz, John, 'Criminal MS-Representation: *Moll Flanders* and Female Criminal Biography', *Studies in the Novel*, 23 (1991), 183–97.

Robert, Marthe, *Roman des Origines et Origines du Roman* (1972), tr. Sacha Rabinovitch (Bloomington, IN: Indiana University Press, 1980).

Rogers, Katherine, 'The Feminism of Daniel Defoe', *Woman in the 18th Century and other Essays*, ed. Paul Fritz and Richard Morton (Toronto: Hakkert, 1976), 3–24.

Rogers, Shef, 'Crusoe among the Maori: Translation and Colonial Acculturation in Victorian New Zealand', *Book History*, 1 (1998), 182–95.

Scheuermann, Mona, 'An Income of One's Own: Woman and Money in *Moll Flanders* and *Roxana*', *Durham University Journal*, 80 (1988), 225–39.

Scheuermann, Mona, *Her Bread to Earn: Women, Money, and Society from Defoe to Austen* (Lexington, KY: University Press of Kentucky, 1993).

Schonhorn, Manuel, *Defoe's Politics: Parliament, Power, Kingship, and Robinson Crusoe* (Cambridge: Cambridge University Press, 1991).

Seidel, Michael, 'Crusoe in Exile', *PMLA*, 96 (1981), 363–74.

Seidel, Michael, *Exile and the Narrative Imagination* (New Haven, CT: Yale University Press, 1986).

Seidel, Michael, *Robinson Crusoe: Island Myths and the Novel* (Boston, MA: G. K. Hall, 1991).

Sherman, Sandra, 'The Secret History of *The Secret History*: Grub Street Decorum in *Robinson Crusoe*', *Prose Studies*, 17 (1994), 1–22.

Sherman, Sandra, *Finance and Fictionality in the Early Eighteenth Century: Accounting for Defoe* (Cambridge: Cambridge University Press, 1996).

Sill, Geoffrey M., *Defoe and the Idea of Fiction, 1713–1719* (Newark: University of Delaware Press, 1983).

Sill, Geoffrey M., 'Crusoe and the Cave: Defoe and the Semiotics of Desire', *Eighteenth-Century Fiction*, 6 (1994), 215–32.

Sill, Geoffrey M., *The Cure of the Passions and the Origins of the English Novel* (Cambridge: Cambridge University Press, 2001).

Sim, Stuart, 'Interrogating an Ideology: Defoe's *Robinson Crusoe*', *British Journal for Eighteenth-Century Studies*, 10 (1987), 163–73.

Singleton, Robert R., 'Defoe, Moll Flanders, and the Ordinary of Newgate', *Harvard Library Bulletin*, 24 (1976), 407–13.

Smith, LeRoy, 'Daniel Defoe: Incipient Pornographer', *Literature and Psychology*, 22 (1972), 165–78.

Sohier, Jacques, '*Moll Flanders* and the Rise of the Complete Gentlewoman–Tradeswoman', *Eighteenth-Century Novel*, 2 (2002), 1–21.

Spencer, Jane, *The Rise of the Woman Novelists: From Aphra Behn to Jane Austen* (Oxford: Basil Blackwell, 1986).

Swaminathan, Srividhya, 'Defoe's Alternative Conduct Manual: Survival Strategies and Female Networks in *Moll Flanders*', *Eighteenth-Century Fiction*, 15 (2003), 185–206.

Swan, Beth, 'Moll Flanders: the Felon as Lawyer', *Eighteenth-Century Fiction*, 11 (1998), 33–48.

Trotter, Davie, *Circulation: Defoe, Dickens, and the Economies of the Novel* (Basingstoke: Macmillan, 1988).

Turley, Hans, 'The Sublimation of Desire to Apocalyptic Passion in Defoe's *Crusoe* Trilogy', in *Imperial Desire: Dissenting Sexualities and Colonial Literature*, ed. Philip Holden and Richard J. Ruppel (Minneapolis: University of Minnesota Press, 2003), pp. 3–20.

Wall, Cynthia, 'Details of Space: Narrative Description in Early Eighteenth-Century Novels', *Eighteenth-Century Fiction*, 10 (1998), 387–405.

Watson, Tommy, 'Defoe's Attitude Toward Marriage and the Position of Women as Revealed in *Moll Flanders*', *Southern Quarterly*, 3 (1964), 1–8.

Wheeler, Roxann, '"My Savage" My Man: Racial Multiplicity in *Robinson Crusoe*', *ELH: A Journal of English Literary History*, 62 (1995), 821–61.

Yahav-Brown, Amit, 'At Home in England, or Projecting Liberal Citizenship in *Moll Flanders*', *Novel*, 35 (2001), 24–45.

Zimmerman, Everett, 'Robinson Crusoe and No Man's Land', *Journal of English and Germanic Philology*, 102 (2003), 506–29.

Zomchick, John P., '"A Penetration which Nothing Can Deceive": Gender and Judicial Discourse in Some Eighteenth-Century Narratives', *Studies in English Literature, 1500–1900*, 29 (1989), 535–53.

CONCLUSION

Blackburn, Timothy C., 'Friday's Religion', *Eighteenth-Century Studies*, 18 (1984–5), 360–82.

Cope, Kevin, 'All Aboard the Ark of Possibility: or, Robinson Crusoe returns from Mars as a Small-footprint, Multi-channel Indeterminacy Machine', *Studies in the Novel*, 30 (1998), 150–63.

Hudson, Nicholas, '"Why God no kill the Devil?": the Diabolical Disruption of Order in *Robinson Crusoe*', *Review of English Studies*, 39 (1988), 494–501.

Llewelyn, John, 'What is Orientalism in Thinking: Facing the Fact in Robinson Crusoe', in *Proximity: Emmanuel Levinas and the Eighteenth Century*, ed. Melvyn New with Robert Bernasconi and Richard A. Cohen (Lubbock: Texas Tech, 2001), pp. 69–90.

Mayer, Robert, *History and the Early English Novel: Matters of Fact from Bacon to Defoe* (Cambridge: Cambridge University Press, 1997).

Suarez, Michael J., 'The Shortest Way to Heaven? Moll Flanders's Repentance Reconsidered', *1650–1850: Ideas, Aesthetics, and Inquiries on the Early Modern Era*, 3 (1997), 3–28.

Svilpis, Janis, 'Bourgeois Solitude in *Robinson Crusoe*', *English Studies in Canada*, 22 (1996), 35–43.

Vickers, Ilse, *Defoe and the New Sciences* (Cambridge: Cambridge University Press, 1996).

APPENDIX

Blewett, David, *The Illustrations of Robinson Crusoe* (Gerrard's Cross: Colin Smythe, 1995).

Novak, Maximillian E., 'Picturing the Thing Itself, or Not: Defoe, Painting, Prose Fiction, and the Arts of Describing', *Eighteenth-Century Fiction*, 9 (1996), 1–20.

Rogers, Pat, 'Classics and Chapbooks' and 'Moll in the Chapbooks', in *Literature and Popular Culture in Eighteenth-Century England* (Brighton: Harvester, 1985), pp. 162–82, 183–97.

Index